POSTCARD HISTORY SERIES

Walker County
ALABAMA

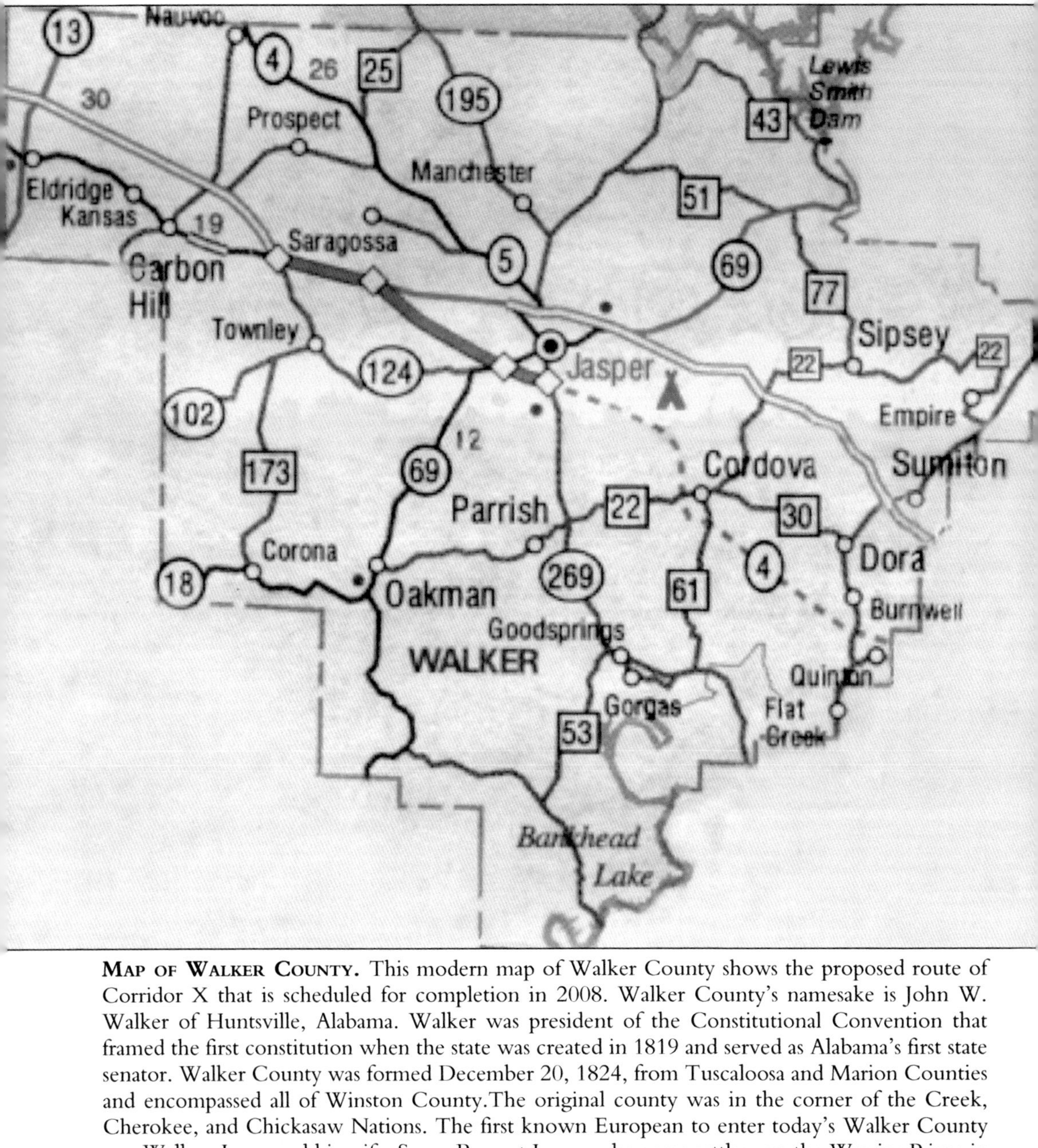

Map of Walker County. This modern map of Walker County shows the proposed route of Corridor X that is scheduled for completion in 2008. Walker County's namesake is John W. Walker of Huntsville, Alabama. Walker was president of the Constitutional Convention that framed the first constitution when the state was created in 1819 and served as Alabama's first state senator. Walker County was formed December 20, 1824, from Tuscaloosa and Marion Counties and encompassed all of Winston County.The original county was in the corner of the Creek, Cherokee, and Chickasaw Nations. The first known European to enter today's Walker County was Wallace Jones and his wife, Susan Beavert Jones, who were settlers on the Warrior River in the late 1700s. Their son, Giles C. Jones, born in 1799, may have been the first white child born in the territory.

POSTCARD HISTORY SERIES

Walker County ALABAMA

Pat Morrison

ARCADIA PUBLISHING

ISBN 978-0-7385-1690-5

Published by Arcadia Publishing
Charleston, South Carolina

Printed in the United States of America

Library of Congress Catalog Card Number: 2004108600

For all general information contact Arcadia Publishing at:
Telephone 843-853-2070
Fax 843-853-0044
E-mail sales@arcadiapublishing.com
For customer service and orders:
Toll-Free 1-888-313-2665

Visit us on the Internet at www.arcadiapublishing.com

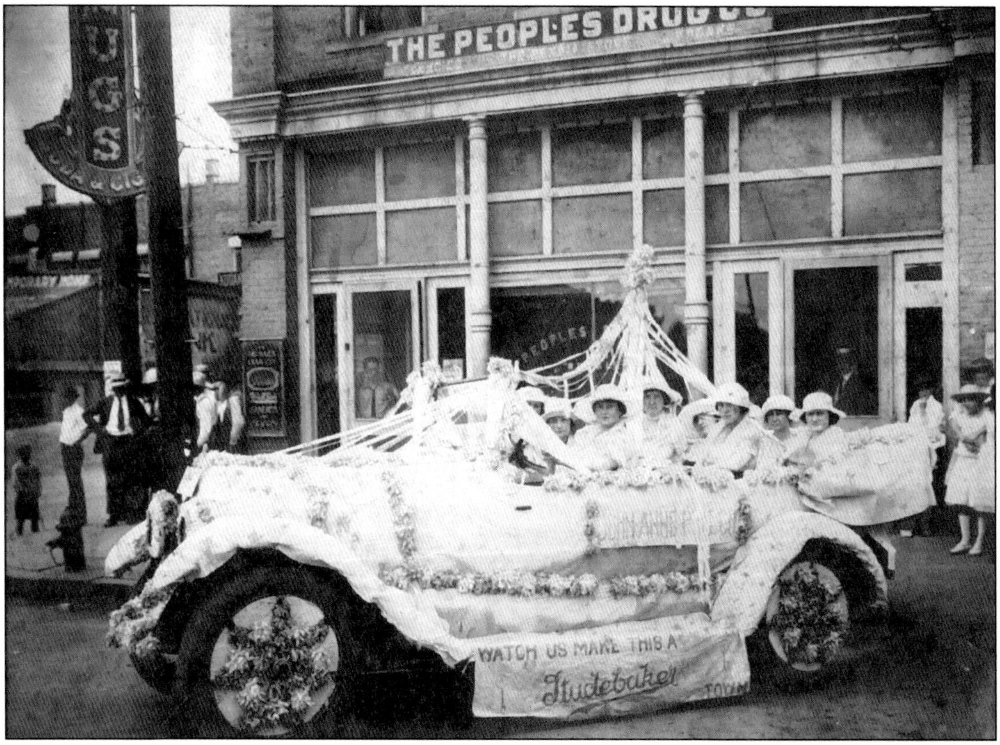

Parade in Downtown Jasper. This parade on November 14, 1924, was in celebration of Walker County's centennial anniversary. The parade included school bands, horseback riders, decorated automobiles, and an ox cart that carried some of the oldest settlers. The county had reached its zenith, and no one could know that less than five years later the Great Depression would bring the darkest days in memory to all of Walker County.

Contents

ACKNOWLEDGMENTS

The publication of this book is possible because of the many people who have aided me in numerous ways. I wish to thank my brother, Billyfrank Morrison, who introduced me to the world of postcards, and Konnie Godfrey, who has a knack for finding those hard-to-find objects, including postcards. Colleen Miller, director of the Jasper Public Library, has dedicated her life to preserving the history of Walker County and is always willing and able to help with photographs, information, and personal knowledge of those early times. Linda Lewis, director of the Walker County Chamber of Commerce, is willing to take on any project that will promote the local area. Bonnie Groves, director of the Alabama Mining Museum, works tirelessly to preserve the mining history of Walker and nearby counties and has lent her expertise, knowledge, and resources to this project.

I wish to express a special thanks to Mrs. Rex (Hilda) Brown for being my tutor and friend throughout this project. She has provided me with postcards, pictures, information, and a glimpse into everyday life of the early 20th century in Walker County. She has also been instrumental in providing an early pictorial history of the Indian Head Mill in Cordova, one of Walker County's largest employers in the early years.

Words cannot express how much I appreciate Bill Songer, who has provided me with the technical assistance that has brought this project together. His knowledge and enthusiasm of many different fields has been invaluable during the entire process of writing and organizing this manuscript.

I wish to extend my sincere gratitude to the following people who have provided me with numerous photographs to help supplement the postcards depicted in this book: Richard Barnes, Horace DeFore, and Floyd Guthrie. I would also like to offer a special thanks to postcard collectors Pat Nelson, Bob Bryan, and Dewayne Crowe for the use of their cards. My appreciation is extended to the following individuals for providing postcards or other important materials or information, which has been helpful in the writing of this local history: Diane Blankensopp, Wendy Sandlin Courington, Felix Files, Mary Virginia Files, Danny Gambrell, Beverly Haddock, Betty Hood, Jennie Jenkins, Ozema Kelley, Rejina Keeton, Fred May, Wayne O'Rear, Alma Lee Ragsdale, Lucy Richardson, Ralph Sandlin, Hazel Scott, Charlotte Sherer, Chris Sherer, Maurice Sherer, Bill Songer, Nancy Stewart, Dr. Buddy Thorne, Perry Vickers, Jerome Weinstein, Della Wilson, Betty Wright, and Charlie Yow.

Many of the images, in both photographs and postcards, were made possible because of the work of local photographers such as Charles Mathis, Capt. William Massey, J.H. Reeves, and Lewis Rushing. The quality of their work is unmatched, and their subject matter plays a vital roll in preserving the history of early Walker County.

Information for the captions came from many individual sources as well as the following books: *The Heritage of Walker County Alabama (1999)*, *City of Sumiton 1952–2002*, *Dora Centennial 1886–1986*, *Daily Mountain Eagle Newspaper*, *Carbon Hill Centennial Scrapbook 1888–1988*, John Dombhart's *History of Walker County (1937)*, Nathaniel Self's *Echoes of the Great Depression*, and various research material from the Jasper Public Library.

I genuinely feel that because of the unselfishness of the aforementioned individuals, we have produced a book that the people of Walker County will be proud to own and show to their friends and family.

INTRODUCTION

We came to Walker County in 1968, expecting to be here for a maximum of 2 years; yet here it is 36 years later, and we're still here. What persuaded us to stay is the same reason I'm writing this book: the people of Walker County. They are unique in their friendliness, sincerity, and work ethic. They epitomize all that is good about the South. They are always willing to lend a hand to those who are less fortunate than they are, and their generosity knows no bounds. They are sincere about their faith, family, and football, and they are willing to make a commitment to all three. Finally, they have a work ethic born out of necessity. They have learned from their ancestors, who lived on the edge of frontier America, how to survive under all conditions.

My interest in postcards began a number of years ago as I occasionally looked to add to my brother Billyfrank's collection. He had been a serious collector for over 25 years. As I looked I would sometimes find a Walker County card, and I would toss it in my desk drawer at school. I had no concrete plan in mind for them, so they were basically forgotten. As I cleared out my desk upon retirement, I rediscovered these cards and a plan gradually began to emerge. My true passion began when I received about 20 Walker County postcards from Konnie Godfrey, an entrepreneur and one of my former students, who had purchased part of the Siddie and Ethel Sellers estate. My passion was ignited, and from that point on I was hooked on local postcards. I am first and foremost a postcard collector, but that passion has flowed over into historic photographs and an interest in the history of Walker County. Out of this passion emerged the desire to author this book.

The whole of Walker County is rich in history, although we sometimes let this fact become obscured by our familiarity with the area. Like most places, when we are young, we cannot wait to get away, but we find that the place we are going has all the same characteristics as the place we left. It is not the place with which we are dissatisfied; it is with ourselves. Then as adults, we come back looking for the things that made us happy in our youth, but they are no longer there either. Places like Sherer's Drive-In, where we had so many good times as teenagers, no longer survive, and Johnny Mack, "Mouth of the South," no longer "toot-a-loos" the passing cars from the window overlooking the parking lot and highway. The old Japer Movie Theatre where we attended the "Popeye Club" on Saturday mornings and later had our first date has been torn down and replaced by a store, and her sister, the Pastime Theatre in Carbon Hill, has been destroyed by fire and not replaced at all. The Tallulah Hotel is falling down, and old downtown Dora is gone completely. Even the legendary Clear Creek Falls where our parents and grandparents "went a Kodaking" now lies beneath 100 feet of water because of the construction of the Lewis Smith Dam.

Railroads came to the county in 1884 and would make or break the small struggling communities, since development followed the railroads. Mining came even earlier to Walker County and has been another main reason for the development of the county. Most were small-scale miners who were trying to eke out a living with a pick, shovel, and if they were lucky, a mule. Most have disappeared over the years. Some have grown into mega-companies, but they all had humble beginnings. We have had our share of strikes, fights, and labor disputes, but we have come out much stronger because of the experience. There was once hardly a family that was not touched by some branch of the coal industry or did not depend on the success of coal. Today we have a much more diverse, industry-based economy with top schools, recreation facilities, parks, shopping malls, and now even two super Wal-Marts and a Home Depot. We've come a long way.

This book will teach you that the first car in Walker County was a 1907 Maxwell, which took 11 hours to drive the 40 miles from Birmingham to Jasper, and that much of Jasper was burned by the Yankees during the Civil War. Discover that Indian Head Mill in Cordova had a day-care program for its working mothers over 100 years ago, and that Walker County was named for Alabama's first United States senator. Learn which town was divided down the middle of Main Street—the east side owned and controlled by one family, and the west side owned and controlled by another.

Enter the penny postcard: with its pictures it awakened our memories of old or educated us about the things that once were. Images of the Sumiton prison camp, President Roosevelt in Jasper, and the Cordova flood fill the pages of this book. Without postcards and postcard collectors to keep these images and memories alive, we risk losing a part of our heritage with each passing generation. Deltiology is the official name of collecting postcards, but I believe it is actually an addiction to the collecting and saving of local history.

I hope that as you look through the pages of this book you will have old memories rekindled, and each one of you will add to the story of Walker County by reminiscing with old friends or telling stories long forgotten to your children or grandchildren. So sit back, relax, and enjoy a ride into the past that might not have been possible had someone not saved that little 3.5 by 5.5–inch piece of paper called the "penny postcard."

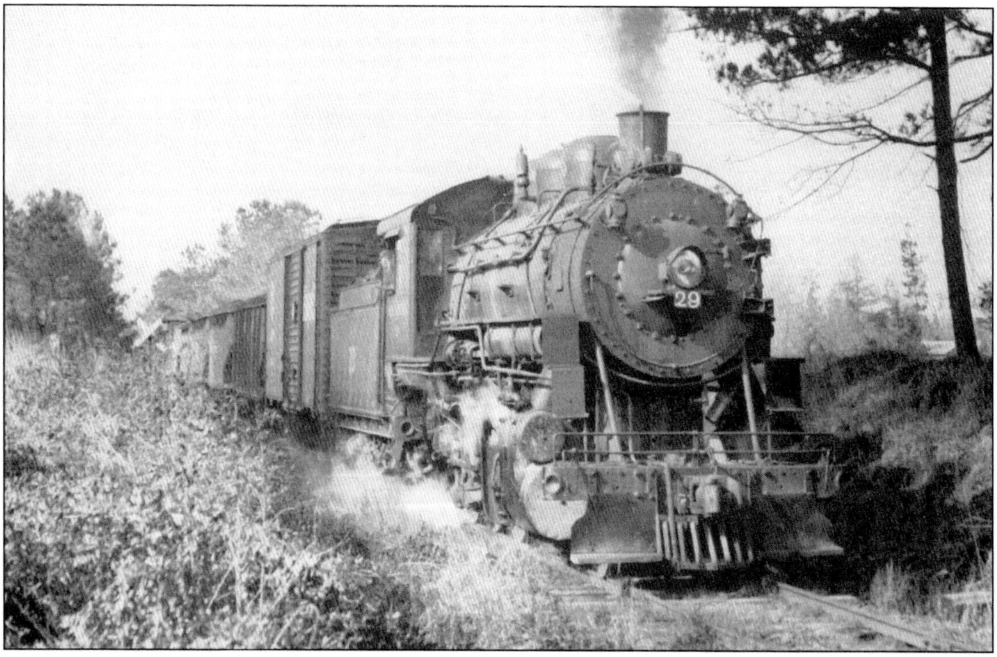

OLD NUMBER 29 LOCOMOTIVE. This steam locomotive, used to haul coal to railheads across Alabama, symbolizes the rail and coal industry in Walker County. During its prime, it steamed busily around the county. Then, in 1957, it made its last run, and for the next 30 years, it was retired to Walker College. In 1987, it moved to its final home at the Alabama Mining Museum in Dora.

One

Downtown and Public Buildings

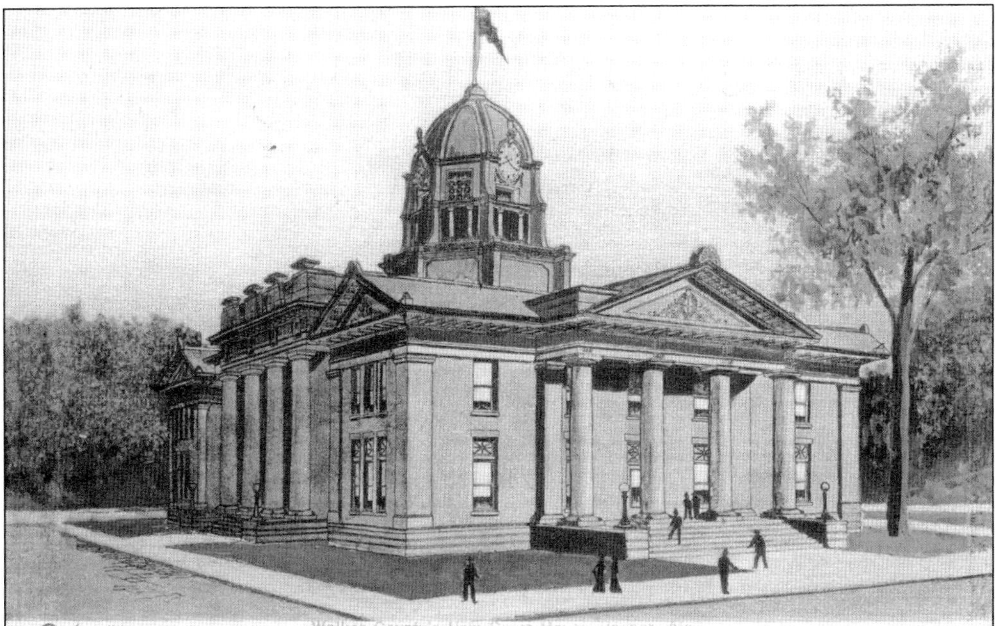

Walker County Courthouse, 1907. This beautiful, domed structure of rough-hewn Georgia marble, designed in the classical Romanesque style, was built at a cost of $200,000, giving Walker County one of the grandest courthouses in the nation. The courthouse prior to this one had burned five times, and this structure was doomed to the same fate just 25 years later in 1932.

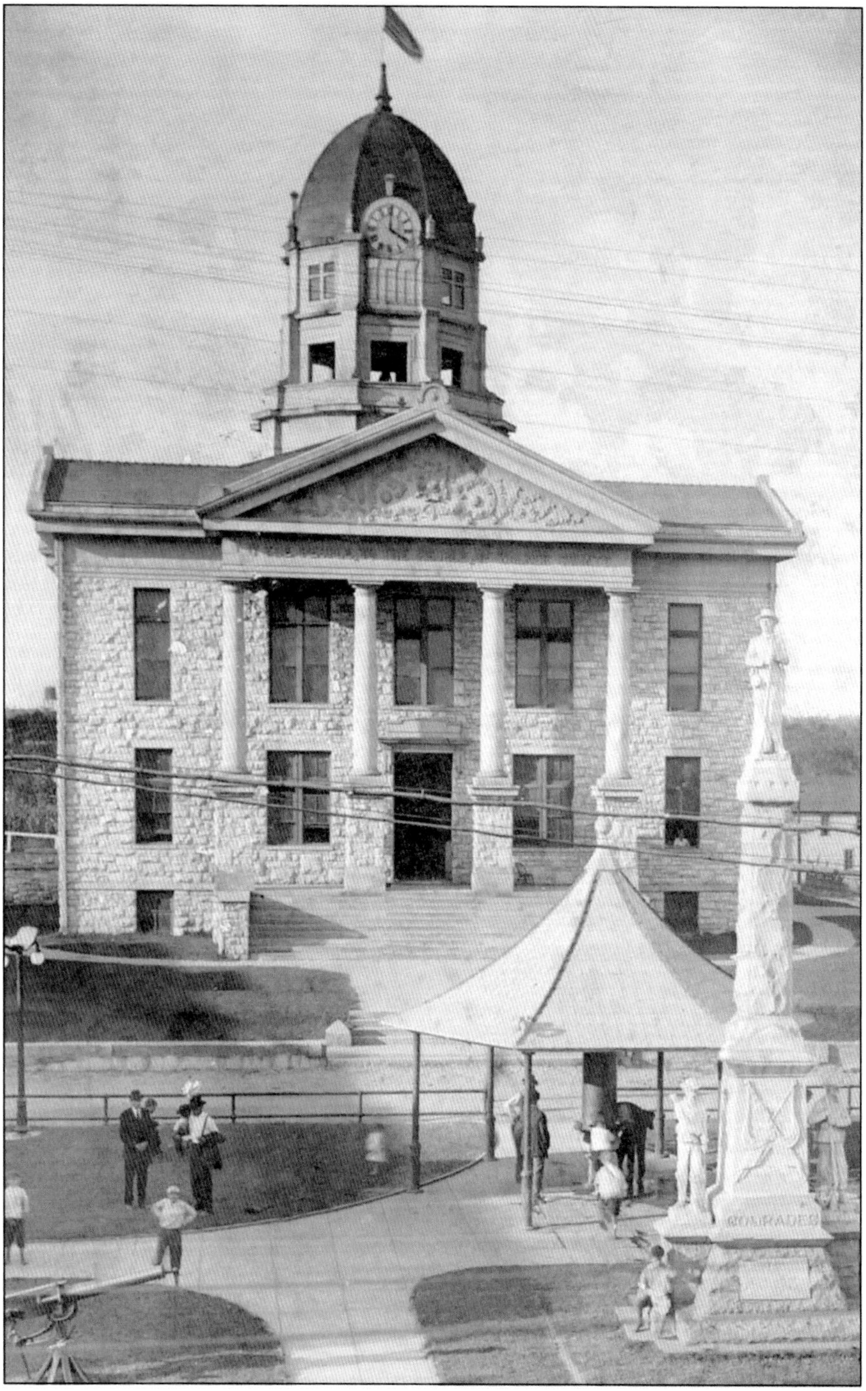

Walker County Courthouse. The pride of Walker County was this beautiful, old building that seemed to symbolize the county. As long as the courthouse stood in all her magnificence, the county seemed to grow along with her, but after she burned down and was reduced to rubble, things were never the same again. This seemed to also spell doom to development in the county. Walker County never seemed to reach the heights to which it had previously soared.

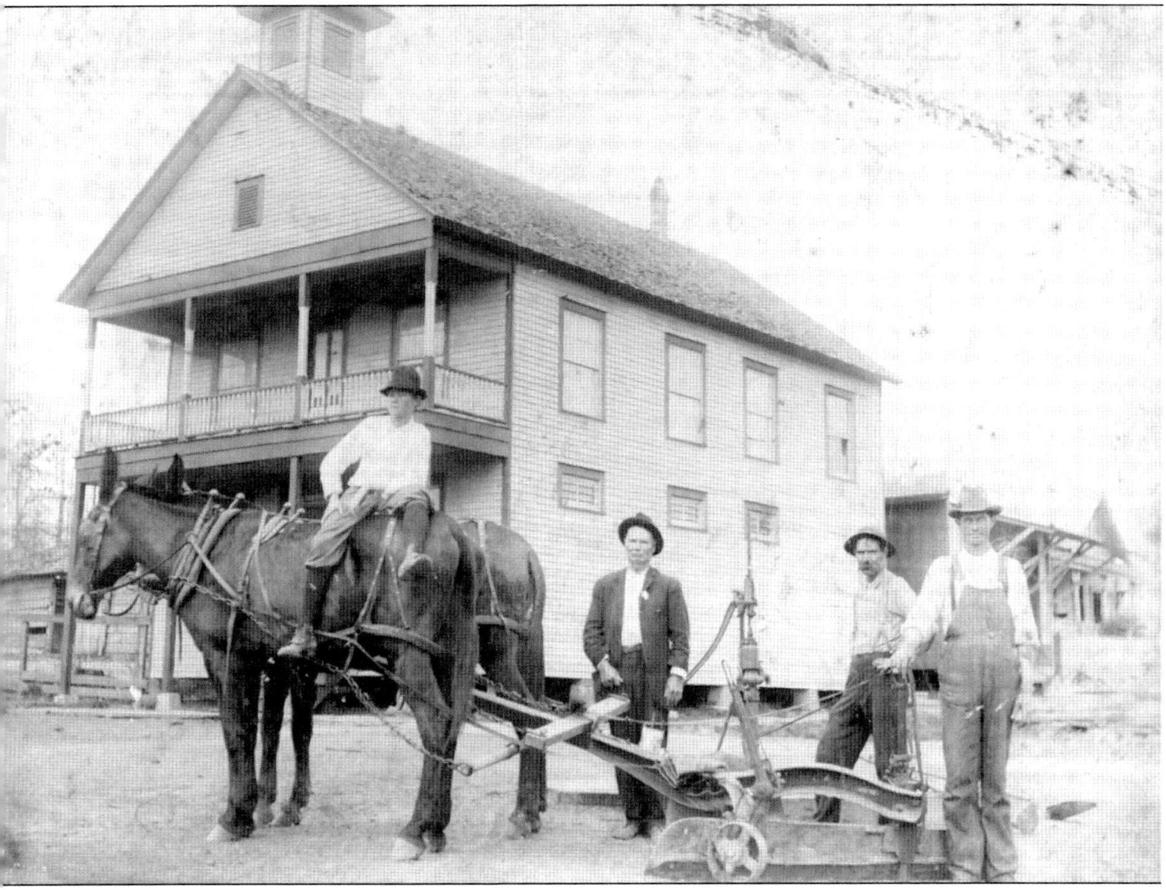

Odd Fellows Lodge, Nauvoo, 1910. Above is the Odd Fellows Lodge that once stood on what is now McDaniel Avenue and Third Street in Nauvoo. The interesting thing in this image is the old horse-drawn road scraper used on the dirt roads. In the background to the right is Dr. Sankey's office. Second from the left, in the dark coat, is the sheriff of Nauvoo, identified by his badge.

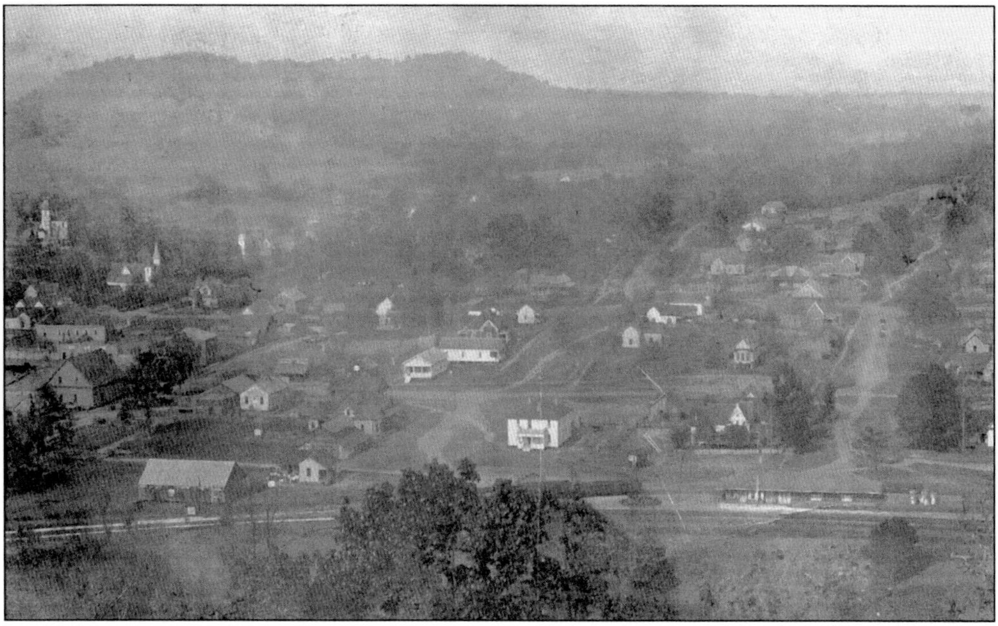

Oakman, c. 1904. The railroad has already made a huge difference in the development of this small town. It was originally known as Day's Gap, then Corry, and then Marietta (to entice Marietta, the wife of a wealthy businessman, to move to this wilderness area). It finally became Oakman in 1894 to honor President Oakman of the Georgia Pacific Railroad Company, who had made a large donation to the town. Notice Day's Gap school in the top left edge of town.

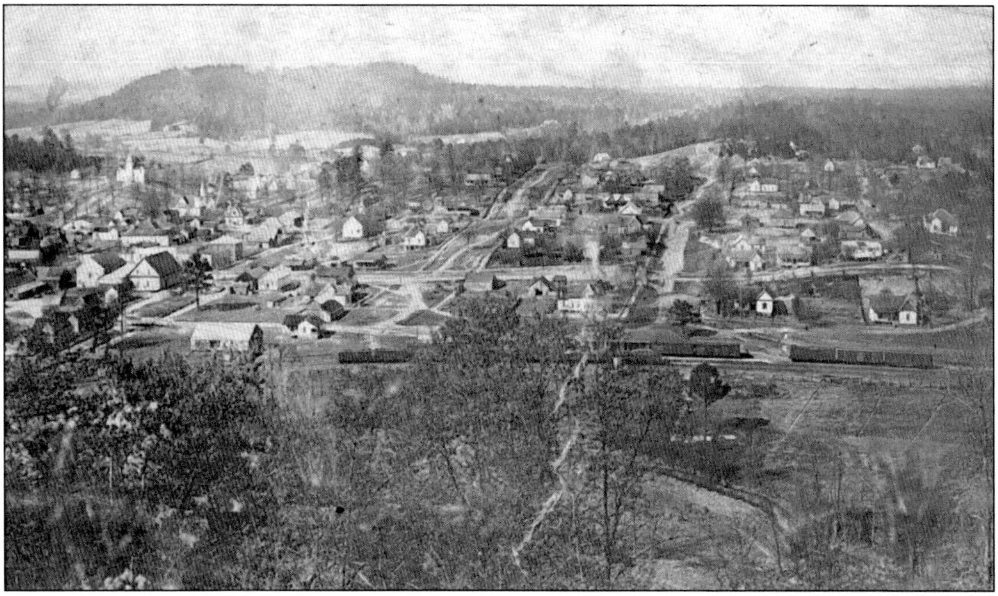

Oakman, Aerial View. This postcard shows the town just five years later, after it had begun its growth spurt brought on by the railroad. It was originally known as Day's Gap in honor of William Byrd Day, who owned the little valley between the mountains. The community was divided down the middle by Main Street; the eastern side was Day's Side and the western side was Corry's Side, named for the "Duke of Day's Gap."

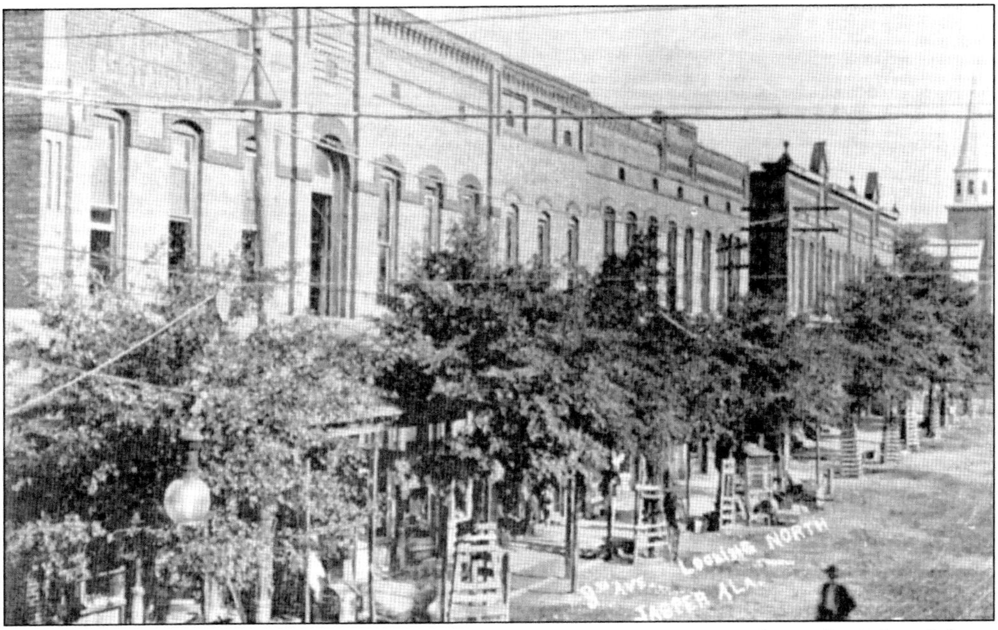

THIRD AVENUE, LOOKING NORTH. This 1908 view of downtown Jasper shows the Palace Saloon & Restaurant (first building on the left) that five years later became Peoples Drug Company. Note the dirt streets and the wooden guards, which kept the horses from eating the trees. The far building on the right is the old Methodist church that was organized in 1826, making it the city's oldest church.

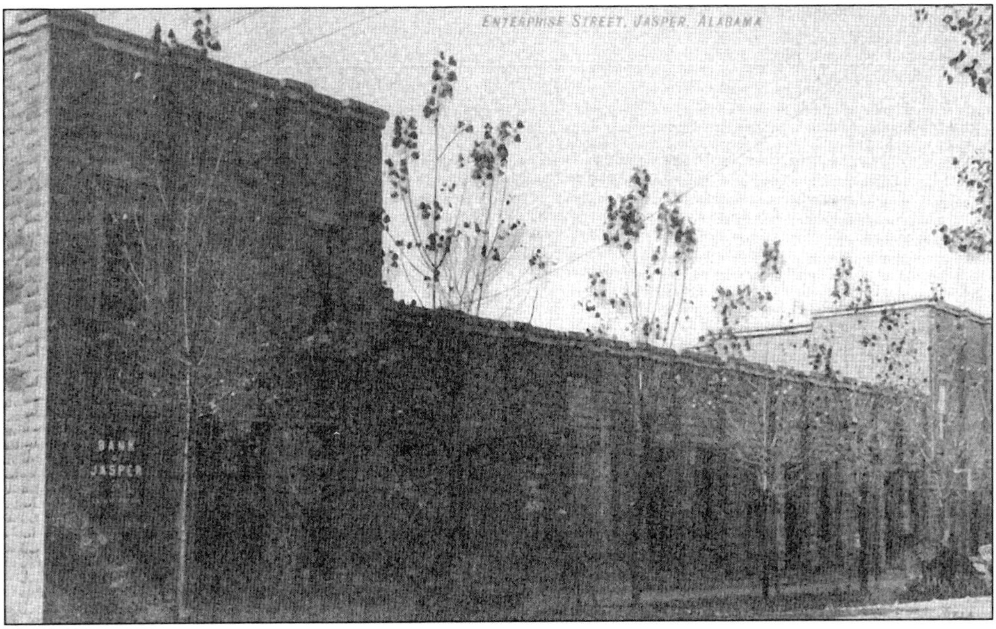

ENTERPRISE STREET, JASPER. The first building on the left is the Bank of Jasper, located on Third Avenue, south of Nineteenth Street. It was organized in 1899 by John H. Cranford, making it the one of oldest banks in the county. He served as the first president of the bank, and his wife served as the first teller. Cranford also opened the First National Bank of Jasper in 1905.

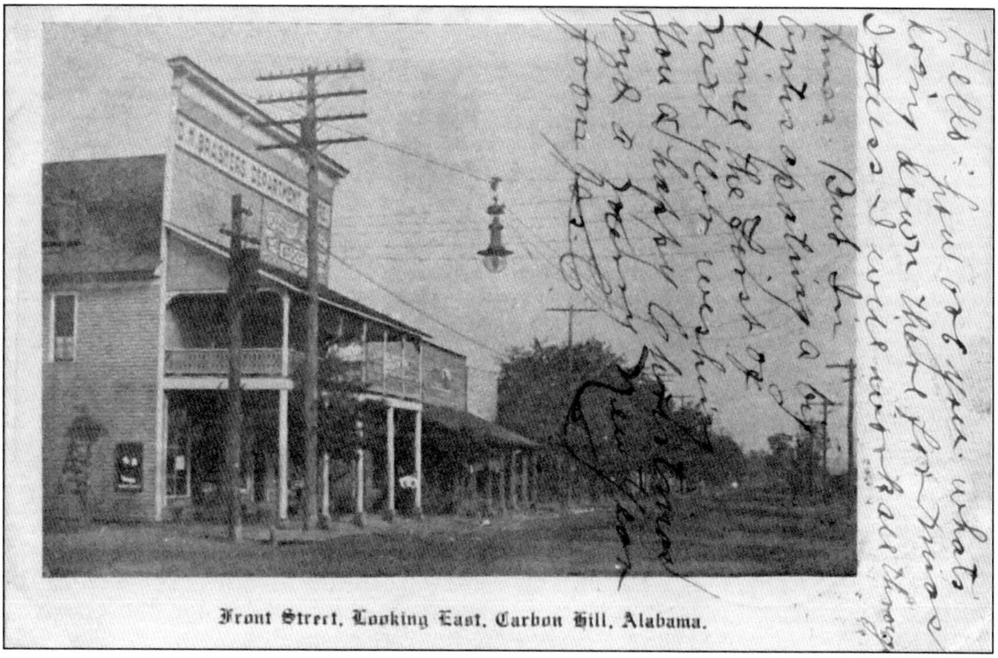

FRONT STREET LOOKING EAST, CARBON HILL. In this view of downtown Carbon Hill, the Brasher Department Store and Hotel is shown on the left. The downstairs was used as a department and hardware store, and the upstairs served as a hotel. Note the unusual street light in the middle of the street. This building now serves as the Front Street Antique Store.

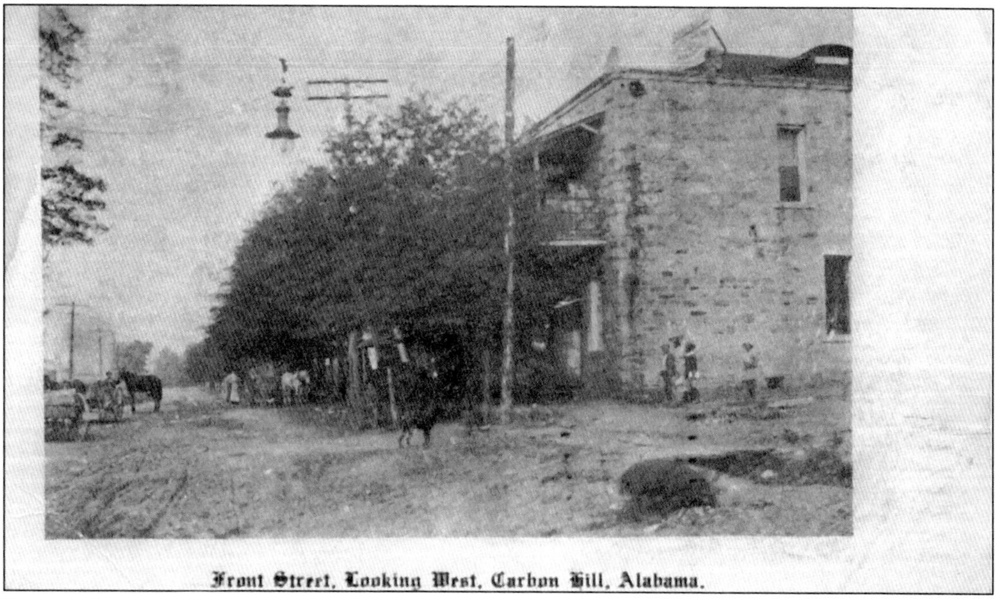

FRONT STREET LOOKING WEST, CARBON HILL. A 1908 postcard of Carbon Hill shows an unidentified building on the right. Many interesting items appear in this picture. Visible are four different wagons, three horses, four children, people on the balcony, a black dog, and most unusual of all, the pig "rooting" in the dirt street in the right foreground. Front Street is now Highway 78 through Carbon Hill.

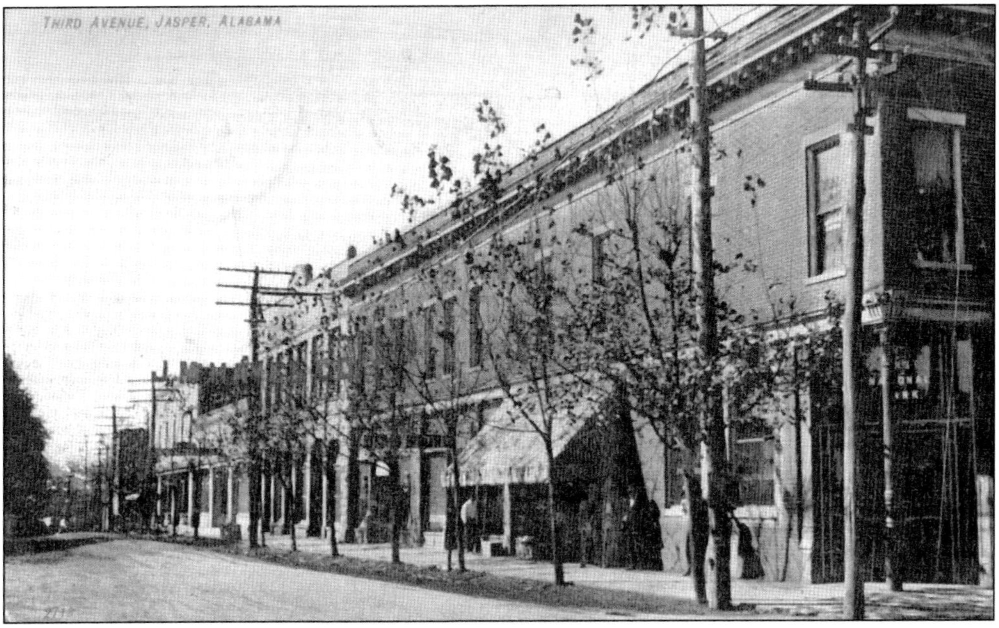

THIRD AVENUE LOOKING SOUTH. The building on the right is First National Bank of Jasper. Located on the southwest corner of Third Avenue and Nineteenth Street, it was formed by "Cap'n" Jack Cranford. Located next to it is Hayes Dry Goods, then Ballenger's Grocery, followed by a number of dentist and doctors' offices. This part of the block is now home to G. May Furniture Company.

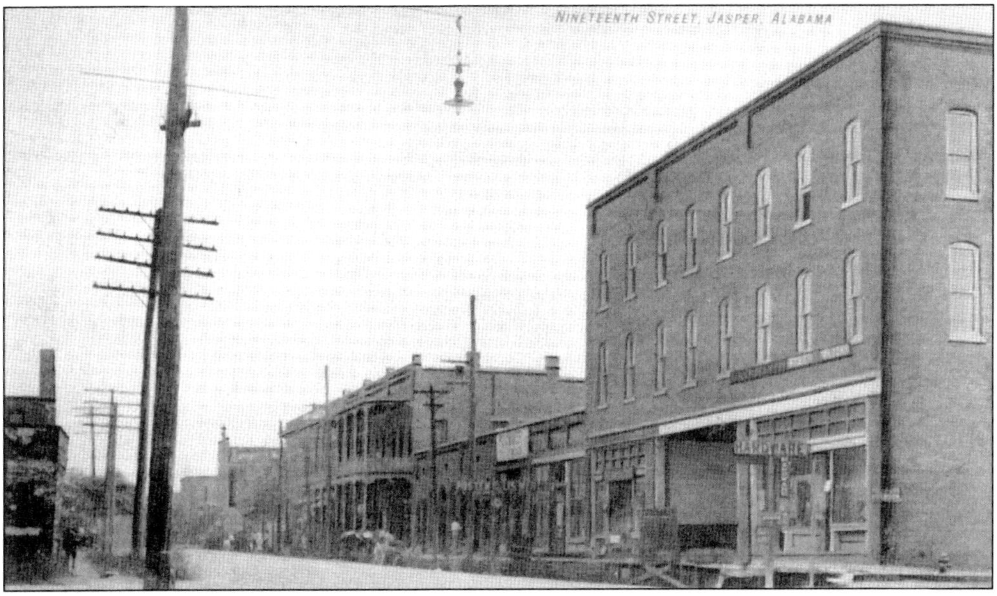

NINETEENTH STREET, LOOKING EAST. The building on the right is a hardware store advertising Weber Wagons and has a pool room located in the back. The next building is the Posten Ellis Mercantile Company. The building in the middle of the card with the balcony is the Jasper Inn, one of Jasper's many hotels, and owned by Jack Cranford. Notice that the streets are still unpaved in 1910.

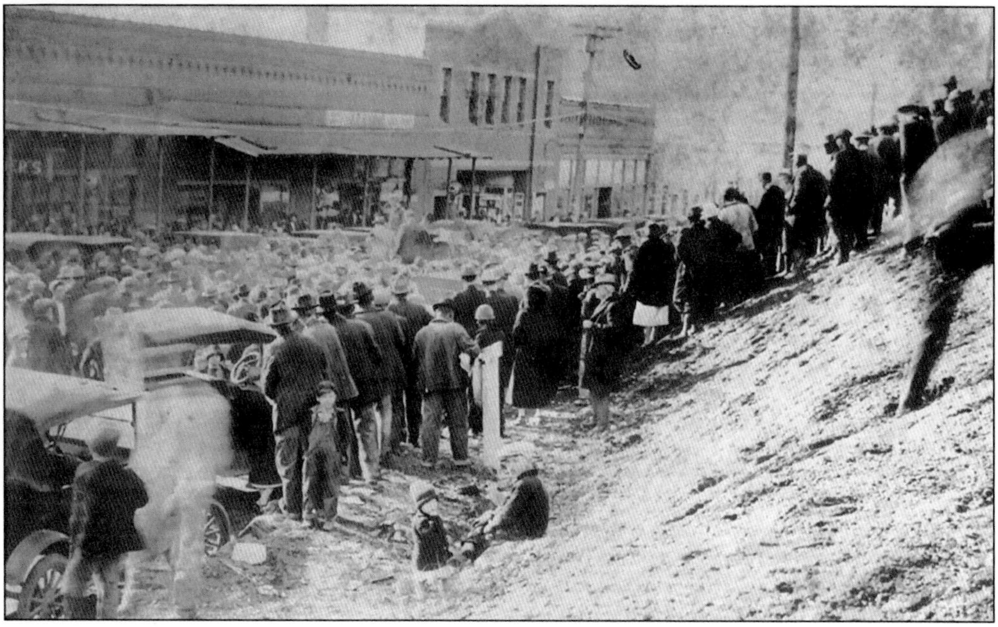

Dora Street Scene, 1925. This huge crowd has gathered in downtown Dora for the give-away of a new Model T Ford. The crowd is gathered in front of Palmer's Mercantile Building on a Saturday morning in 1925, with dreams of owning the new automobile, which is being given away by Dora Motor Company's owner George A. Averitt. People have overflowed the street all the way up the hill to the railroad tracks.

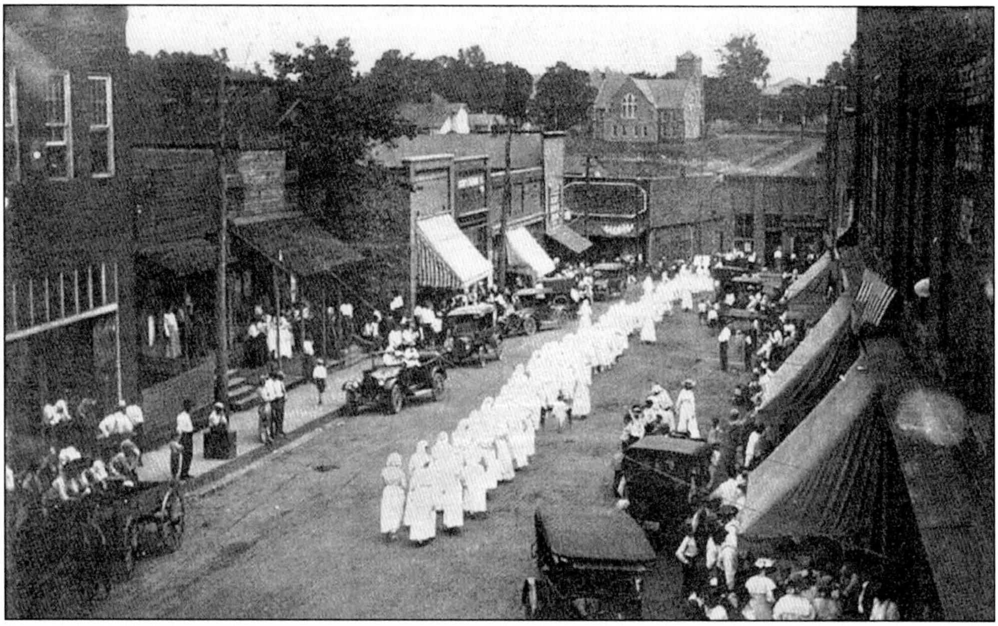

Armistice Day Parade, Cordova. Red Cross nurses from Walker County march in a parade on November 11, 1918. They are part of the festivities celebrating the end of World War I. This parade is headed south down Main Street, and the Long Memorial Church can be seen in the background. The large building on the left is the old Tallulah Hotel.

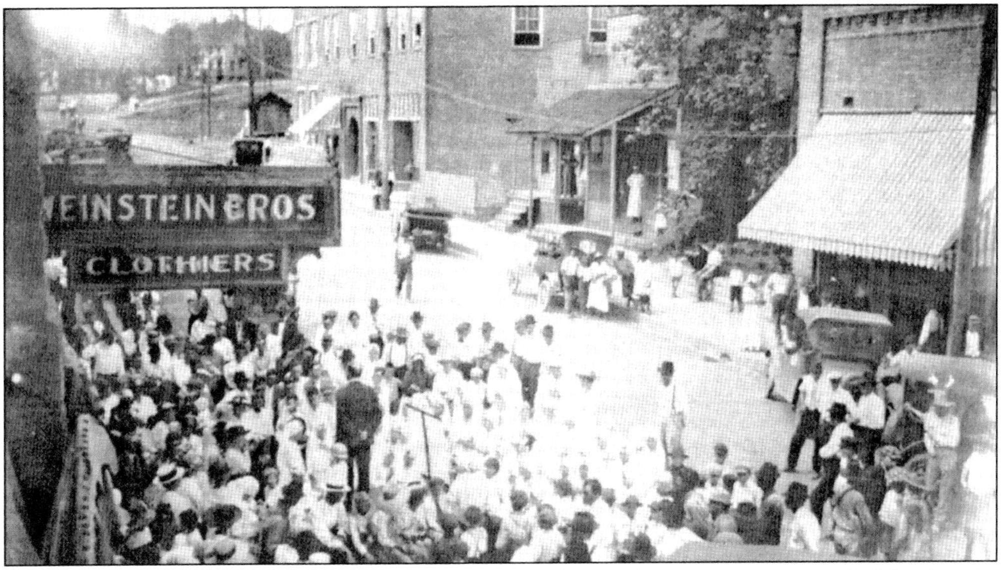

DOWNTOWN GATHERING, CORDOVA. This card shows the Armistice Day Celebration in Cordova. A large crowd has gathered outside the Weinstein Brothers Clothiers Store to listen to political speeches on the future of America. Will the victory in the Great War bring an end to war in the 20th century? The beautiful old Tallulah Hotel, seen in the top middle, is now in complete disrepair and in desperate need of restoration.

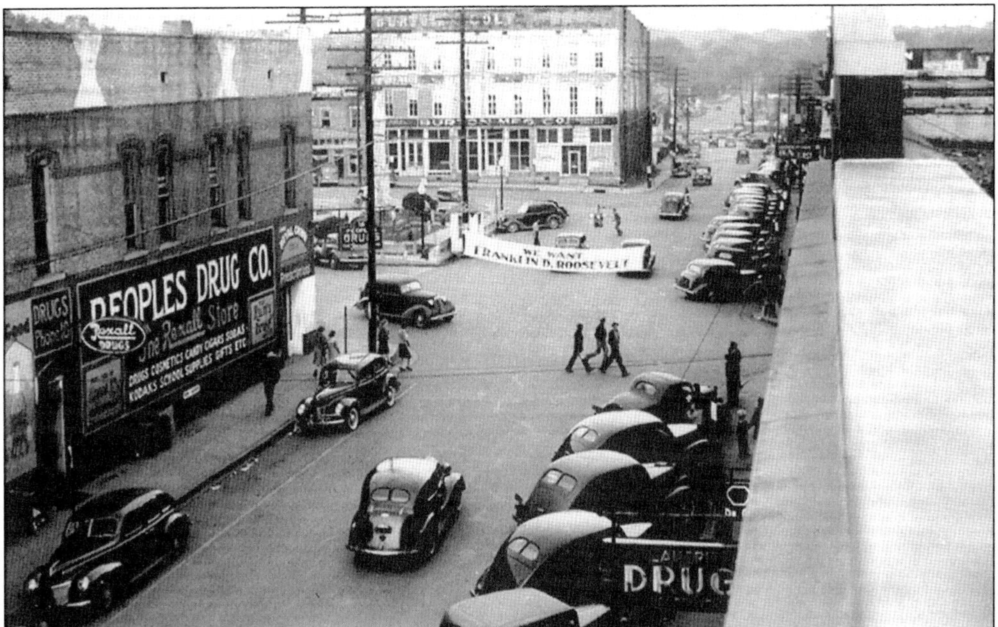

ELECTION TIME, JASPER. A view of Nineteenth Street looking east shows a banner supporting the Democratic nominee for President. The sign reads, "We Want Franklin D. Roosevelt." Pictured on the left is the Peoples Drug Company, the Burton Building is in the middle background, and on the right is Landrip's Drug. Landrip produced many Walker County postcards. Note the choice of colors in cars.

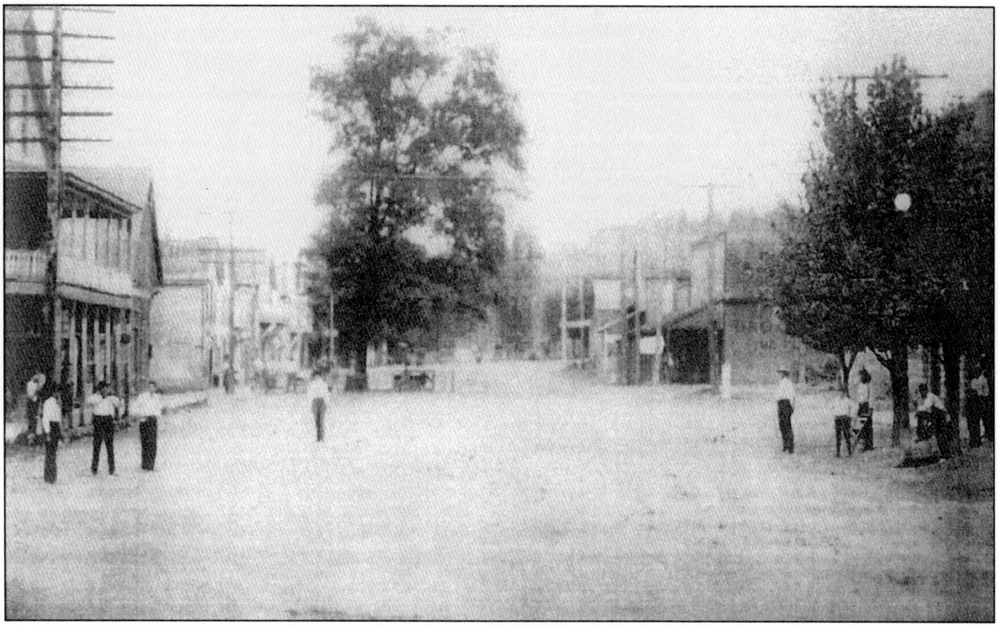

MAIN STREET, OAKMAN. This early 1900s picture shows the unpaved Main Street through Oakman. Note the man in the middle on the left side of the street: is he pointing a rifle at the men on the right side of the street? This thriving town had a stagecoach route running from Oakman to Jasper to South Lowell to Birmingham, carrying goods and people in all directions.

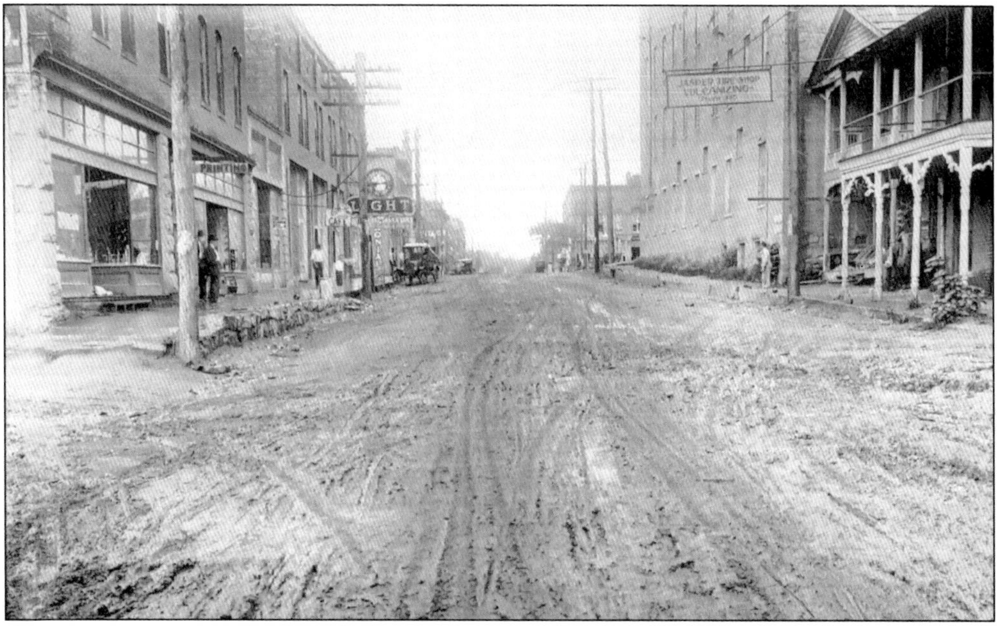

NINETEENTH STREET, JASPER. This gives a glimpse into the past of what Jasper's busiest street looked like in the early 1900s. Note the numerous wagon and buggy tracks in the mud of the street. Identifiable on the left are the Barber Hand Printing Shop and a café. On the right are the Jasper Tire/Vulcanizing Shop and the Jasper Inn. Note the phone number of the Vulcanizing Shop—335.

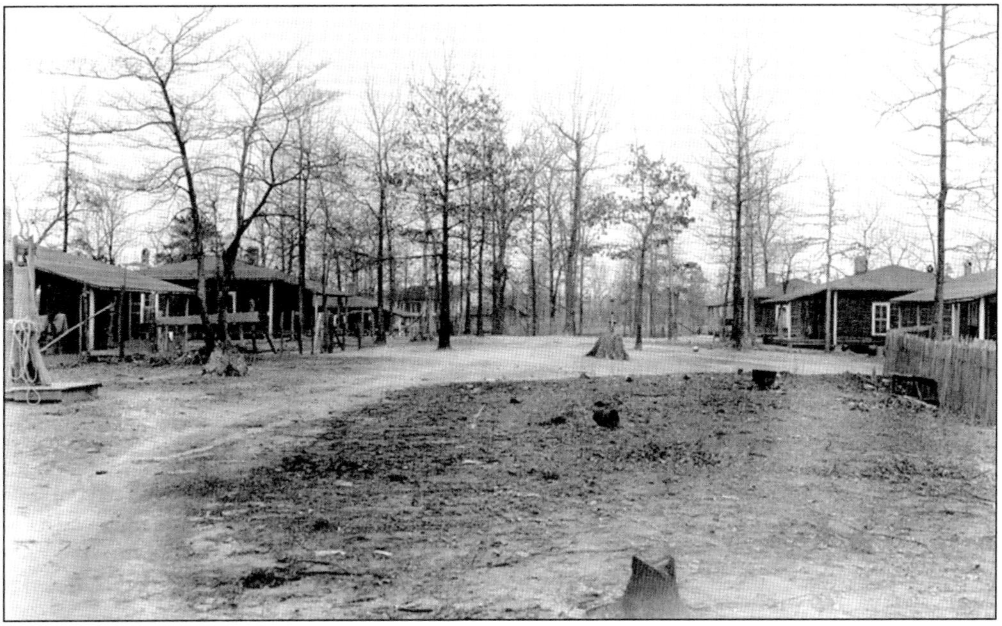

Coal Company Village, Empire. A street scene from the white employees' section of the company town is shown here. The company provided equal but opposite facilities for the black and white workers. They had separate housing, churches, schools, and even movie houses. The only place they were together was in the mines, where both races were treated equally and worked long, hard, backbreaking hours digging the coal.

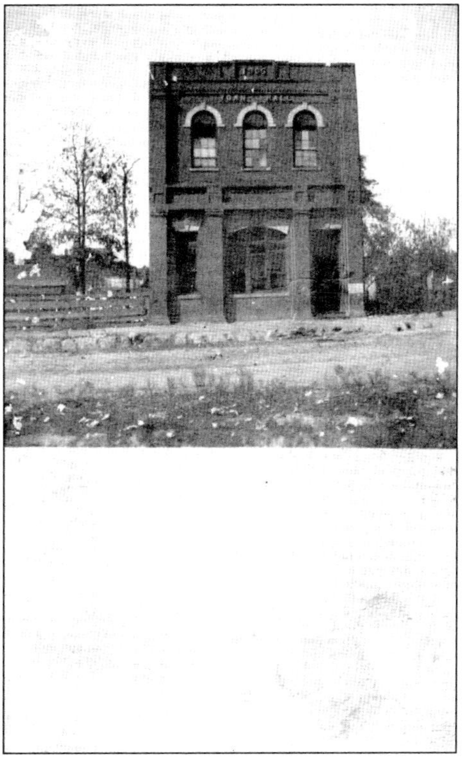

Town Hall, Carbon Hill. The town hall was built in 1906 on Second Avenue in downtown Carbon Hill. The upstairs was used as the city jail, and the downstairs was the police chief's office. It was later used as the city library, and the last librarian was Mrs. Elsie Collins. The building was damaged by a tornado in 2002, and it was then torn down in April 2003.

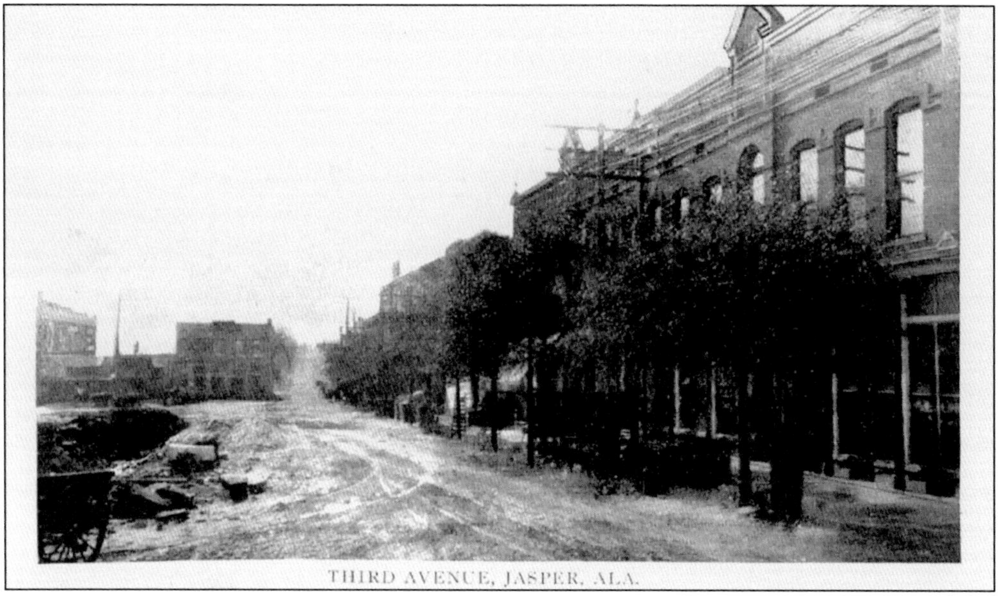

THIRD AVENUE LOOKING SOUTH, JASPER. This 1908 view of Jasper shows the condition of the roads all over the county at that time. The roads became terrible as the weather worsened. The construction area on the left side of the photo shows the new courthouse as it nears completion. The building facing us at the end of the street is the Long Drug Store and Telephone Exchange.

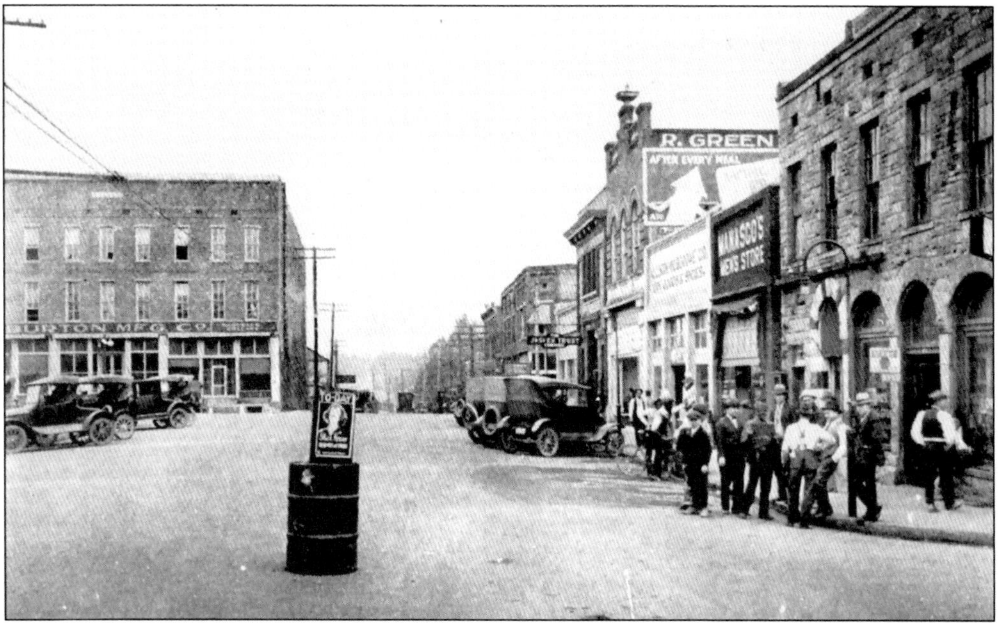

NINETEENTH STREET LOOKING EAST, JASPER. This view was taken in the mid-1920s from the looks of the cars lining the street. The crowd of men may be discussing the weather, economy, or politics. The building on the left is the Burton Building, and on the right are Manasco's Men Store, R. Green's Store, and the Jasper Trust Company. The barrel is used as a street divider and for advertising.

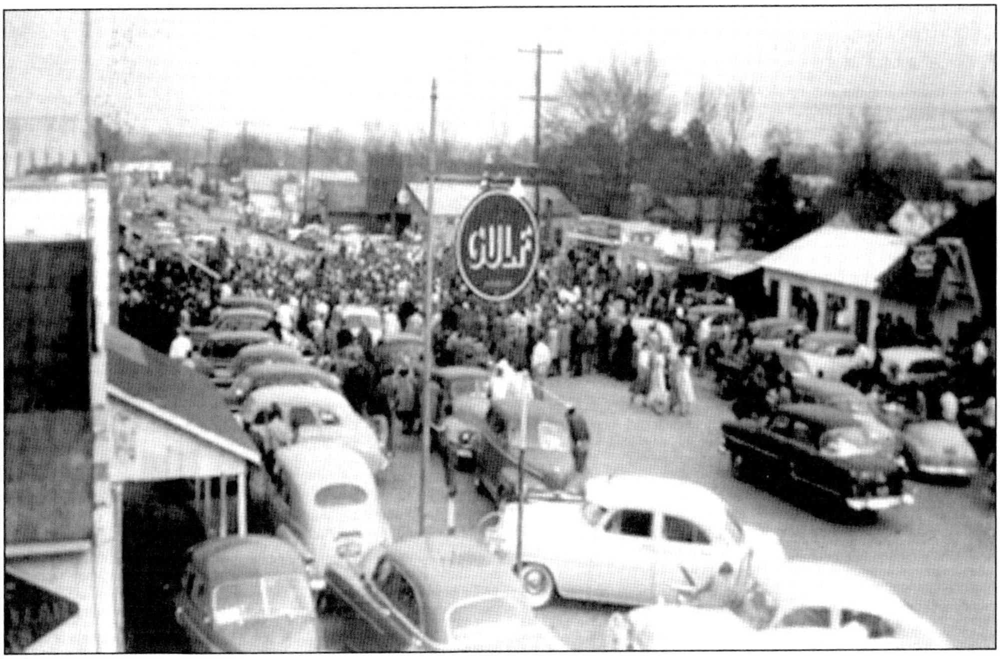

STREET SCENE, SUMITON. This scene of downtown Sumiton in the 1950s shows a huge crowd gathered on a Saturday morning in the middle of Highway 78 for a give-away by local merchants. The crowd would block the main route from Memphis to Birmingham for two hours, and all traffic would come to a standstill, irritating many truck drivers.

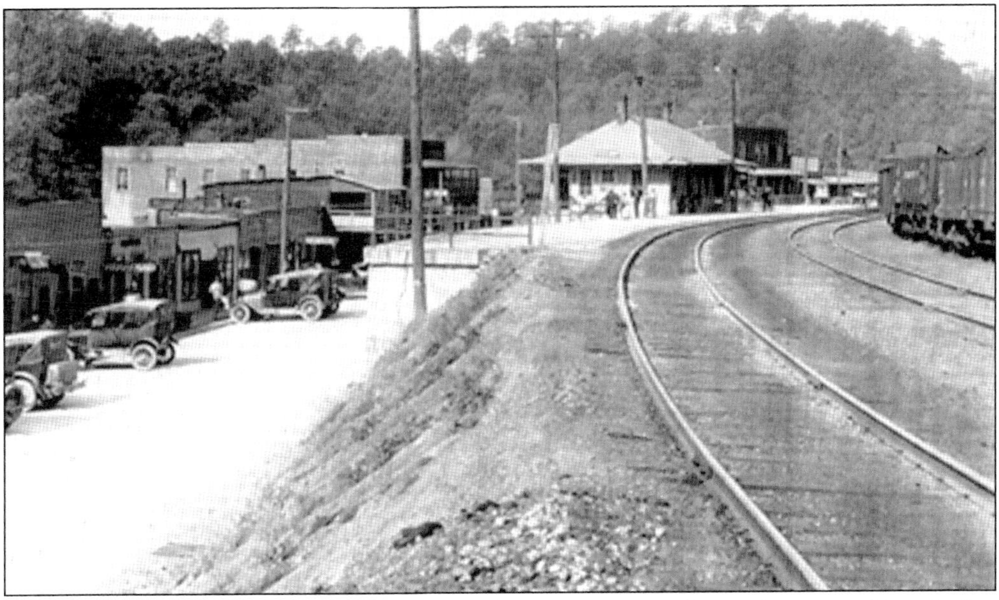

DOWNTOWN DORA, *c.* 1920. This post–World War I picture shows downtown Dora in her glory days. The building in the middle, at the top of the hill, is the old Dora Train Depot, built in 1912 after the original depot burned. Main Street, shown here, would become a hive of activity every Saturday when the people came to town to celebrate their day off work. Of course, no one worked on Sundays.

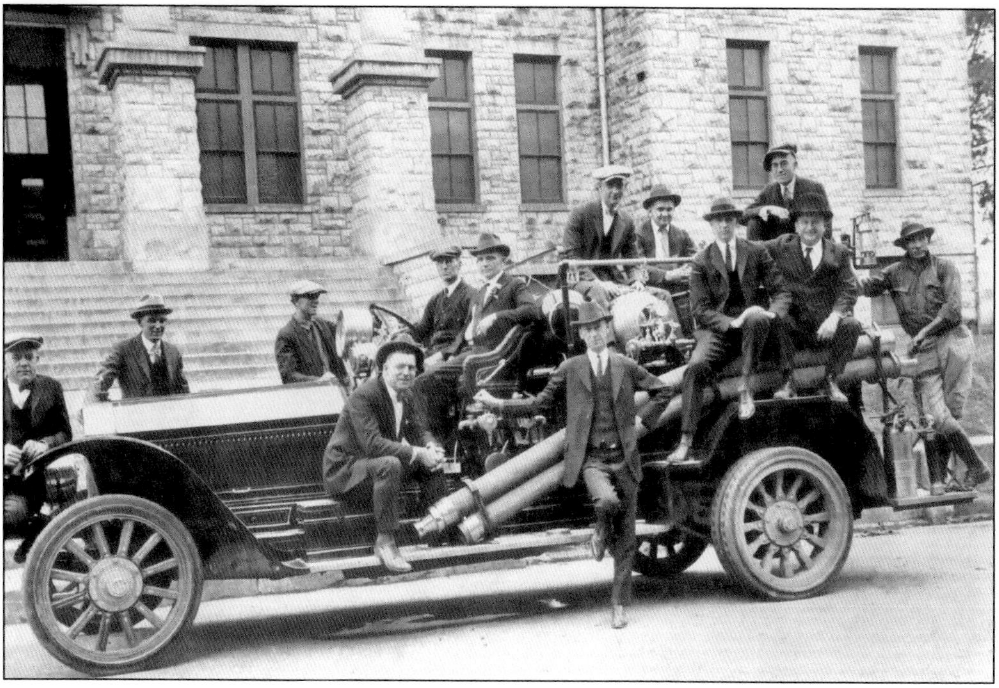

New Fire Truck, Jasper. Here is the new fire truck purchased in 1924 displayed in front of the 1908 Walker County Courthouse. The city officials pictured are, from left to right, J.D. McDaniel, John Hutto, E.V. Lewis, Howard Turner, Chief Lee Palmer, Charlie Long, Jim Christian, Charles R. Cranford, Tom Edgil, W.G. Clapp, Mose Newburger, and George Blevins.

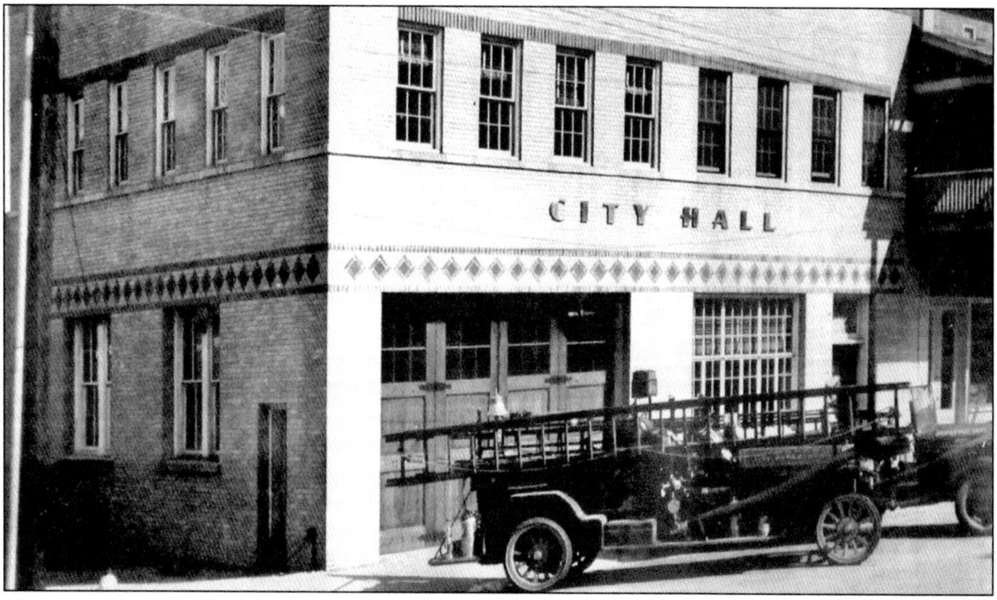

City Hall and Fire Department, Jasper. Two hook-and-ladder trucks are parked in front of city hall, located on the east side of Second Avenue. Fire was one of the deadliest forces the early citizens faced, and a well-equipped fire department was a necessity to keep fire from spreading from one structure to the next and perhaps destroying an entire block of businesses.

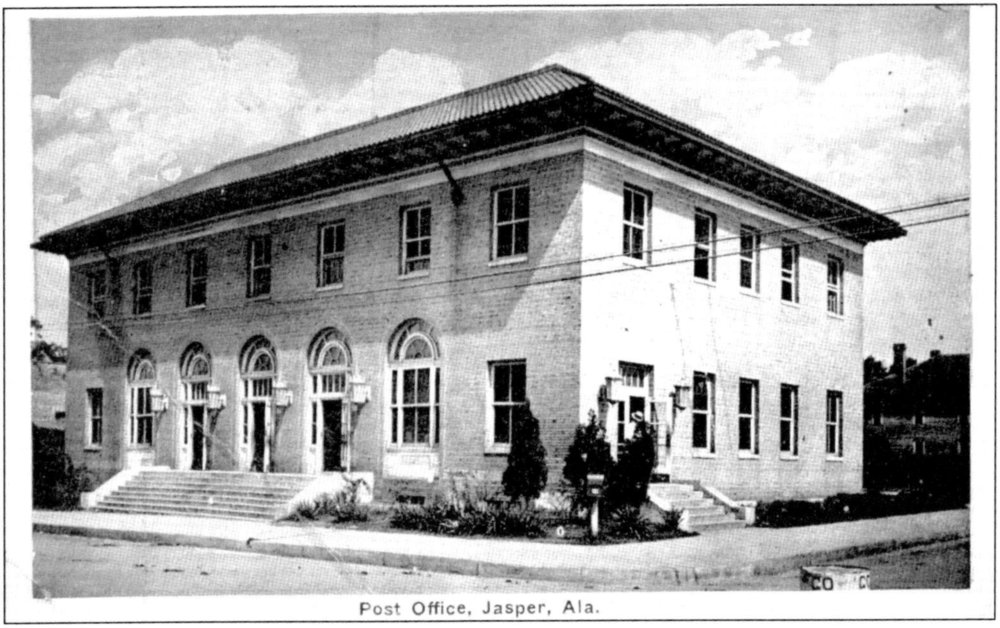

U.S. Post Office, Jasper. The cornerstone for the post office was laid in 1917 during the administration of President Woodrow Wilson, and the building was completed in 1919 at a cost of $100,000. It was erected on the northwest corner of Fourth Avenue and Nineteenth Street and served as the post office until 1968, when the City of Jasper purchased the building to use as the new city hall.

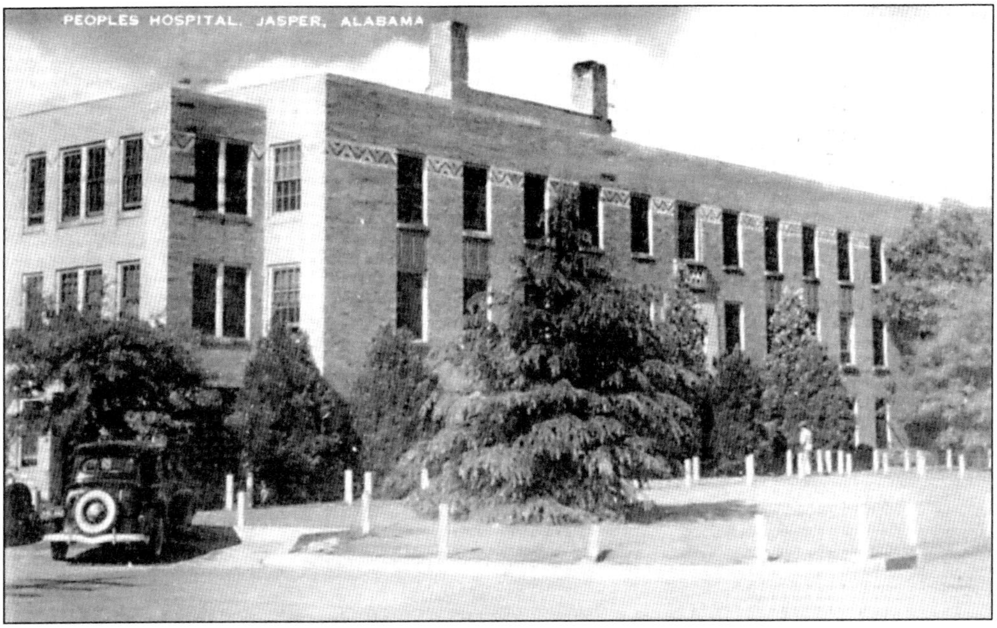

Peoples Hospital, c. 1940. This hospital, built by the Works Project Administration (WPA), was completed in 1936, thanks to President Franklin D. Roosevelt's New Deal and the never-ending work and support of Dr. Roy Hare. Peoples Hospital was located on Eighteenth Street. It was torn down and has now been replaced by the Community Health Services Inc. building.

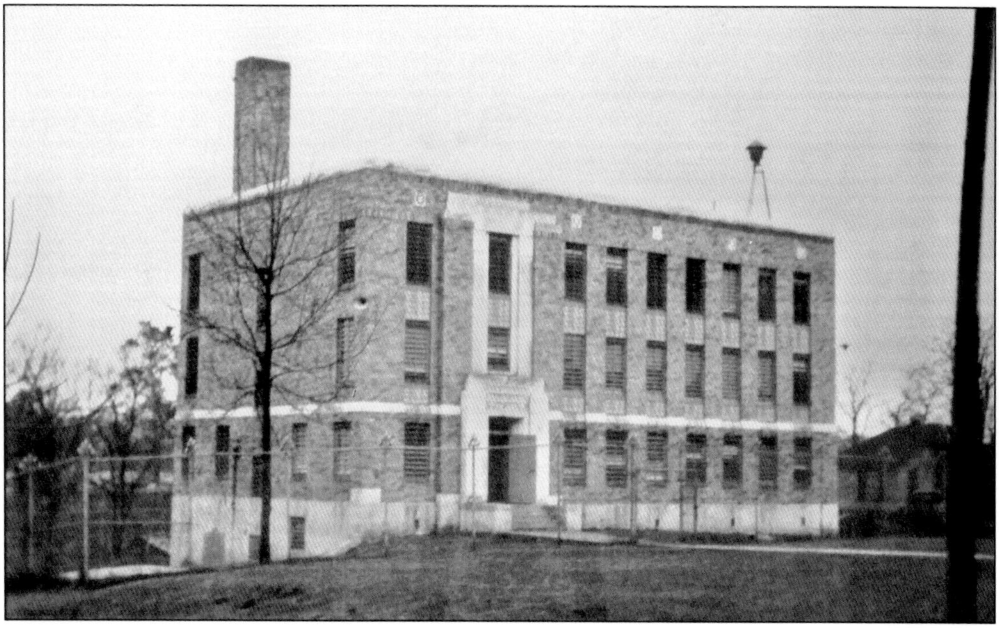

WALKER COUNTY JAIL, JASPER. This old county jail was built in 1936 as part of the WPA (Works Projects Administration). It was used until 1974 when the prisoners were moved to the jail annex at the Walker County Courthouse. They were then moved into the new county facility on Second Avenue across from the post office. Jasper's original jail was located on the west side of First Avenue.

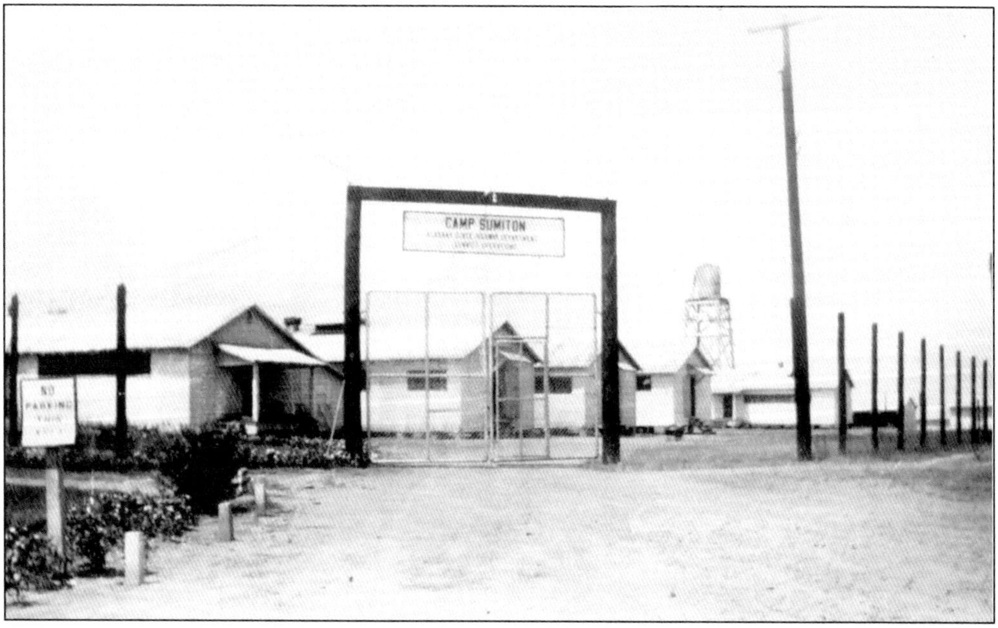

PRISON CAMP, SUMITON. The Sumiton Prison, located on Convict Road in Sumiton, was established in 1948 to be used as a minimum-security prison. The City of Sumiton purchased it from the Walker County Commission, and it is now used as the Sumiton City Maintenance Department. Part of the property is now in the process of being developed as an athletic field.

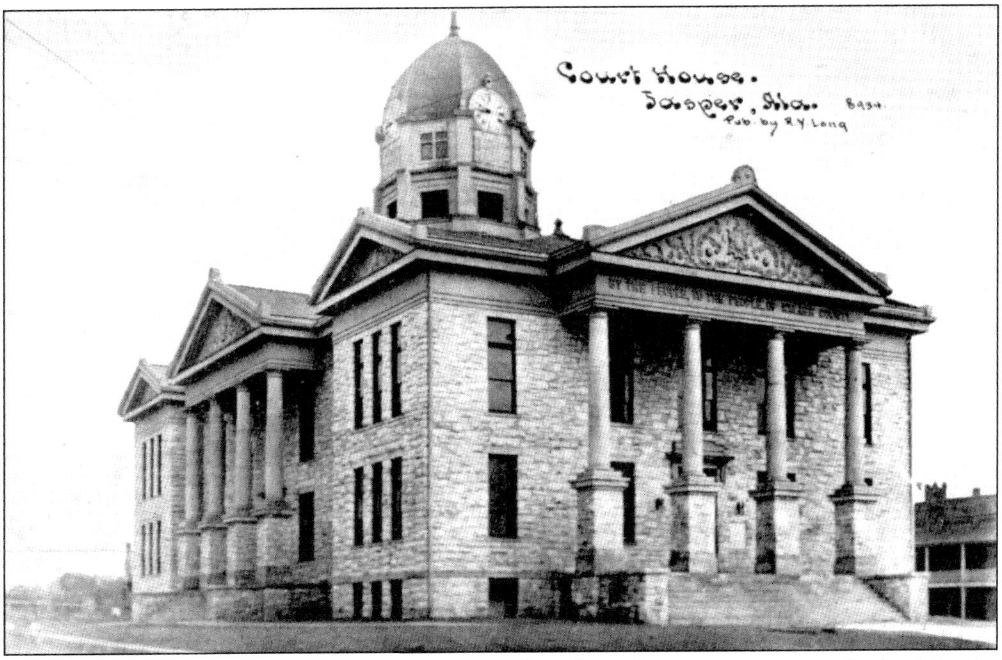

WALKER COUNTY COURTHOUSE, *c.* 1910. Dr. Edward Gordon Musgrove gave the land for the entire city of Jasper in exchange for it becoming the county seat. Part of this land was used for the construction of a courthouse, a church, and numerous businesses. The original land given by Musgrove has served as the location for four different courthouses, including the present one.

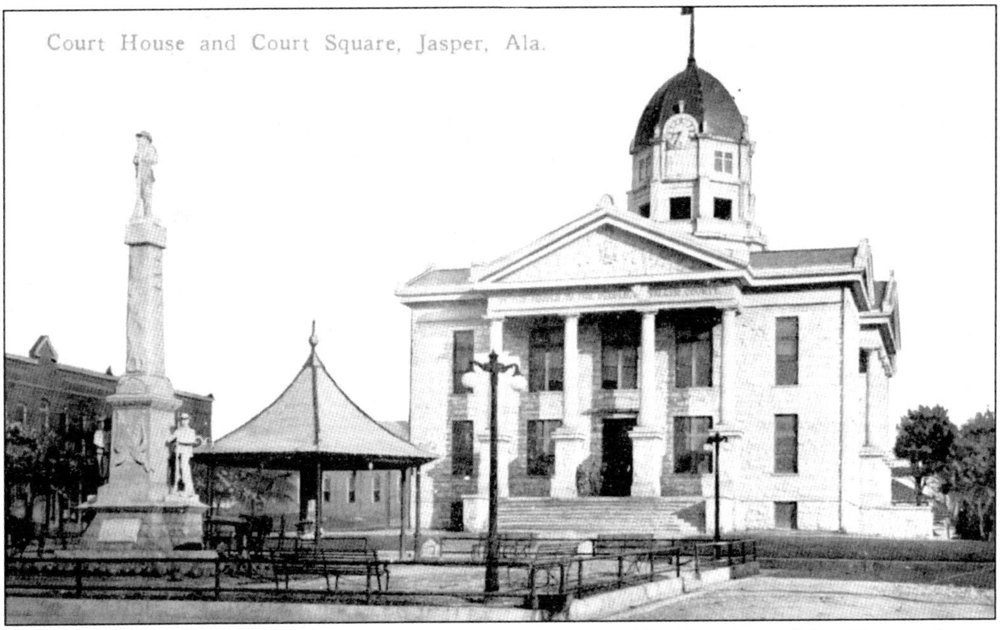

COURTHOUSE, GAZEBO, CONFEDERATE MONUMENT, 1914. The beautiful old courthouse is shown in 1914 with two new additions. The gazebo, with an artesian well beneath it, and the Confederate Monument, placed on the square in 1908 by the United Daughters of the Confederacy, gave Walker County a town square that was second to none in the South.

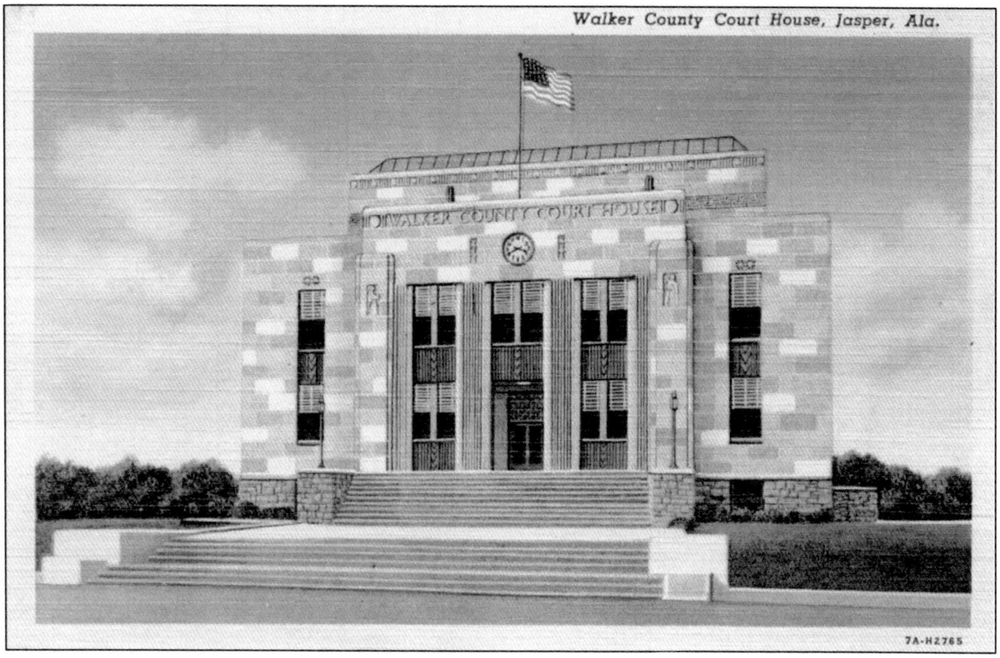

NEW WALKER COUNTY COURTHOUSE, 1933. The old Romanesque courthouse burned on January 12, 1932. This new building was built upon the foundation of the previous one. The new courthouse was described as "an awkward lumpish square of limestone in the heart of the town." It definitely does not compare aesthetically with the old courthouse building.

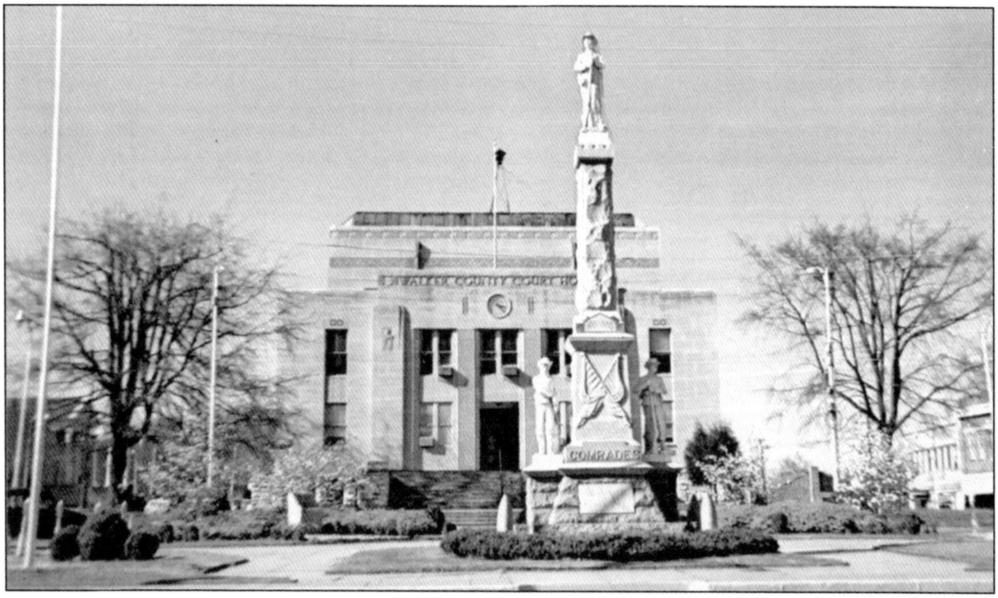

MODERN WALKER COUNTY COURTHOUSE, *c.* 1990. This modern view of the courthouse shows the building and the square as they appear today. The building was substantially damaged in the tornado of 1974 but was rebuilt. The only thing that remains of the former courthouse's glory is the Confederate Monument. Gone are the gazebo (to Walker College) and the artesian well (to Fourth Avenue).

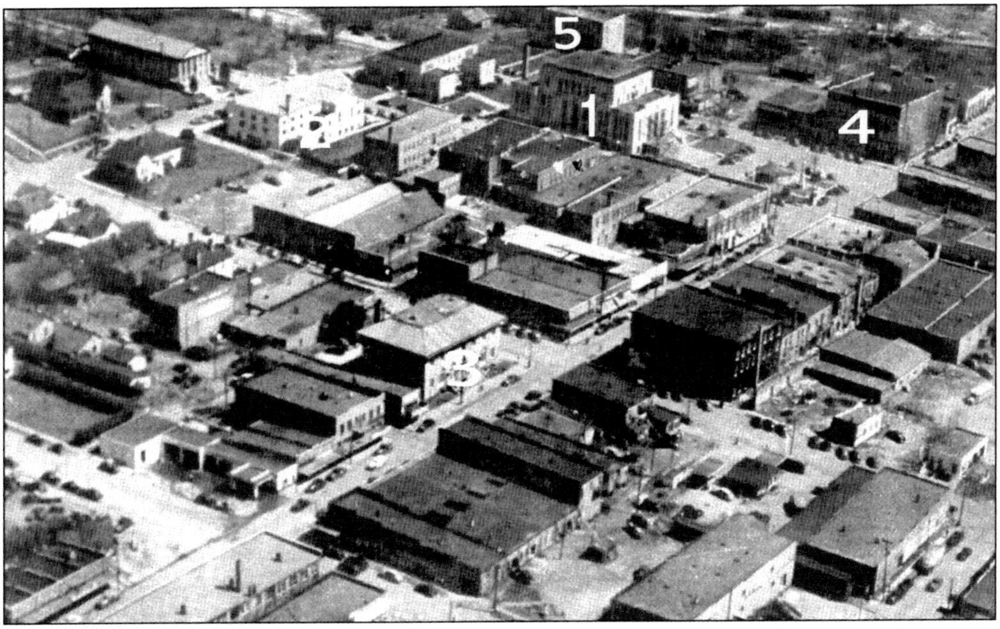

AERIAL VIEW OF JASPER, 1946. A view in 1946 shows the progress and growth of the city. The (1) Walker County Courthouse, (2) United Methodist Church, (3) post office (now city hall), (4) Burton Building, and the (5) county jail (which no longer exists) are clearly visible. An aerial view of Jasper today would show a much different picture because of fires, tornadoes, and progress.

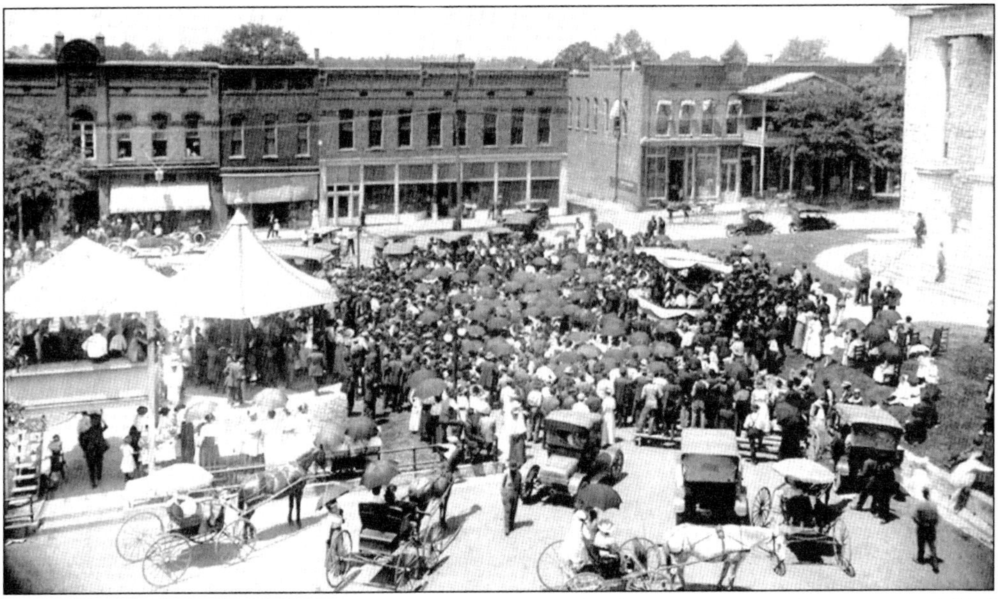

CROWD IN THE SQUARE, *c.* 1910. This classic view is looking west across the square to Third Avenue. From an early map of Jasper, it is known that the building on the left is a grocery and meat market. Then, to the right, are two general stores and, finally, a drug store. The building with the covered porch is thought to be a hotel. Note the two-story bandstand, gazebo, horse and wagons, and old automobiles.

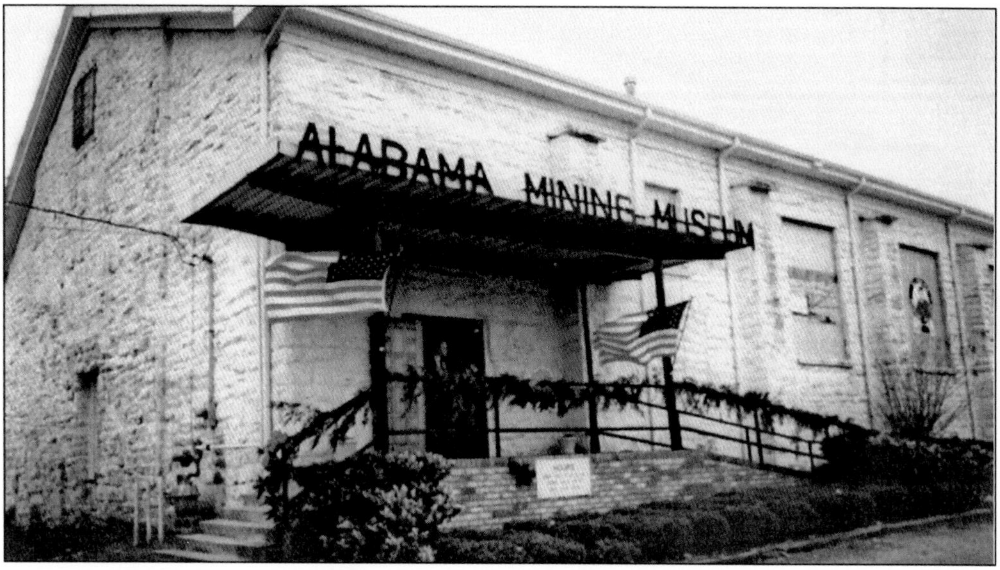

ALABAMA MINING MUSEUM, 2001. The Alabama Mining Museum is housed in the old Dora High School gymnasium that was built in 1930. The museum opened in 1964 and is an authentic representation of the history of mining and related industries. Numerous exhibits include the old #29 steam locomotive, the Oakman Depot, and the Wyatt Elementary School. The director of the museum is Bonnie Groves.

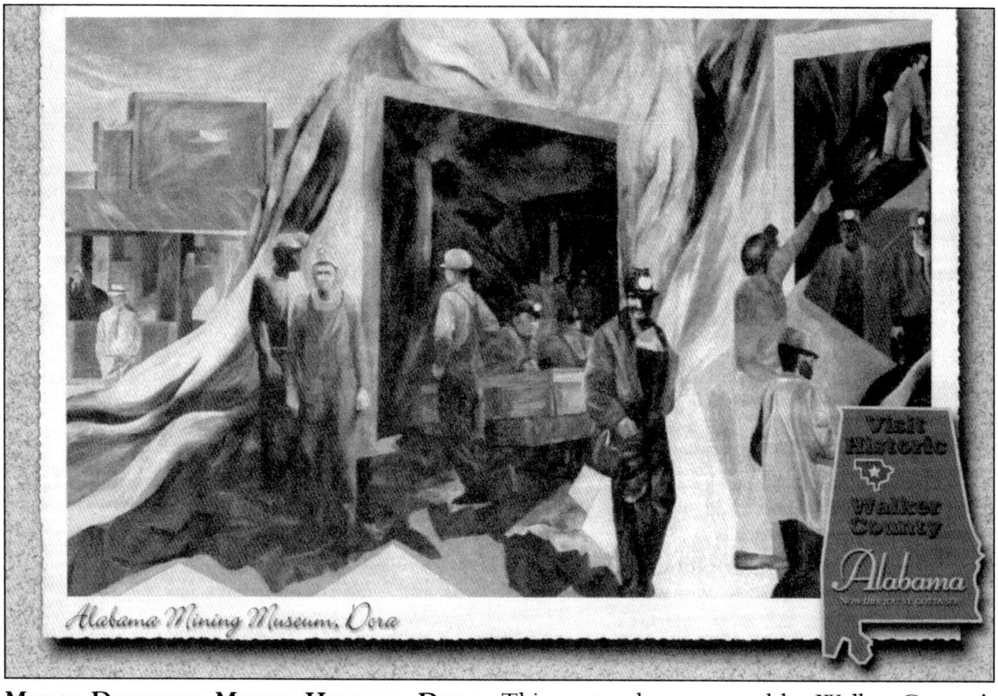

MURAL DEPICTING MINING HISTORY, DORA. This postcard was created by Walker County's Chamber of Commerce in 2003 as one of a group of six that were representative of the county. The mural shown here, painted by Vince Wasson, depicts the history of mining from 1890 to 1940. The director of the Walker County Chamber of Commerce is Linda Lewis.

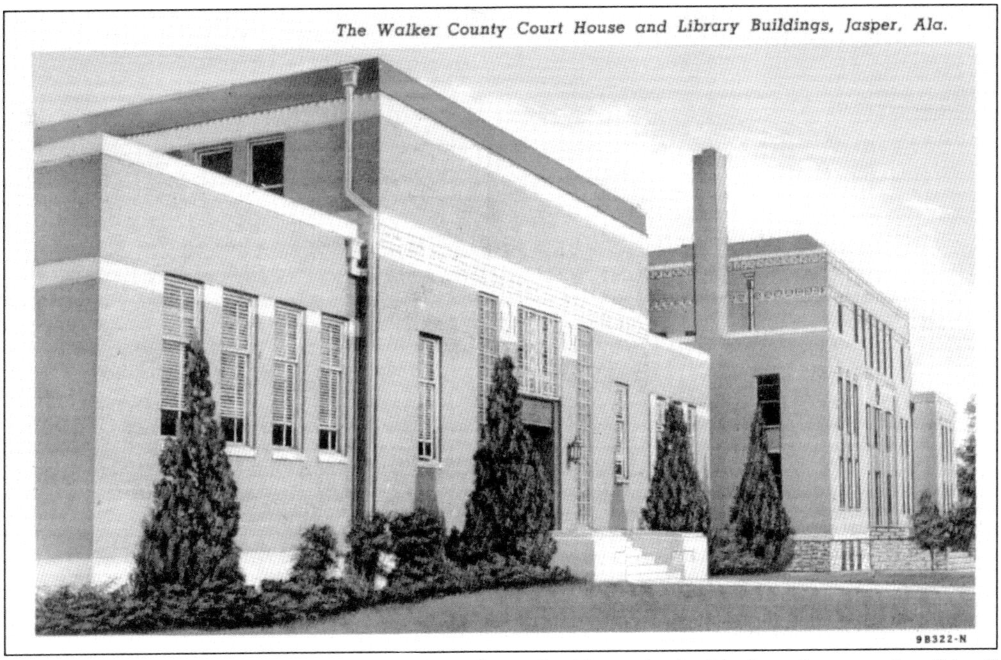

WALKER COUNTY LIBRARY, *c.* 1965. This is how the library looked before the tornado of April 3, 1974, damaged it so severely that it could not be repaired. The library was built in 1937 by the WPA and was called the Walker County Public Library, but it later changed its name to the Jasper Public Library, which also houses The Carl Elliott Regional Library. The director of the present library is Colleen Miller.

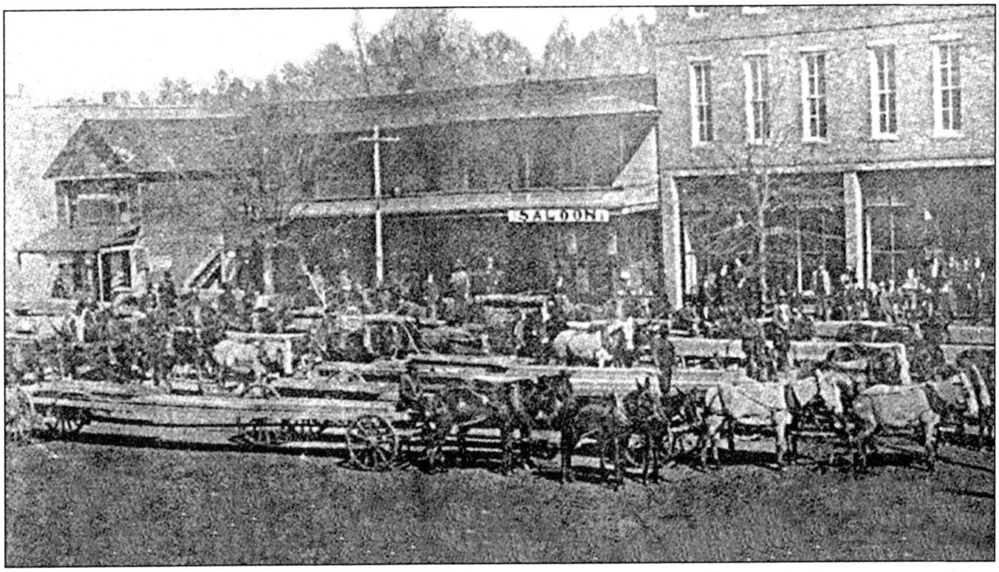

DOWNTOWN JASPER, 1900. This is a scene of a typical Saturday gathering in Jasper across from the county courthouse. Shown from left to right are the Hogue Hotel, Saxon Hotel (which later became the Green Top Hotel), and the Long Building (which later became the Burton Building). Mule power brought timbers into town, where the wood was sold to mills or to individuals who were constructing downtown buildings and homes.

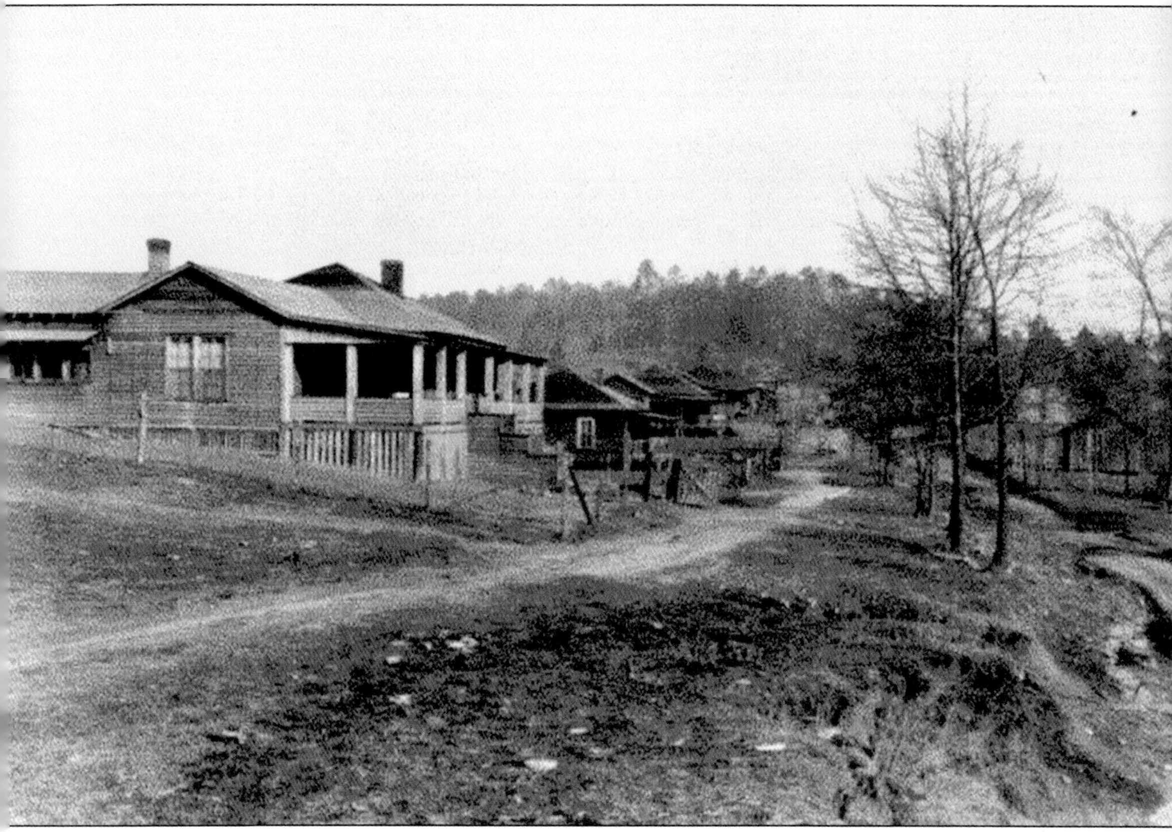

Mining Camp Street Scene, Sipsey. This street scene of the DeBardeleben Coal Mining Camp at Sipsey in the early 1920s shows the white housing section of the camp. The name of this mining community, "Sipsey," is a Choctaw word meaning "poplar tree" that was probably derived from the numerous poplar trees that grew along the banks of the Sipsey River. Henry T. DeBardeleben, the founder of the company, and his two partners Newton Hanson and Milton H. Fies, operated the company that mined the Black Creek coal seam. The company built 200 homes to be rented by the miners, who earned $1.50 to $3 for a 10-hour day, a much higher wage than the other mines paid. The camps had segregated but equal facilities, as was the custom of that day. The four-room houses rented for $6 per month, and white meat was 5¢ a pound. Many families supplemented their food supply with wild animals and fish from the surrounding woodlands.

Two

Businesses

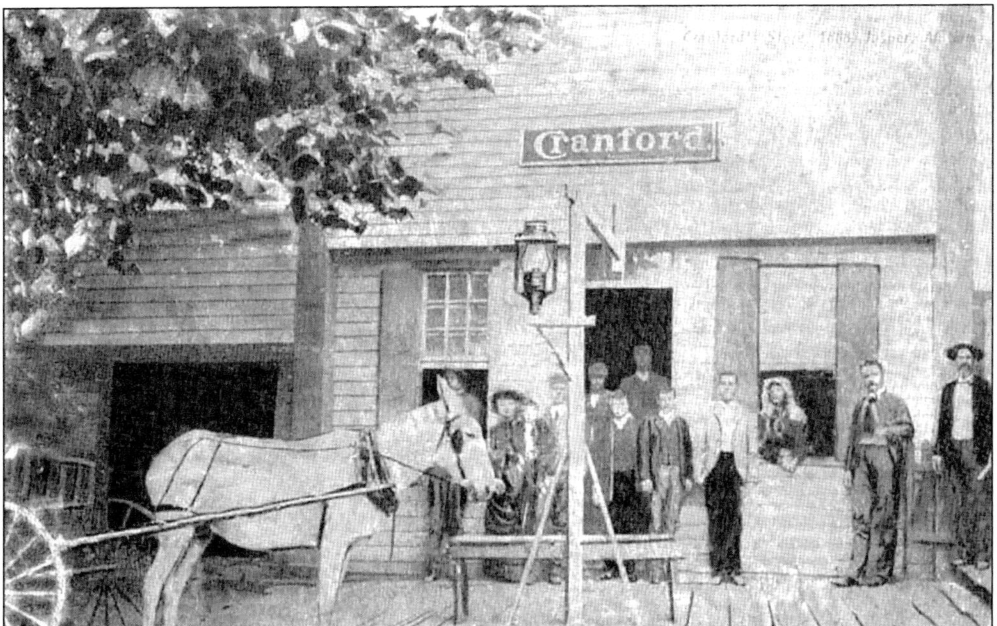

Cranford's Store, 1888. John H. Cranford got his start in Jasper as a clerk in B.M. Long's Mercantile Store. After teaching for a short while, he opened the above store in 1888 on Third Avenue and was one of Jasper's most successful businessmen. Many of Jasper's older citizens have worked in one of his businesses at some time. This is the oldest postcard in the author's collection.

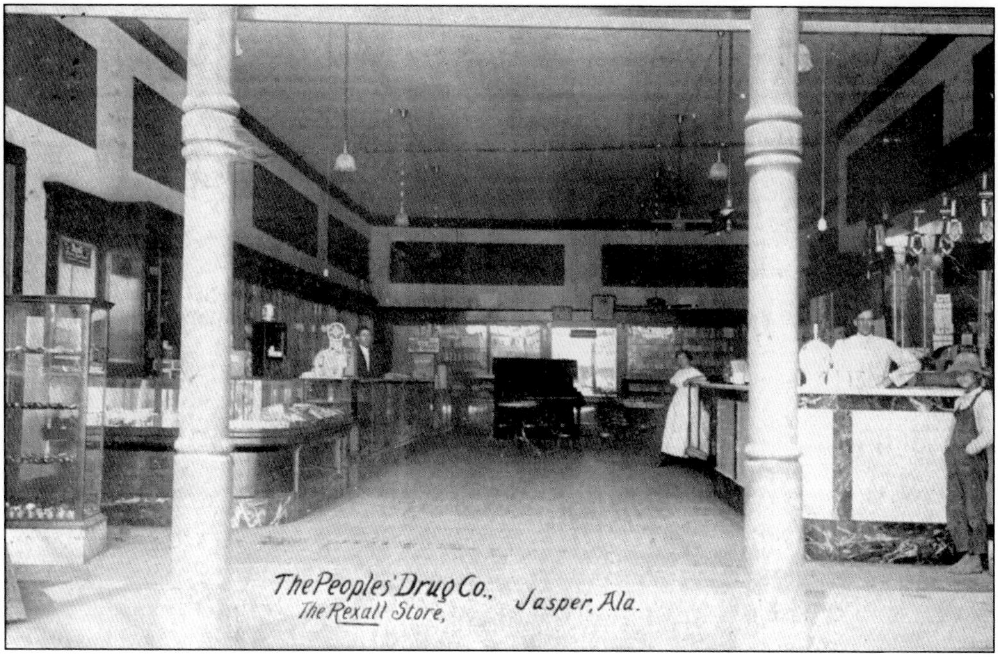

Interior of People's Drug Company, 1913. Shown in the postcard above is one of Jasper's most popular places to shop, socialize, visit the soda fountain, listen to the piano, and even get medicine. In 1927, George Hiller purchased the store, and his family operated it for 65 years. He was a two-term mayor and a lieutenant colonel in the army reserve.

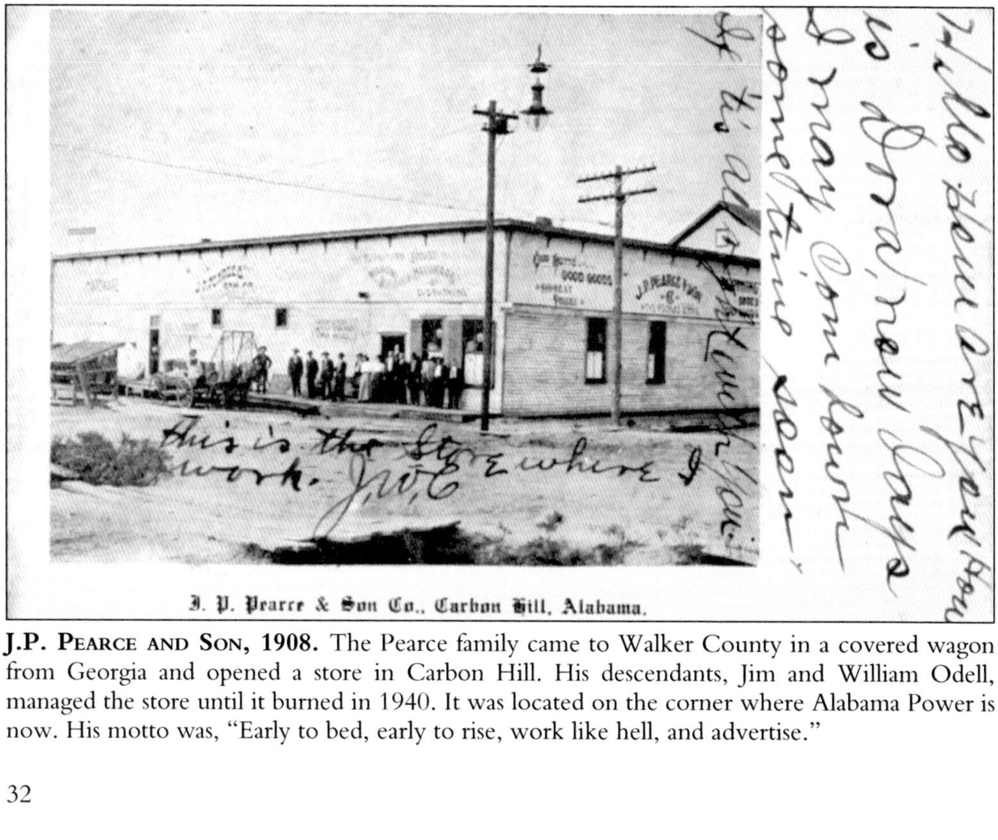

J.P. Pearce and Son, 1908. The Pearce family came to Walker County in a covered wagon from Georgia and opened a store in Carbon Hill. His descendants, Jim and William Odell, managed the store until it burned in 1940. It was located on the corner where Alabama Power is now. His motto was, "Early to bed, early to rise, work like hell, and advertise."

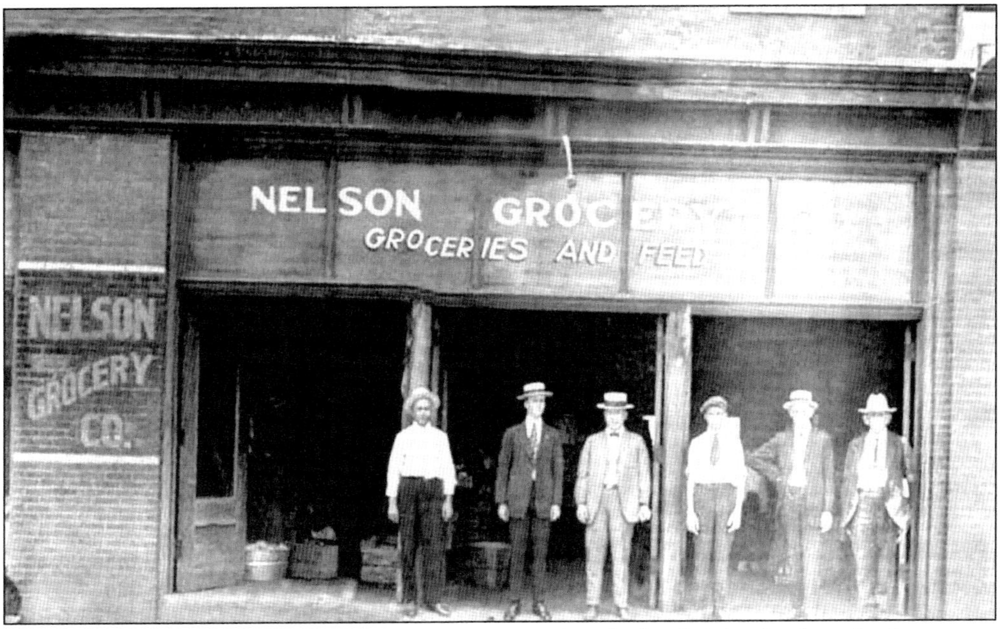

Nelson Grocery Company, Cordova. Frank Nelson had a thriving business in downtown Cordova in the 1920s. His store was located at the corner of Main and Mill Streets. Pictured from left to right are J. Spencer Black, Rube Carpenter, Frank Nelson (owner), Clarence Ellis, Charlie Nations, and Dan Nations. J. Spencer later had his own grocery and meat store located on Mill Street.

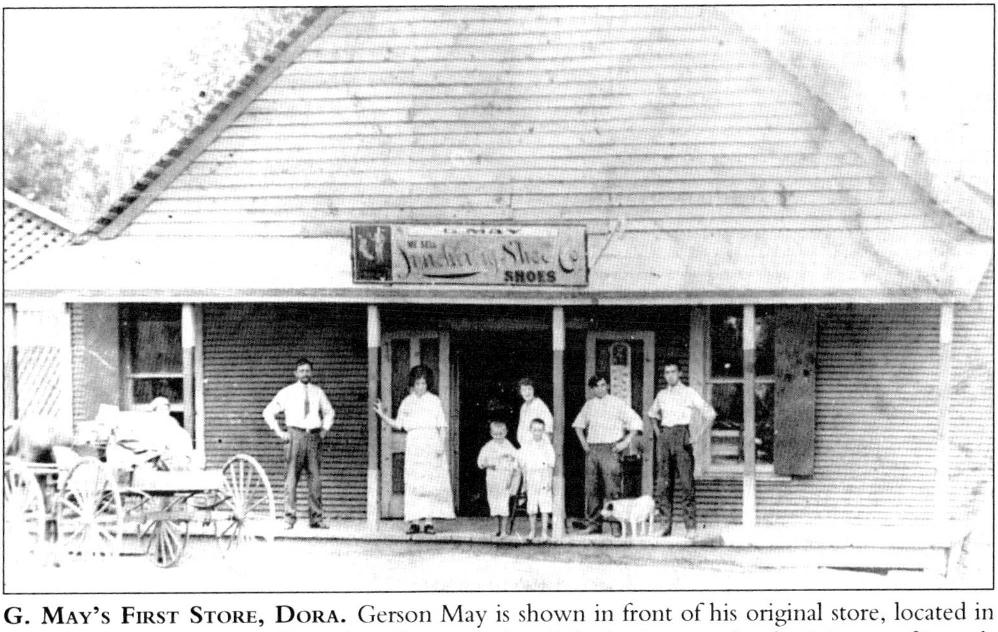

G. May's First Store, Dora. Gerson May is shown in front of his original store, located in Dora, in 1913. His sons and grandsons have continued the business, and today it is one of Jasper's leading enterprises. Pictured from left to right are Mike Gill (in the wagon), Gerson May, his wife Fannie May, Babe May, Celia Denaburg, Ike May, Harvey Mennen, Leon May, and their dog named "Pup."

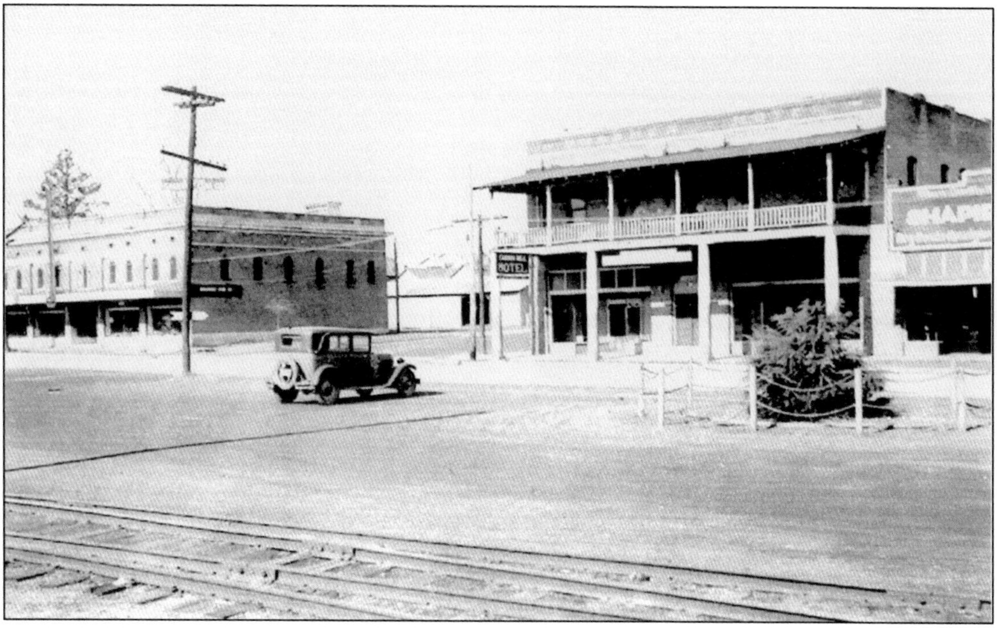

CALLOWAY COAL COMPANY, CARBON HILL. The two-story building on the right is the Carbon Hill Hotel, which was formerly known as the Brasher Hotel. On the left is the Calloway Coal Company mine headquarters. They were recognized as "The South's Standard in White Ash Coal" and have been one of the leading factors in the growth of Carbon Hill.

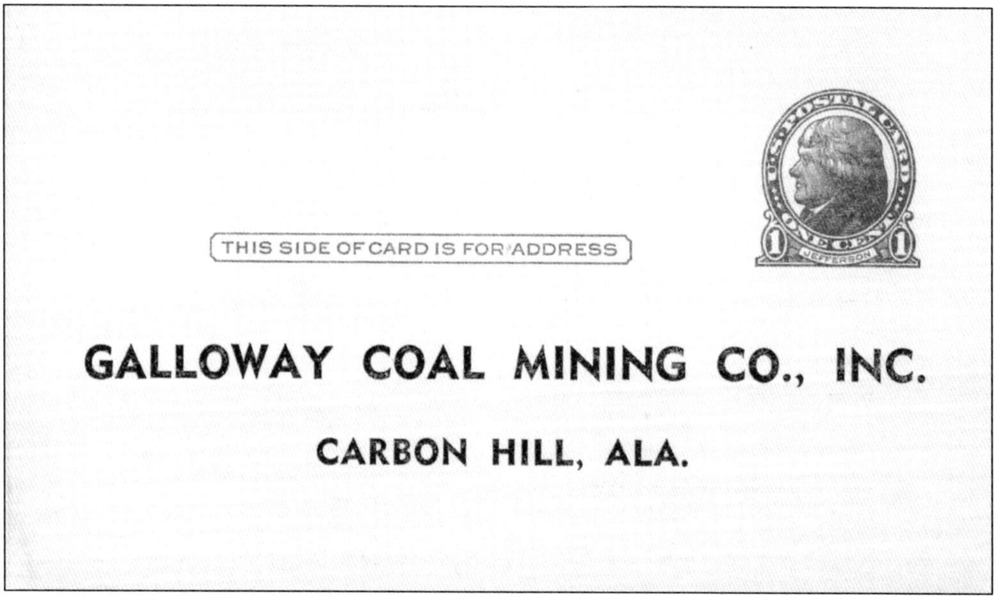

CALLOWAY COAL MINING COMPANY, CARBON HILL. This mailing card, distributed by the Calloway Mining Company in Carbon Hill, was used for company business. The back of the card has a place for the date, gross, tare, and net to be used when loading or transporting coal from one of their company mines. Every pound of coal was hand picked and washed by modern machinery.

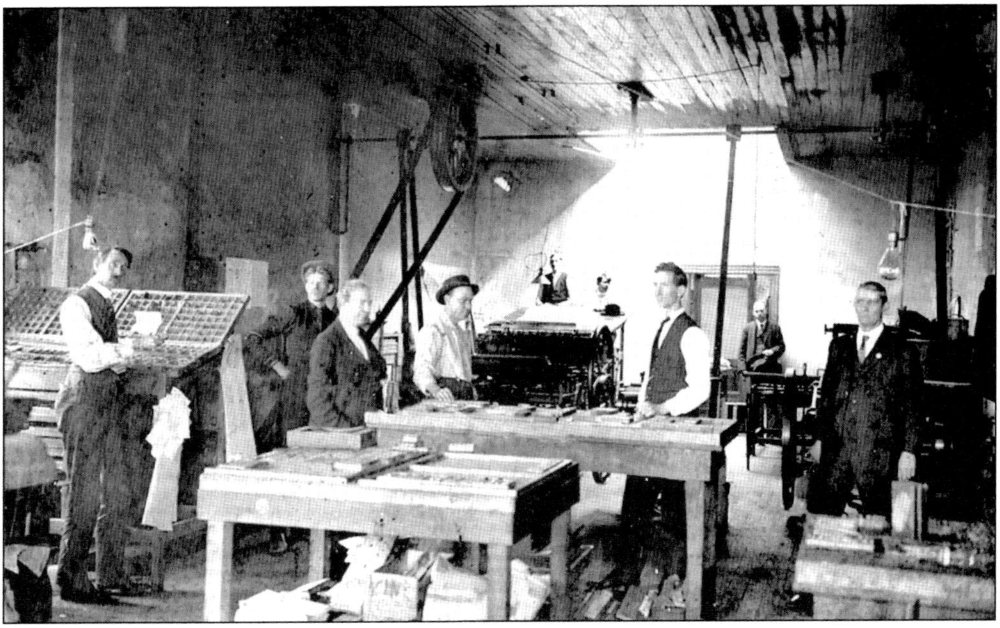

MOUNTAIN EAGLE, JASPER. Shown here is the *Mountain Eagle* as it appeared in the early 1900s. The fire that burned the courthouse in 1878 also destroyed the building that served as the office of the *Mountain Eagle*, and all the equipment was lost. Included in this picture are (far left) preacher E.C. Butler, (fourth from left) Tom Gunter, and (sixth from left) Pete Gunter. The *Mountain Eagle*, at this time, was owned by John Whitt Long.

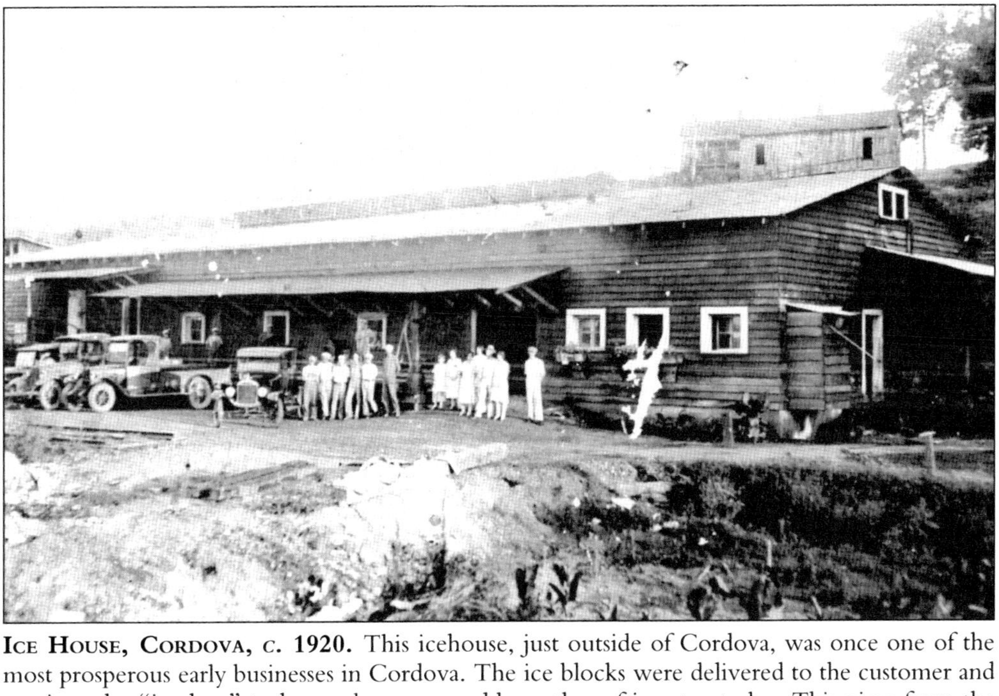

ICE HOUSE, CORDOVA, C. 1920. This icehouse, just outside of Cordova, was once one of the most prosperous early businesses in Cordova. The ice blocks were delivered to the customer and put into the "ice box" to be used as we would use the refrigerator today. This view from the railroad track shows two houses above the icehouse; the one on the left is still standing today.

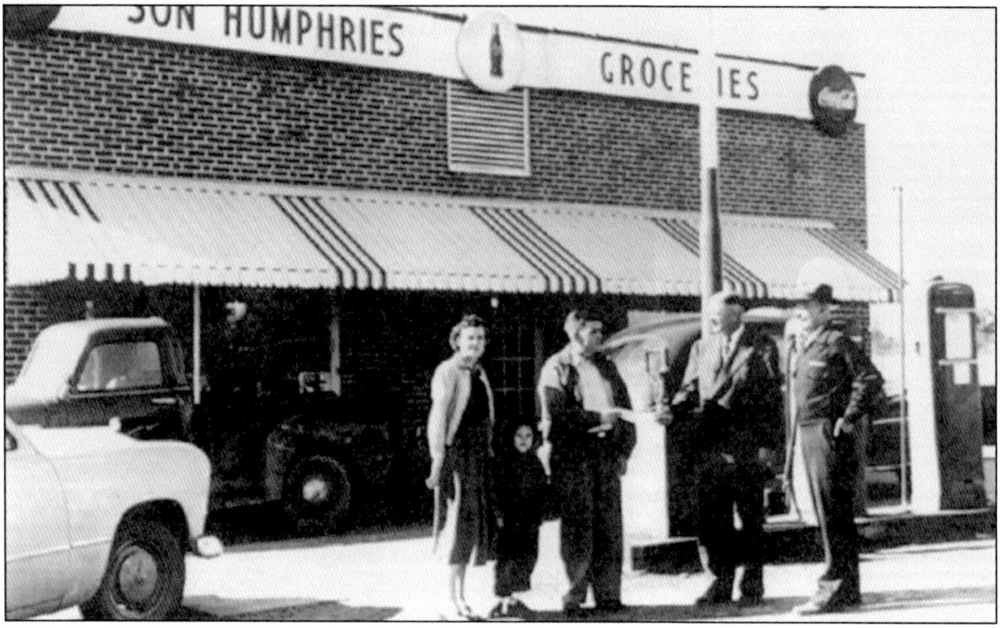

Son Humphries Grocery, 1953. David "Son" Humphries opened Son's Store in 1936. The store pictured above replaced the original store. A third store is presently at this same site on Ninth Avenue. The store served as a grocery and filling station. Pictured from left to right are Alta Humphries, Sandra Humphries Lee, Son Humphries, Manley L. Matthews, and an unknown executive of the Standard Oil Company.

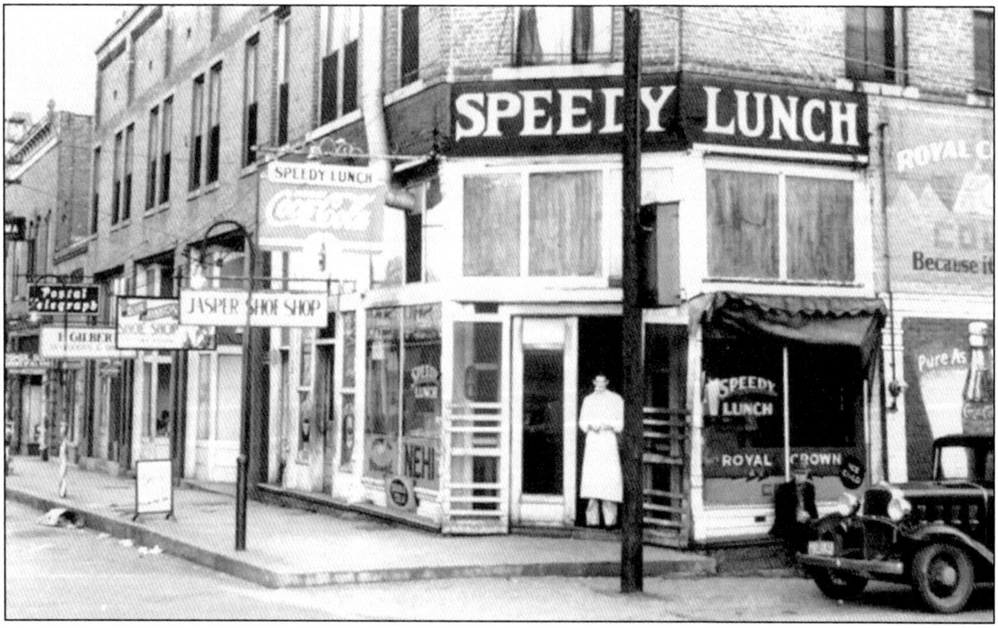

Speedy Lunch, c. 1935. Speedy's was owned by Cain O'Rear. Sitting on the ledge in front of the window is Charlie Gunter, and standing in the doorway is Coke Lindsey. Visible down Nineteenth Street is the Jasper Shoe Shop (owned by Mr. ? Killingsworth,) Blue Ribbon Shoe Shop, E. Gilbert Dry Goods, and the Postal Telegraph Office.

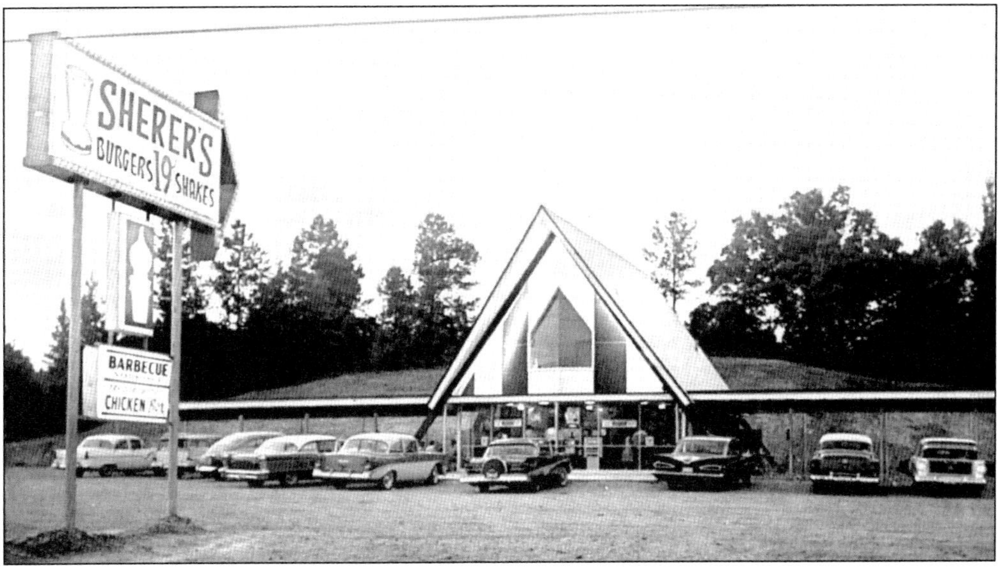

Sherer's Drive-In, 1959. Maurice Sherer opened the Jasper youths' favorite hangout. He added local disk jockey Johnny Mack, "Mouth-of-the-South," as well as a great steak sandwich, broasted chicken, and a 19¢ hamburger or shake to create one of the most successful businesses in Walker County. He went on to have 14 drive-ins in Alabama and Mississippi. It became the favorite eatery on the route between Birmingham and Florence.

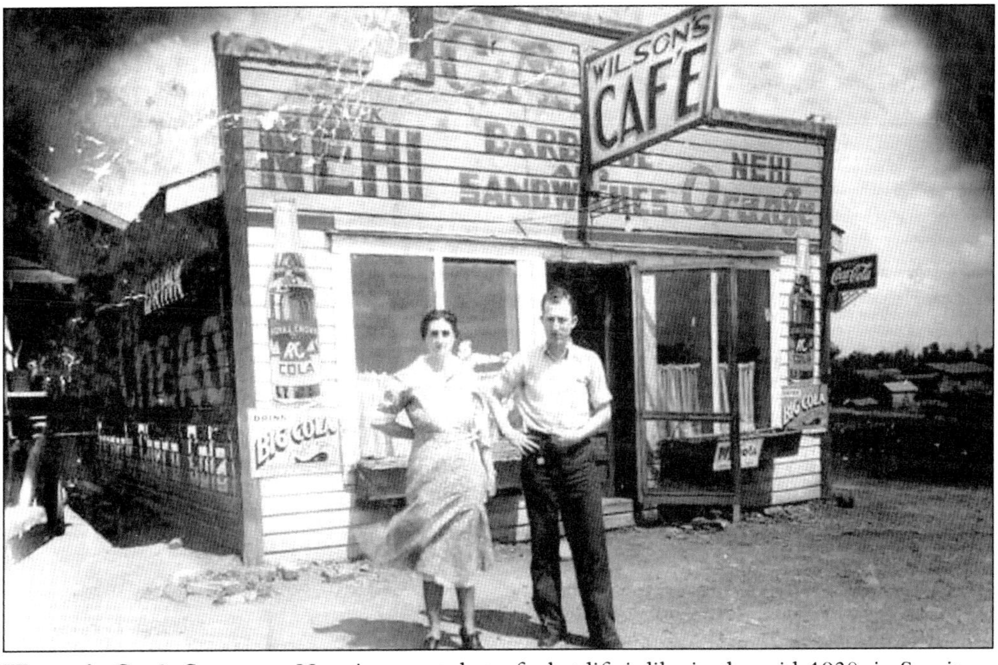

Wilson's Café, Sumiton. Here is a great shot of what life is like in the mid-1930s in Sumiton. Notice all the drinks advertised on the outside of the café owned by William Clay Wilson. Pictured are Ludie Wilson (the owner's wife and cook) and their son Glen Wilson. Their home (seen at the extreme left) and the café were located on Main Street where Scurlock's Furniture is today.

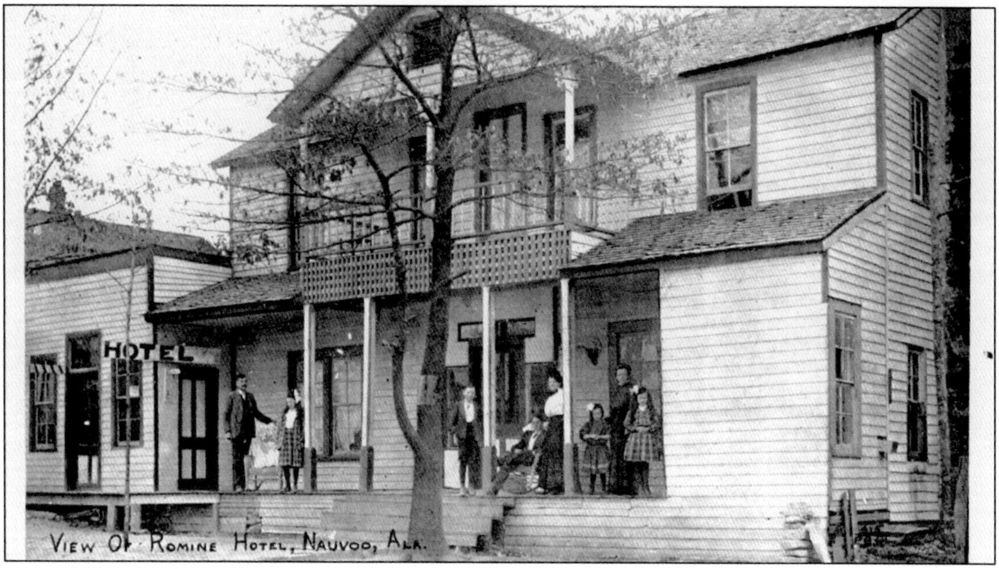

Romine Hotel, Nauvoo. This 1910 view of the old Romine Hotel shows the small city during its prime. It was a Pony Express stop and later a main stop on the Southern Railroad. This hotel survived the devastating tornado of March 7, 1938. It was located on the Carbon Hill-Nauvoo Road, just west of the Harbin Hotel, about where the Quick Shop is today.

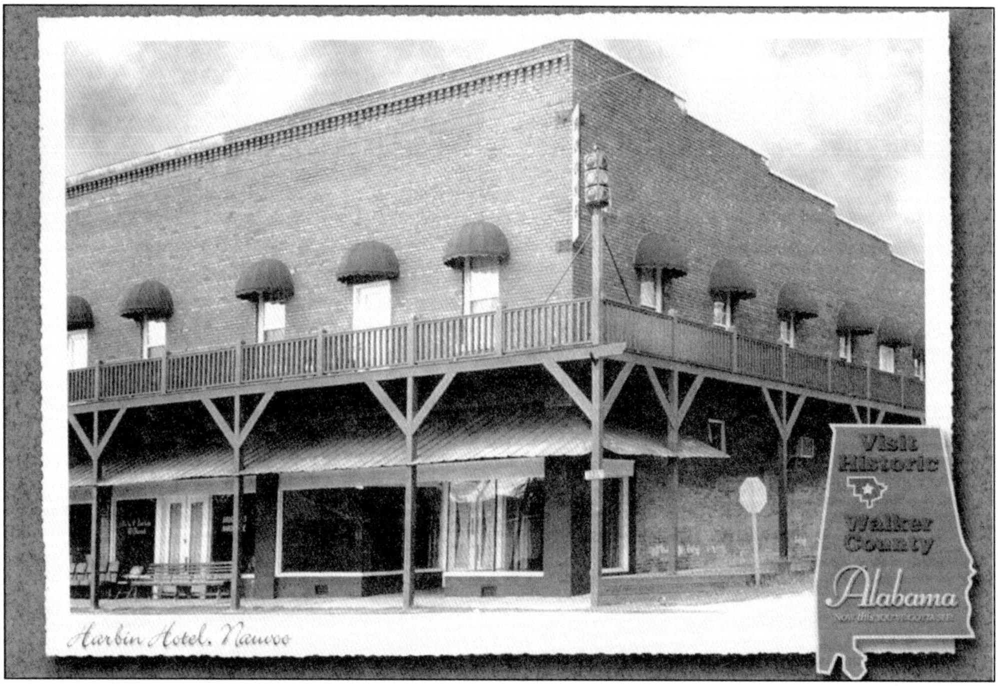

Harbin Hotel, Nauvoo. In 1923, W.O. Harbin built the Harbin Hotel at a cost of $24,500. The downstairs part of the building served as a mercantile store, drug store, parts store, and garage with a gas pump, and the upstairs served as living quarters for the Harbin family. It also served as a hotel for the railroad workers and drummers. Gene and Earlene McDaniel own this Alabama landmark today.

Walker Tourist Court, Carbon Hill. This late 1930s card shows Walker Tourist Court, located on Highway 78 on the eastern edge of downtown. It was owned by Mr. and Mrs. J.G. Walker. They advertised year-round air-conditioning, private baths (a relatively new convenience), and a dining room on the premises. The motel later became the P&M Motel and is now unoccupied.

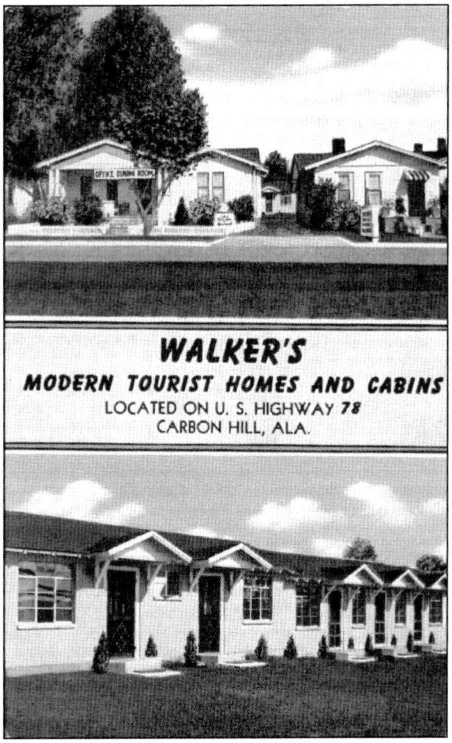

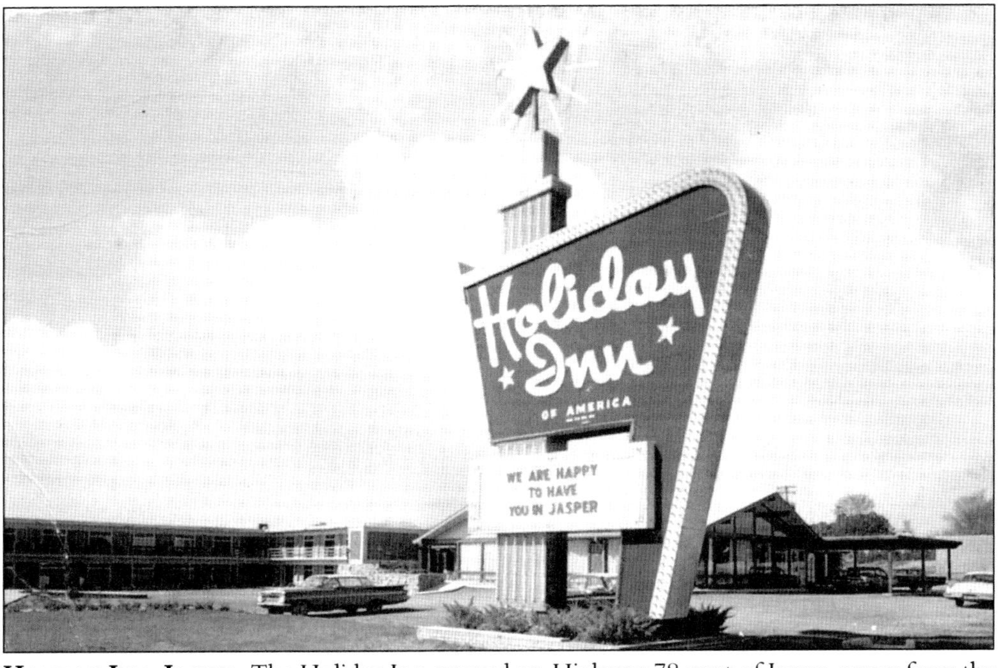

Holiday Inn, Jasper. The Holiday Inn opened on Highway 78 west of Jasper, across from the location of the old Wal-Mart, on November 25, 1961. Jasper mayor Herman Maddox and Sen. John Sparkman were the guest speakers at the opening ceremony. This inn served Jasper for over 20 years but now has been replaced by a Budget Inn.

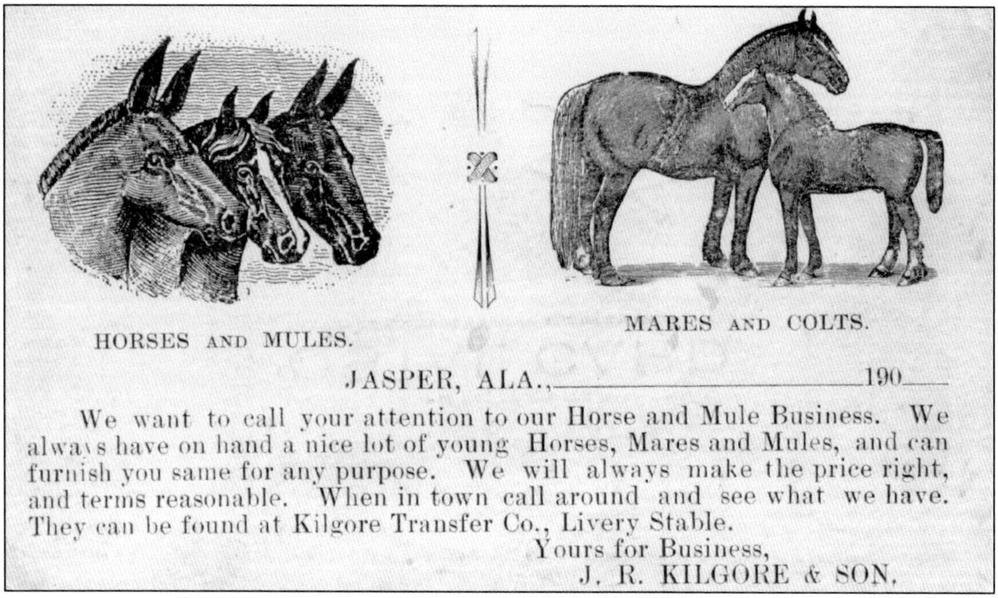

Kilgore Transfer Company and Livery Stable, Advertising Card. J.R. Kilgore and his sons, John, Brack, and Grady, owned this huge business that covered the entire block west of Sixth Avenue between Eighteenth and Nineteenth Streets. The business consisted of a mule barn and cotton gin. An African American named Shorty was the head wrangler, salesman, and expert on the animals.

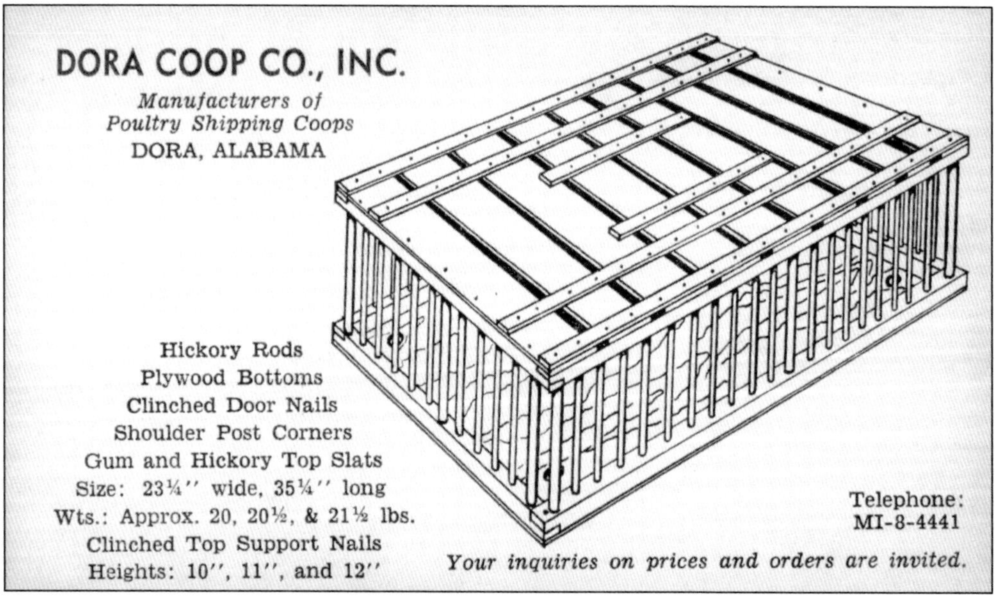

Dora Coop Company, Inc. This advertising card for the Dora Coop Company tells that they manufacture poultry coops of various sizes to be shipped or picked up at the store. The coops were made of the best materials available. They used hickory rods, plywood bottoms, and gum and hickory top slats. This business was located just east of the downtown business district.

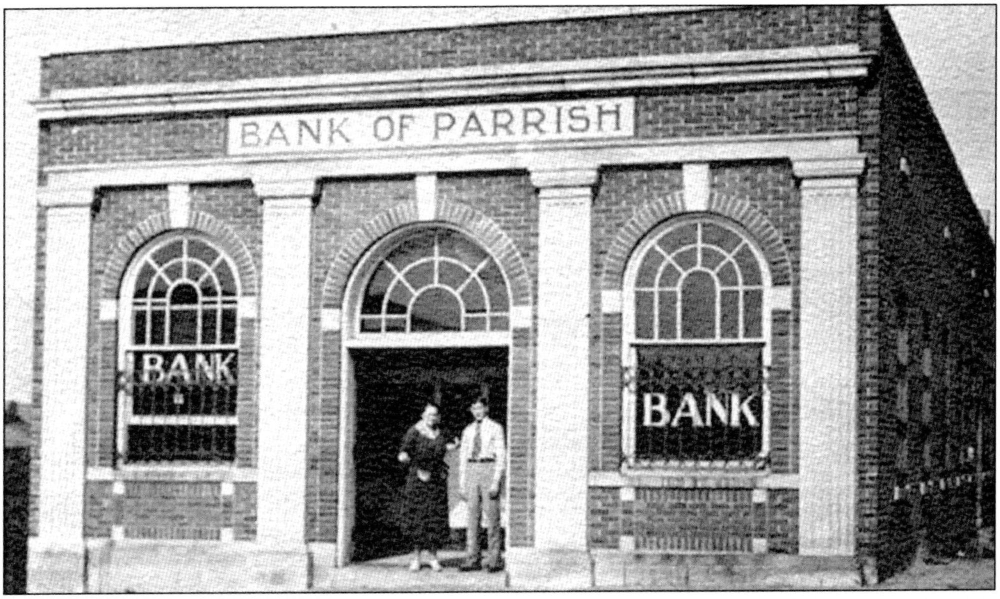

Bank of Parrish, c. 1930. In 1919, John C. Shepherd of Berry established the Bank of Parrish and became its first president. He served in that capacity until his death in 1949. The first building was located on Bank Street just north of the railroad tracks. It was moved to the location shown in the above card in 1929, and in 2000, it moved to its present location on Highway 169.

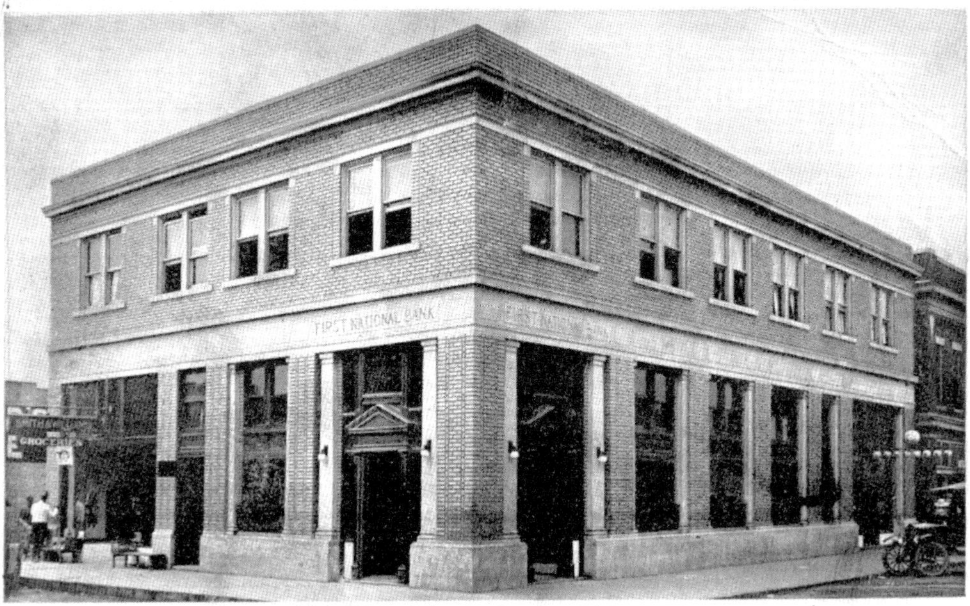

First National Bank, Jasper, Alabama.

First National Bank, Jasper. On April 20, 1905, the First National was incorporated and became Walker County's oldest banking establishment. John H. Cranford had started the bank in 1899 in the office of his mercantile store and called it the Bank of Jasper. The above building is located on the southwest corner of Third Avenue and Nineteenth Street. Judge E.W. Long was the president of the bank in 1925.

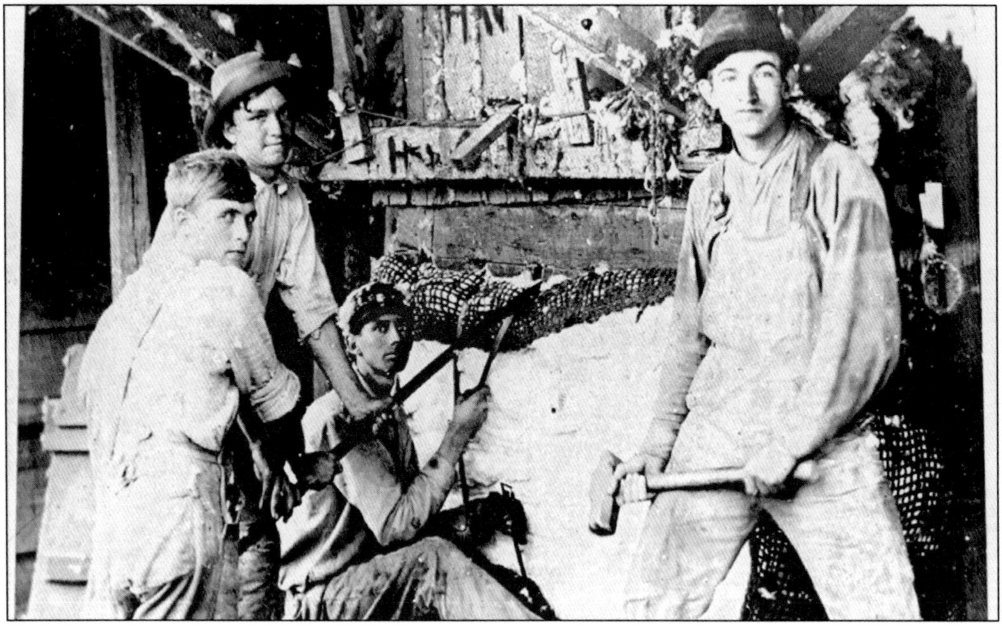

Sam Gardner's Gin, 1910. This gin, located on what is now Gardner's Gin Road between Jasper and Cordova, was opened in 1891, and the last bale was ginned in 1912. The view above was taken inside the gin at the cotton press. From left to right are Sam Evans, Manley Evans, Oscar Gardner (seated), and Lee Minor (holding the hammer). Three teams of mules powered the gin.

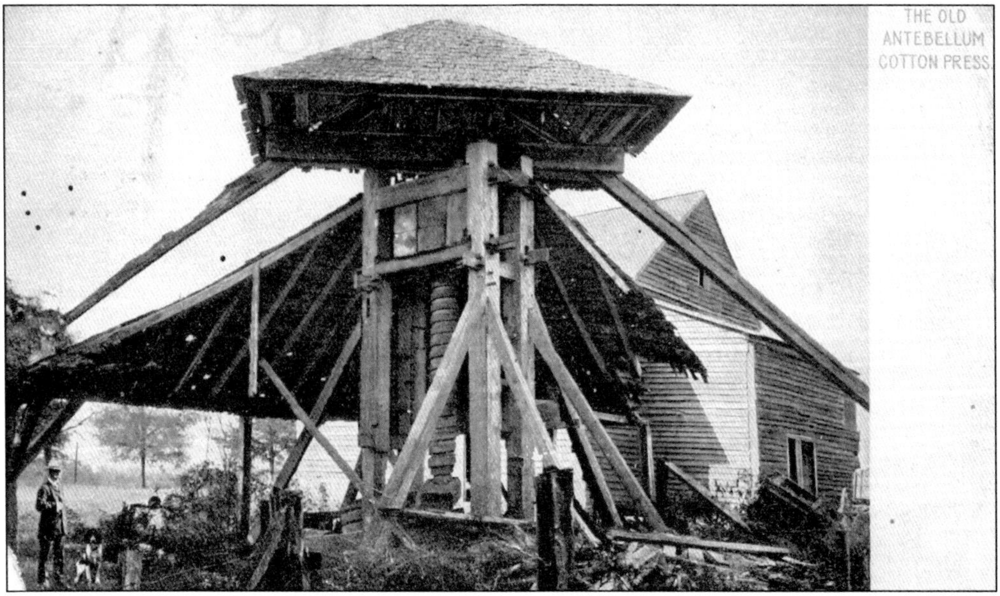

Cotton Press, 1908. The power for this cotton press was provided by mule teams, which turned the press. The seeds were separated from the fiber after it went through a cylinder covered with bristles that took the lint from it. The lint was then pressed into bales. Later this process was performed by a 300-horsepower mechanical compress. This card is from the "In the Land of Cotton" series.

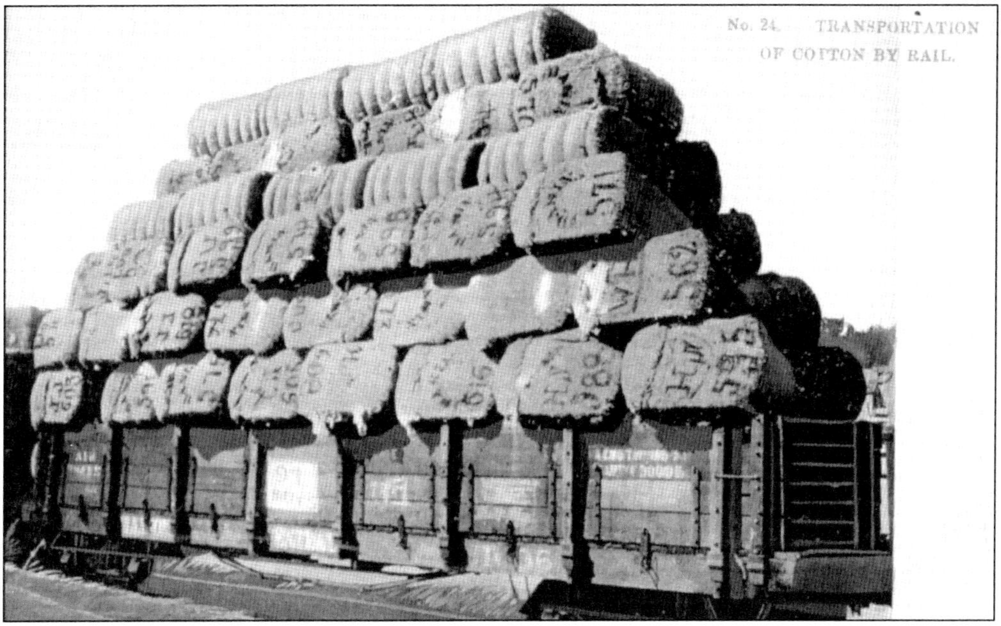

COTTON BY RAIL, c. 1910. The railroad car shown above is filled with local cotton and was shipped to markets across America. Much of the cotton that was pressed in Walker County went to the Indian Head Mill in Cordova. At the mill, the cotton was turned into various products that were sold in the mill store, but much of the cotton was shipped to other markets outside the county.

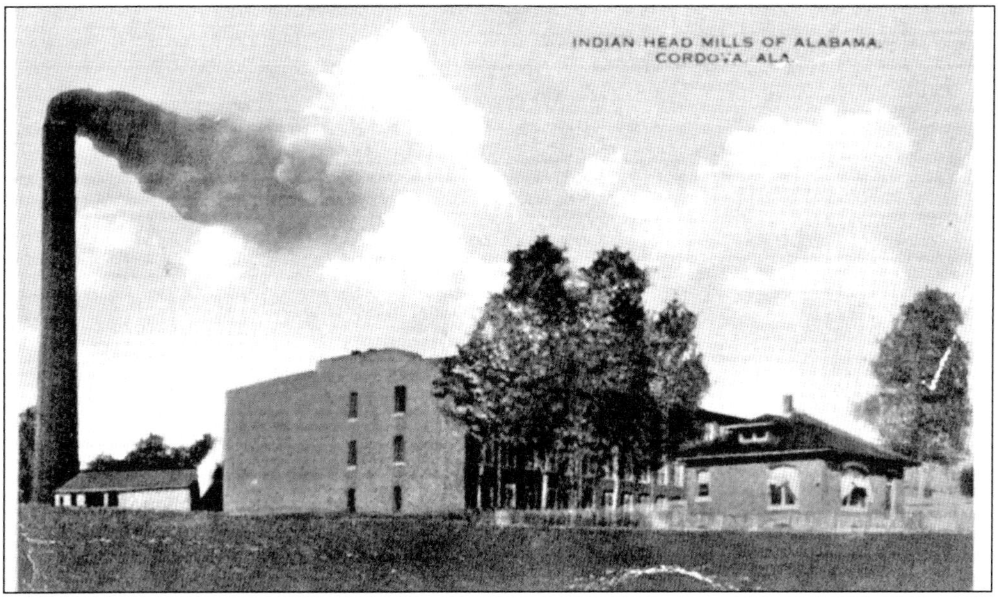

INDIAN HEAD MILL, CORDOVA. Capt. Benjamin M. Long persuaded Eastern Capitol to invest in the construction of a cotton mill in his beloved Cordova. The mill opened in 1898 and employed about 500 local laborers, making it the county's largest employer. The raw cotton was brought into the mill and was made into usable products. In 1962, the mill closed, causing a loss of $2 million to the county's economy.

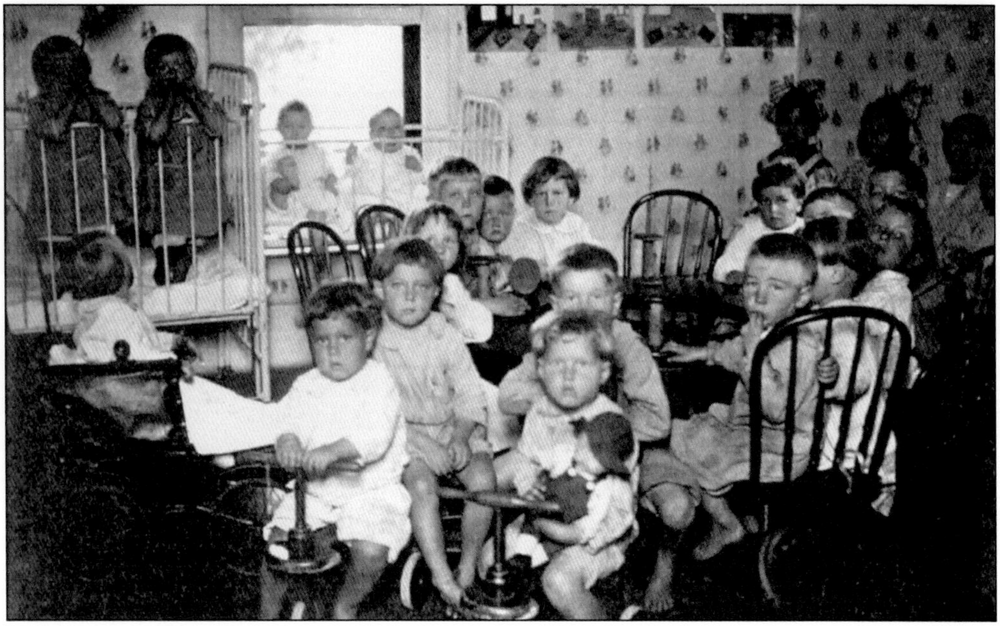

INDIAN HEAD MILL DAY CARE, CORDOVA. Over 100 years ago, the mill had a day-care and nursery program for the working mothers. Many husband and wife teams worked in the mill and utilized this program, thus allowing the wives to supplement the family income, even with small children to care for. Pictured are some children of Walker County whose parents took advantage of this program.

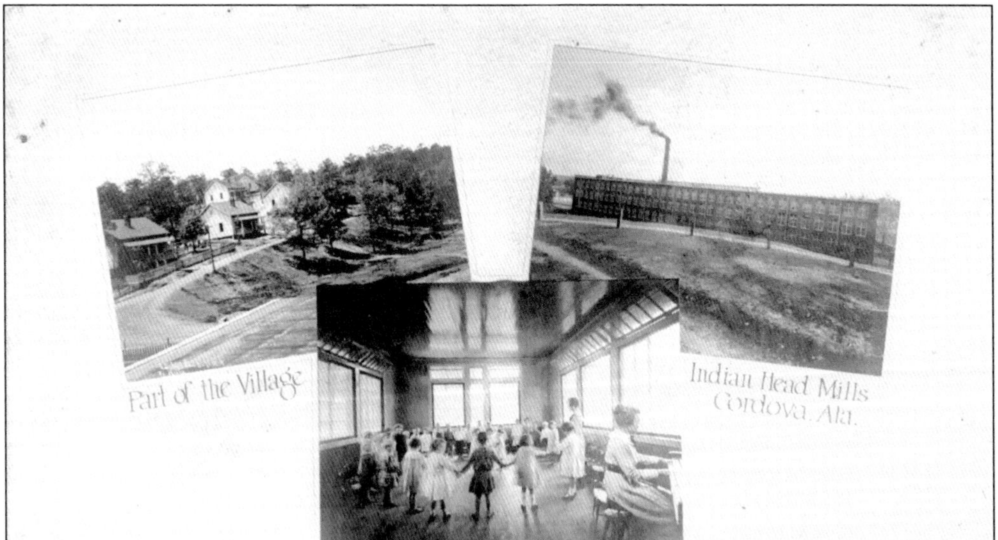

TRI-VIEW OF INDIAN HEAD MILL, CORDOVA. This three-photo view of Indian Head Mill shows some of the facilities available to the employees from "the company." Pictured are the mill village, the kindergarten, and the mill. Other facilities available were a park, nursery, day care, school, church, company store, and even a hotel.

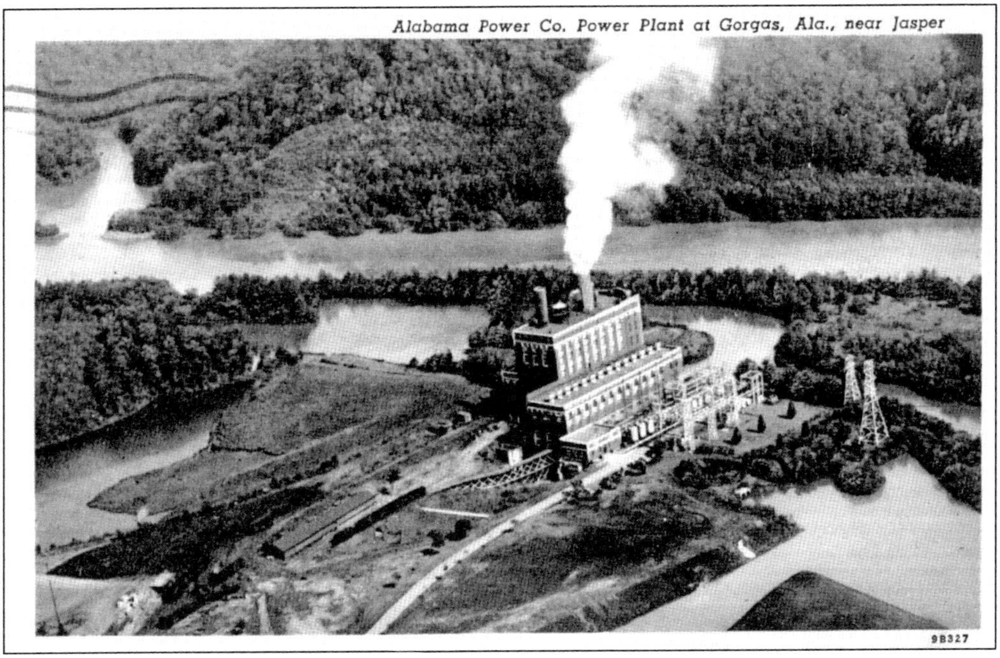

GORGAS STEAM PLANT, 1956. Located near Parrish, 18 miles south of Jasper, this modern power plant is owned and operated by the Alabama Power Company. It is the second of three power plants named in honor of Alabama native Gen. William Crawford Gorgas. His successful fight against yellow fever and malaria insured the completion of the Panama Canal.

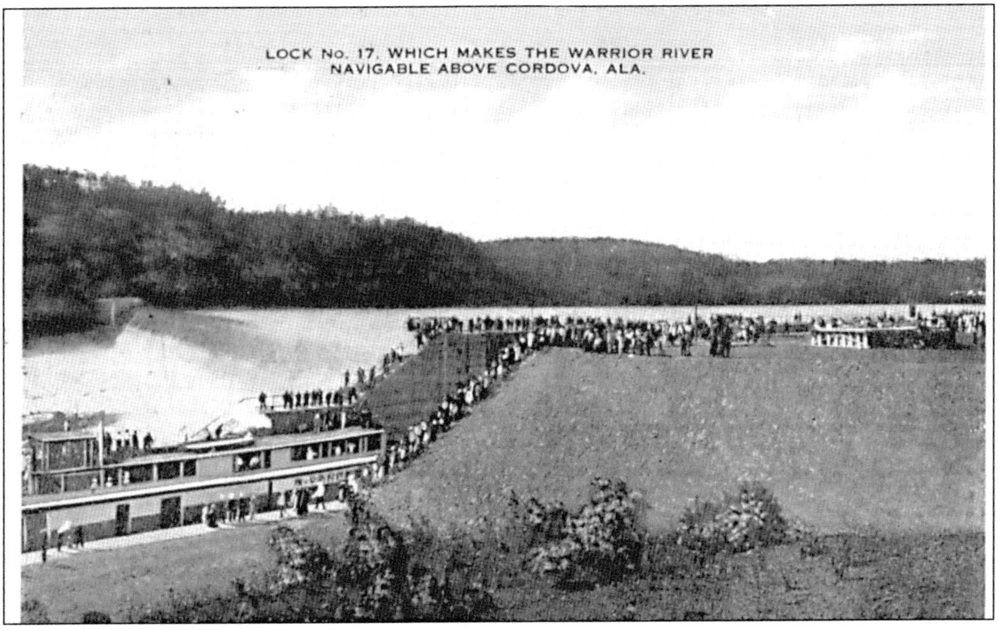

LOCK 17 DEDICATION, 1915. The completion of Lock 17 was attended by over 5,000 people, which included Gov. Charles Henderson and Walker County's Sen. John H. Bankhead. Senator Bankhead did the actual ceremonial dedication of this dam, which made the Warrior River navigable above Cordova. The first steamboat, *The Nugent*, arrived there in May of 1915.

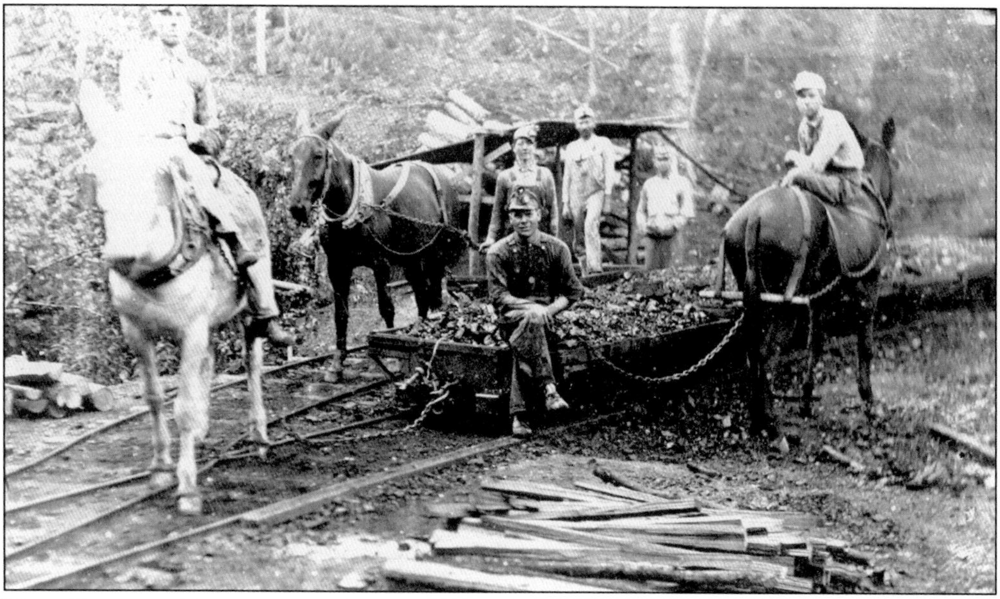

Mule Powered Mine, Dora. Shown above is an early mine in Walker County. This is a family mine near Dora where the coal was dug out by hand using a pick and shovel. The town started out as Sharon in 1886, became Horse Creek in 1890, and eventually was renamed as Dora in 1906. With the decline of mining, Dora gradually began to decline, and most businesses have now moved to Highway 78.

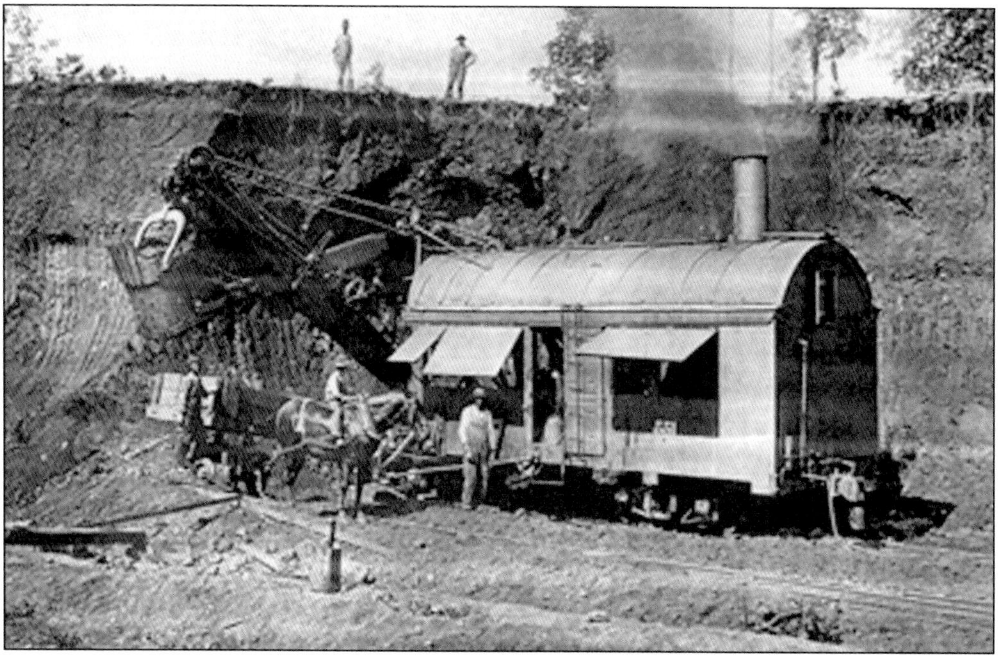

Steam Shovel, Walker County. The advent of the steam shovel allowed mine owners and operators to move huge amounts of coal. This early Walker County mine (thought to be near Sipsey) shows the steam shovel loading a mule-pulled coal cart. The coal was pulled to a railhead to be stacked and then shipped by train to waiting markets.

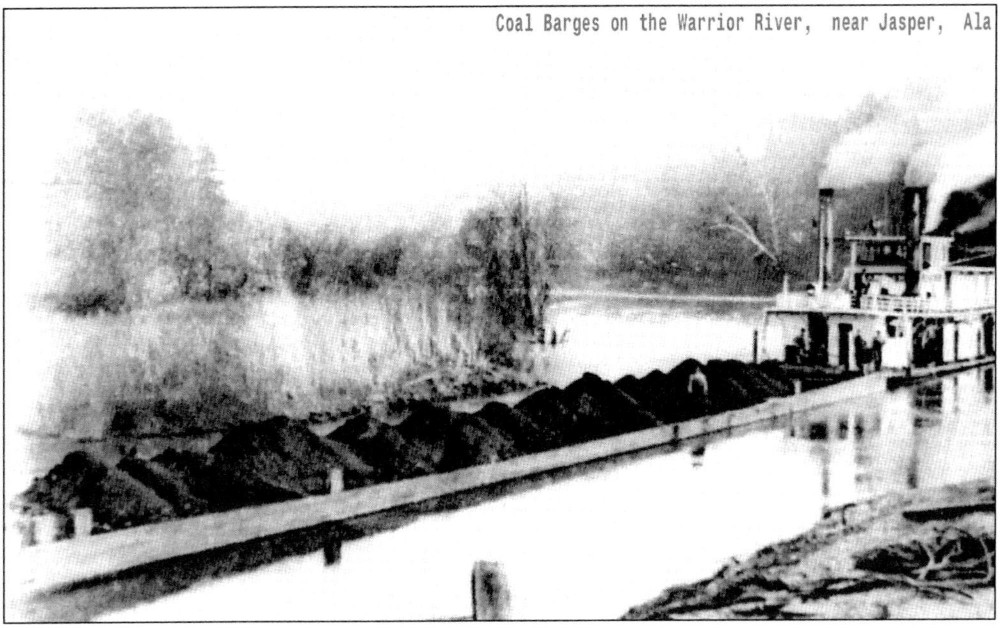

COAL BARGE, WARRIOR RIVER. Originally, coal had to be carried to the Warrior River in Tuscaloosa by wagon, at which point it was floated through the dangerous rapids to southern markets. After the completion of Lock 17 in 1915, coal could be shipped directly from Walker County down the Warrior River. Here, a stern-wheel steamboat pushes a coal barge down the Warrior.

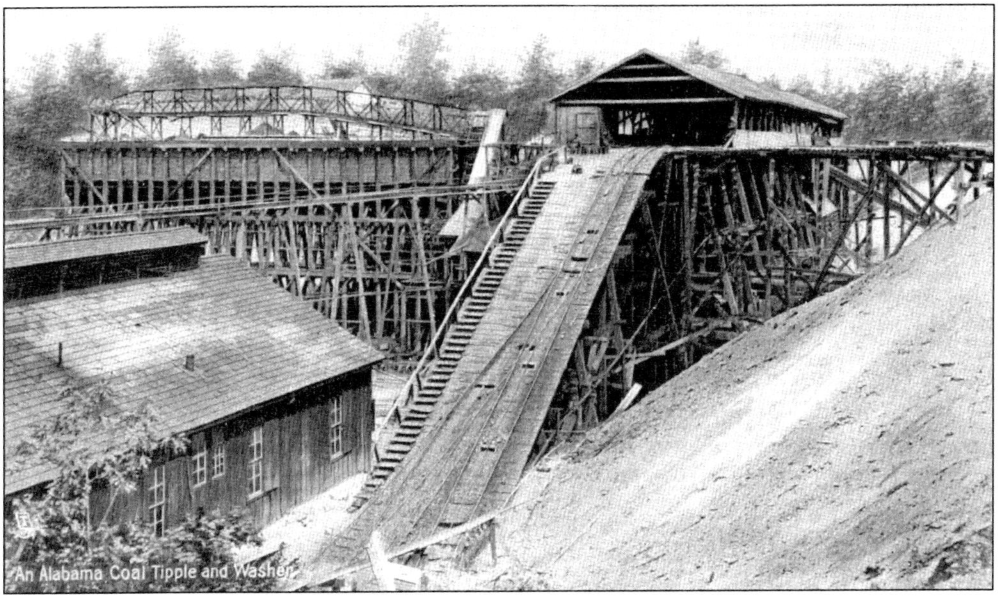

COAL TIPPLE AND WASHER. Tipples and washers were used in the heyday of coal production in Walker County. Coal was pulled from the mine and "tipped over," hence the name "tipple." The coal was then graded, washed, and moved into waiting rail cars, or onto beltlines, to be shipped to numerous markets across the state or nation. Numerous old tipple remains can be seen across Walker County today.

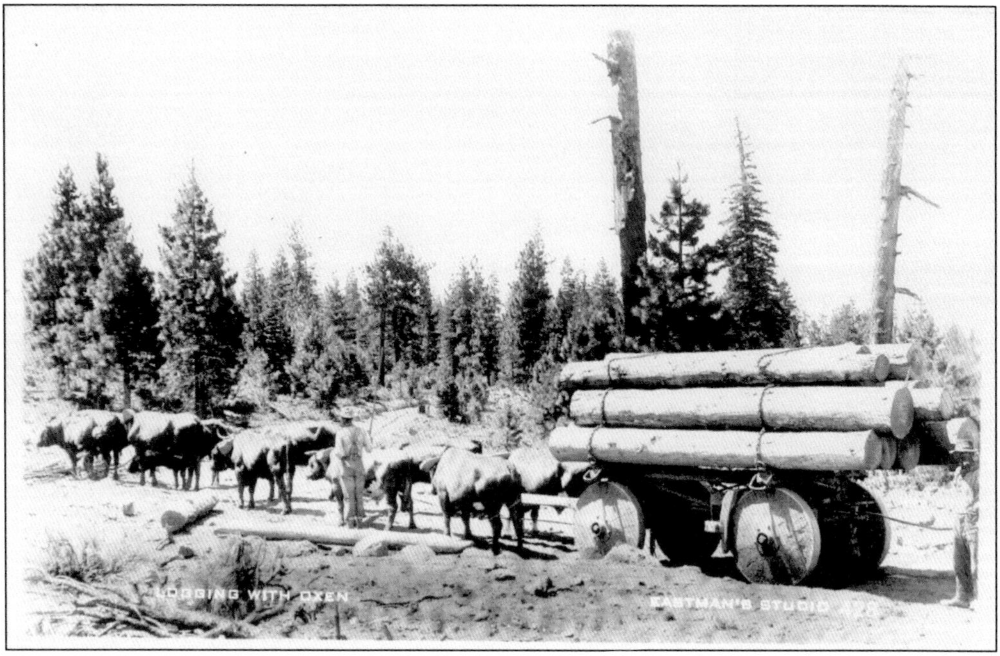

EARLY LUMBER TRANSPORT. Walker County was covered by old-growth timber that made it a valuable potential for lumbering. Manchester became the center of the lumber industry in Walker County. In the mid- to late 1800s, as shown above, the lumber was hand-cut and pulled to market by horses, mules, or oxen. The advent of the railroads in the county made this a much more lucrative business.

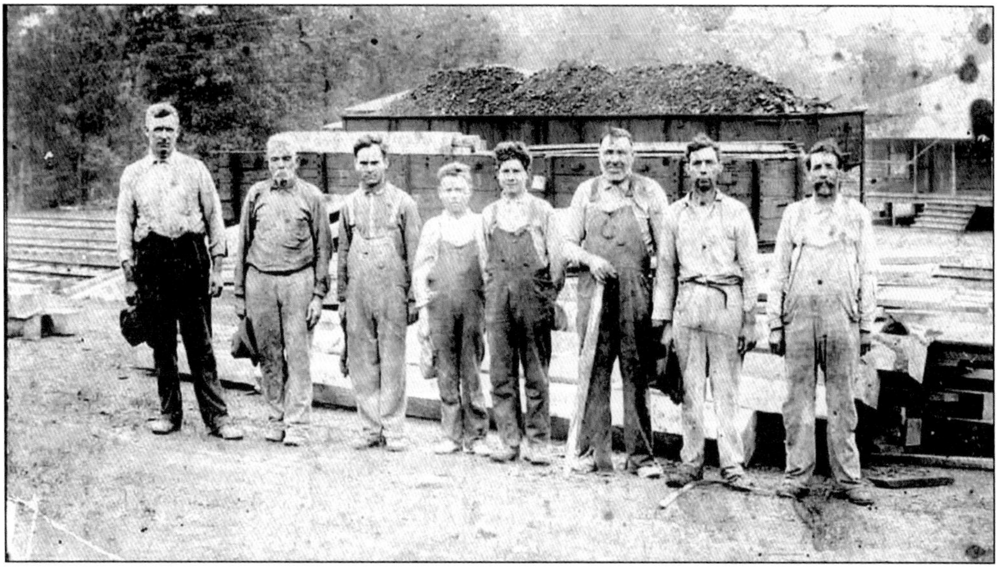

STEAM SAWMILL, MANCHESTER, *c.* 1910. Lumber became an important product in Walker County because of the need for mine timbers and logs, which were used in flatboats for floating the coal down the rivers. The above card shows Andrew Jackson O'Rear on the left, and third from the right with a stick is Bill Alexander. Notice the timbers on the ground and in the rail car behind the men, as well as the coal used to power the sawmill.

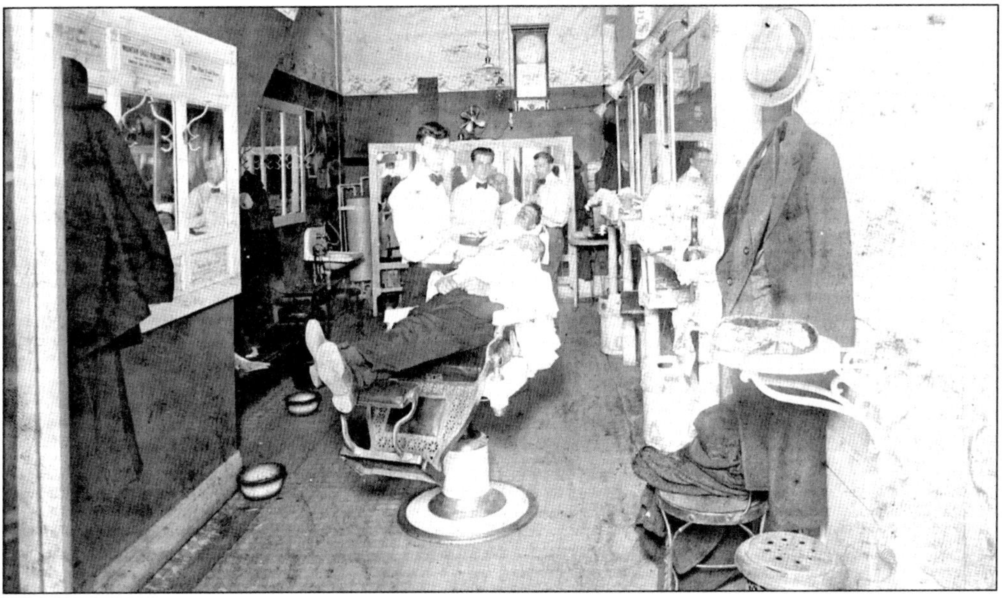

HERRON'S BARBER SHOP, JASPER. Herron's Barber Shop was located behind the Peoples Drug Company on Nineteenth Street. This view shows many interesting items, such as the heater in the foreground, spittoons in the floor, *Mountain Eagle* advertisement above the mirror on the left, and the clock on the back wall. The barber in the middle is Grady Herron. The others are unidentified.

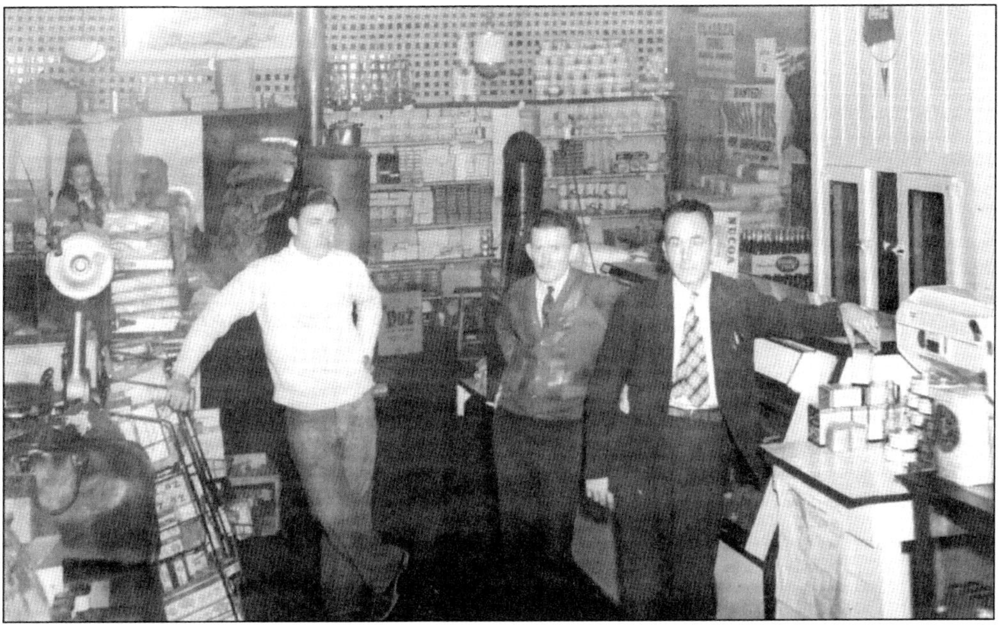

J. SPENCER BLACK GROCERY, CORDOVA. The interior view of Black's Grocery Meat and Food Store depicts, from left to right, Hilda Black Brown (in back), L.I. Hadany, Lee Sides, and J. Spencer Black. Interesting items in the store include (on back wall) coal oil lamp globes, a Clabber Girl advertisement, and a case of Double Cola. This store was located where the bank parking lot is today.

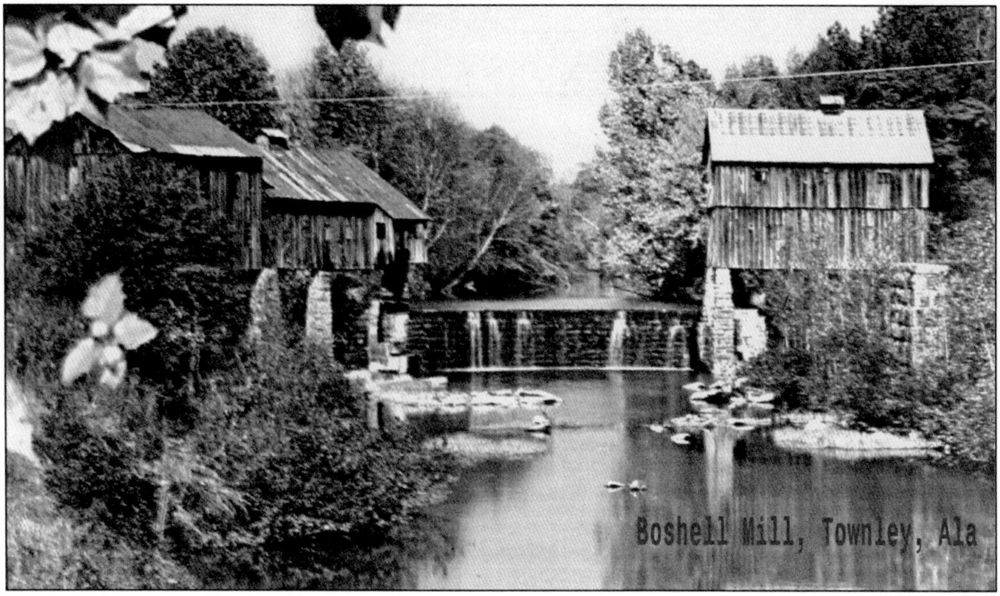

BOSHELL MILL, TOWNLEY. W.R Boshell built the original sawmill in Townley in 1885. It was operated by steam until 1901, when it was converted to a water-driven mill. The mill served as a sawmill, gristmill, and a cotton gin. The mill closed in 1963, and the gristmill burned in 1976. In 1986, the sawmill burned, leaving only its native Lost Creek sandstone foundation.

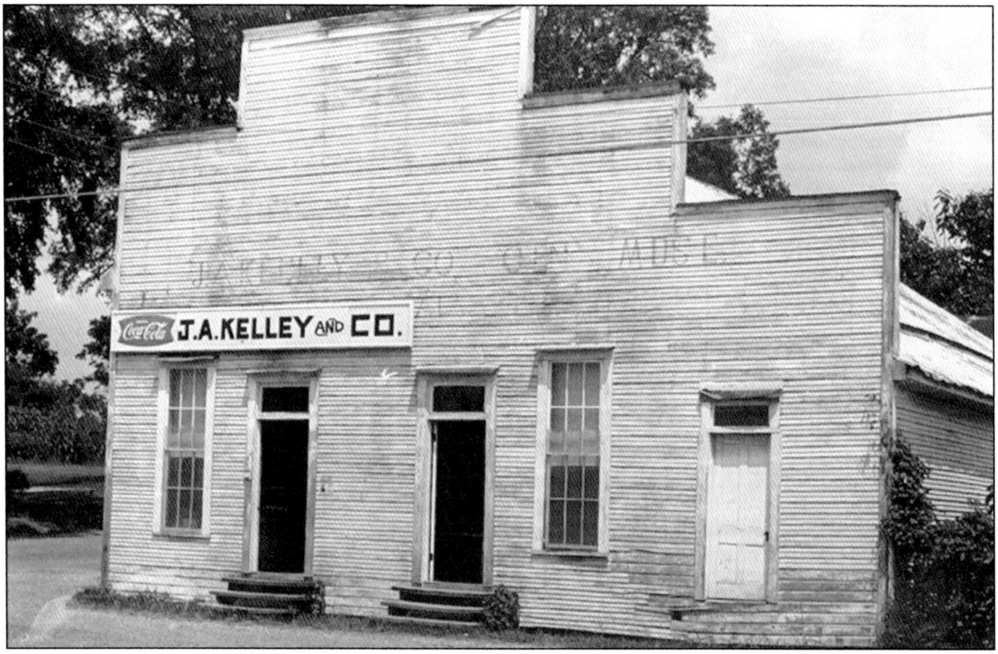

J.A. KELLEY STORE, ELDRIDGE. Walker County's oldest surviving business is pictured above. J.A. Kelly built this store in 1898, at the same location it stands today. It is a one-story, wood-frame structure with a false front. Mr. Kelley's store became the social center of Eldridge, complete with discussions of politics, crops, and weather, as citizens gathered around the pot-bellied stove.

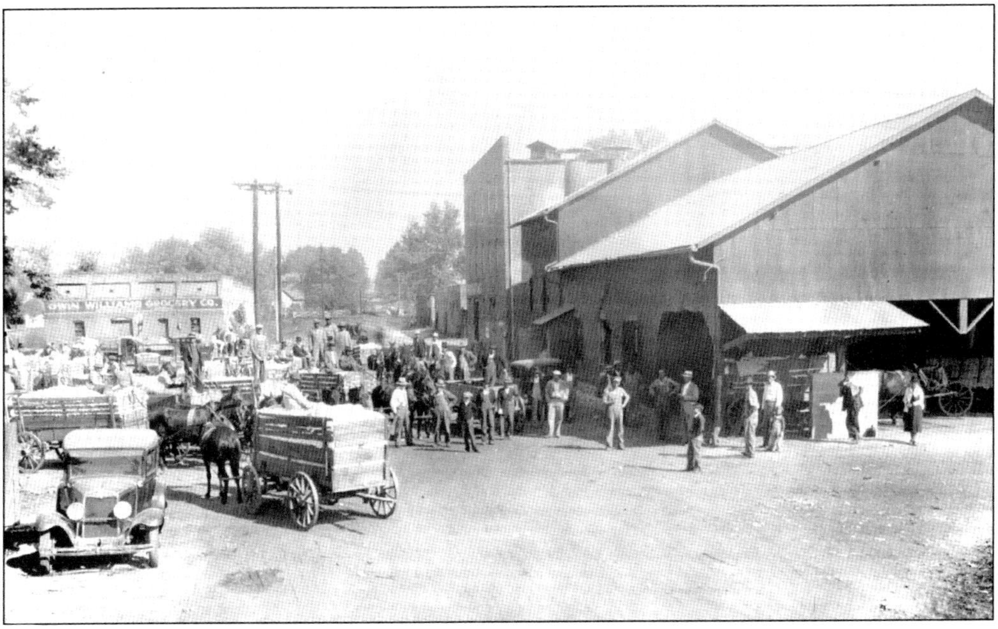

COTTON GIN, JASPER. This view of Jasper in the early 1900s shows the Phillips cotton gin that was located on Seventh Avenue between Nineteenth and Twentieth Streets. The three-story building was on the site of the old Studdard Cabinet Shop and was owned by J. Phillips. To the east of the gin was a small black community called Bear Mash.

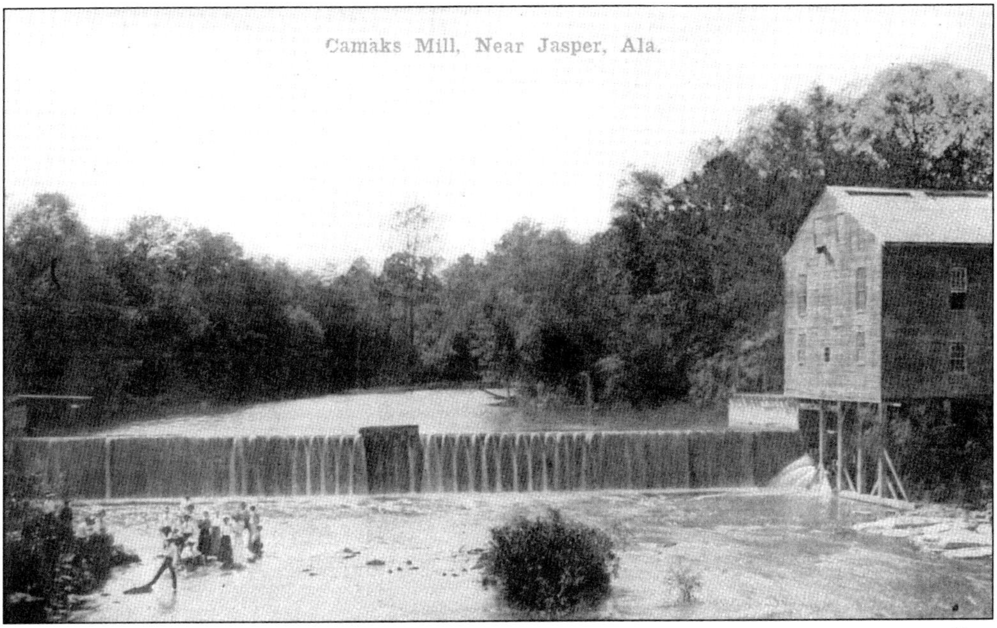

CAMAK'S MILL, NEAR MANCHESTER. A native of South Carolina, Moses Camak came to Walker County in 1835 and built a mill on Black Water Creek. The mill and the dam were constructed of wood, so there is nothing left of either today. It was located just west of the Musgrove Country Club near today's old metal bridge. Moses Camak also owned the Camak-Ryan Hotel in Jasper.

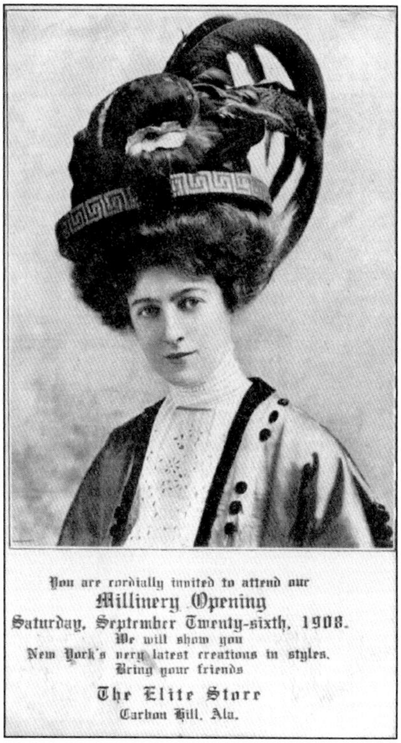

The Elite Store, Carbon Hill. On Saturday, September 26, 1908, the Elite Store opened on Front Street in Carbon Hill, and they had a grand opening with everyone invited to attend. The store was a millinery shop that had the very latest creations in styles from New York. This is an example of an advertising card from the early 20th century. Hats today do not compare with this one.

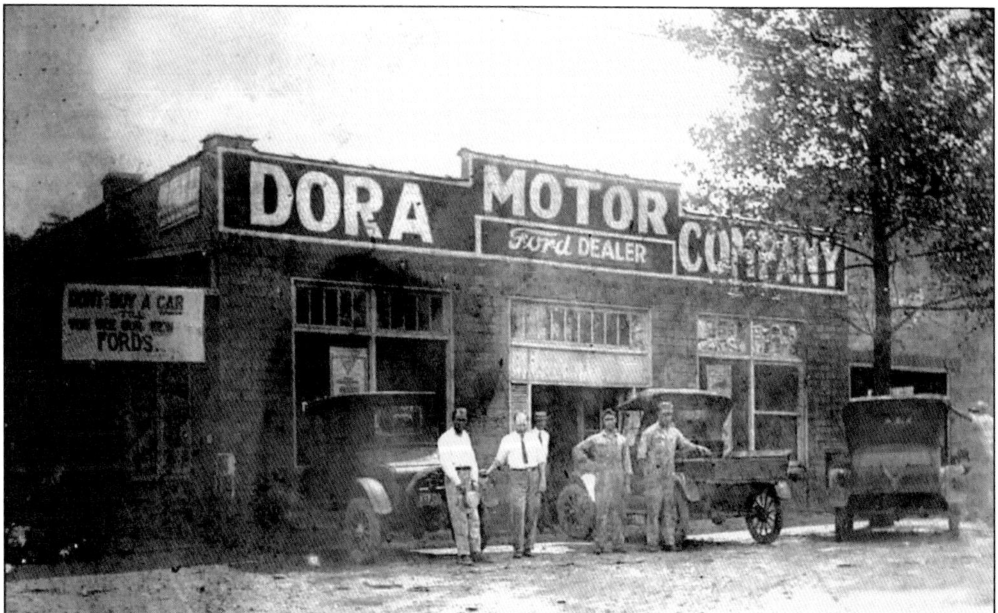

Ford Motor Company, Dora. George A. Averitt purchased the Ford Motor Company in 1925 from Lewis Odom. George married Willie Lou Shepherd in 1926, and they then purchased another larger brick building that had previously been the Chevrolet dealership. This new store was across the railroad tracks from their first location. Averitt was also a two-term mayor of Dora.

Three

Churches and Schools

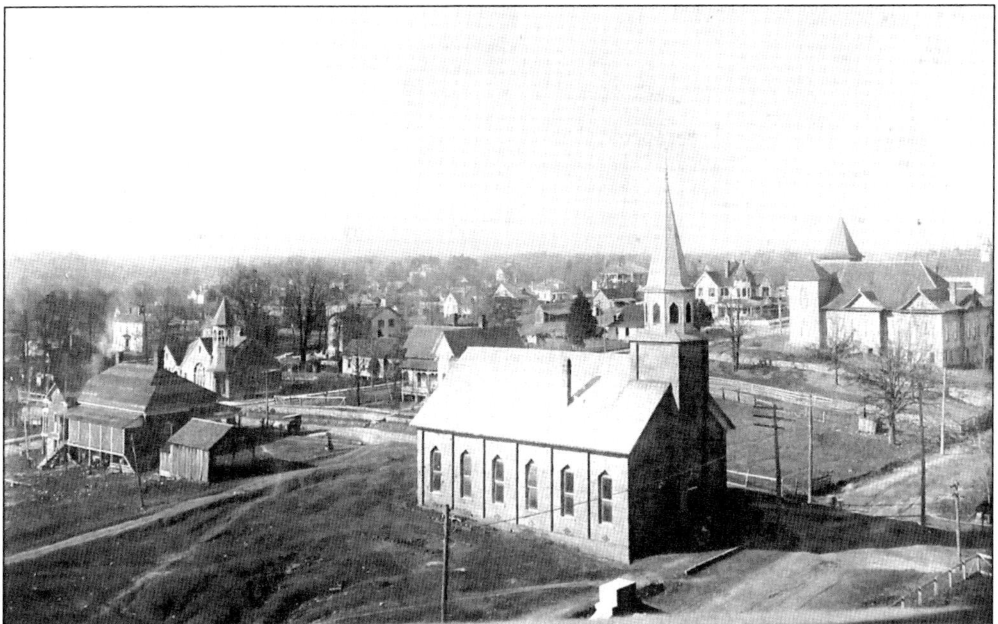

Downtown Jasper, 1913. A spectacular view of Jasper shows all four downtown churches. The First Christian Church is on the left, visible above the top of the infirmary; the old First Methodist Church is in the middle foreground; the First Baptist Church is at right with numerous peaks and steeples; and at the extreme right, barely visible above the Baptist church, is the First Presbyterian Church.

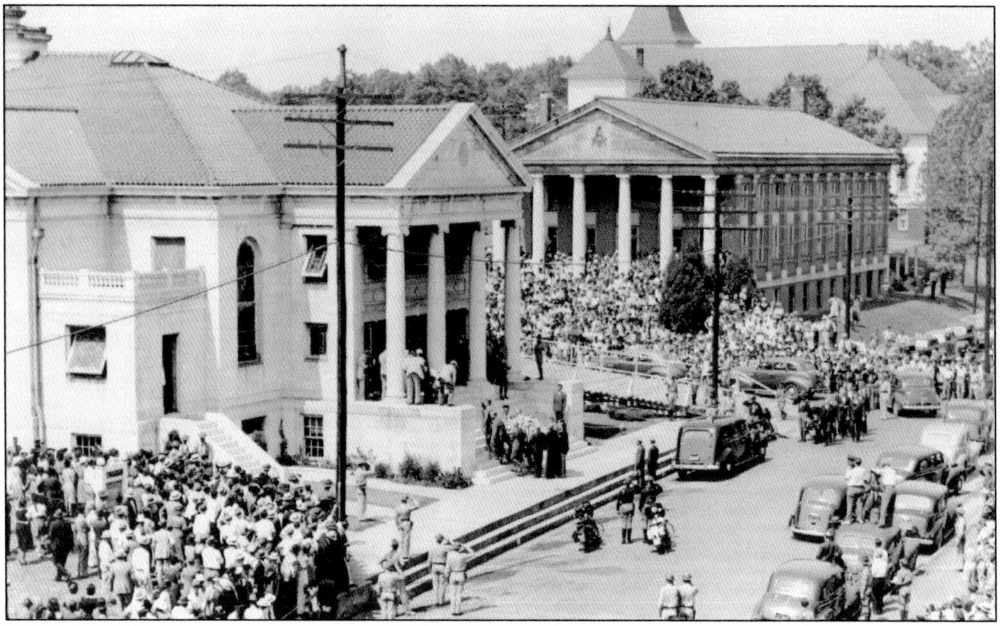

Bankhead Funeral, First Methodist Church, 1940. William Brockman Bankhead died on September 15, 1940, and his funeral in Jasper was attended by President Franklin D. Roosevelt and hundreds of dignitaries from Washington, including a relatively unknown senator from Missouri named Harry S Truman. There was an estimated crowd of 30,000 mourners lining the street from the depot to the church.

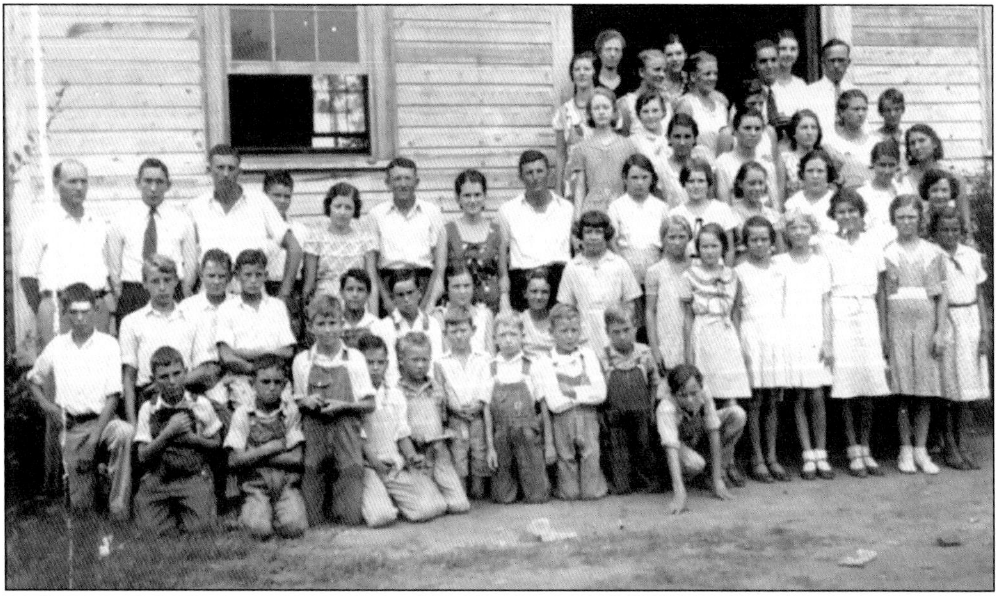

New Prospect Singing School, c. 1940. This singing school, located at New Prospect Baptist Church, was a very popular event, which started in the 1800s in Walker County. The school members are gathered in front of the second New Prospect Church building, the first being a log cabin built in 1857. Luther Drummond, standing far left, taught this "Fa-Sol-La" singing school.

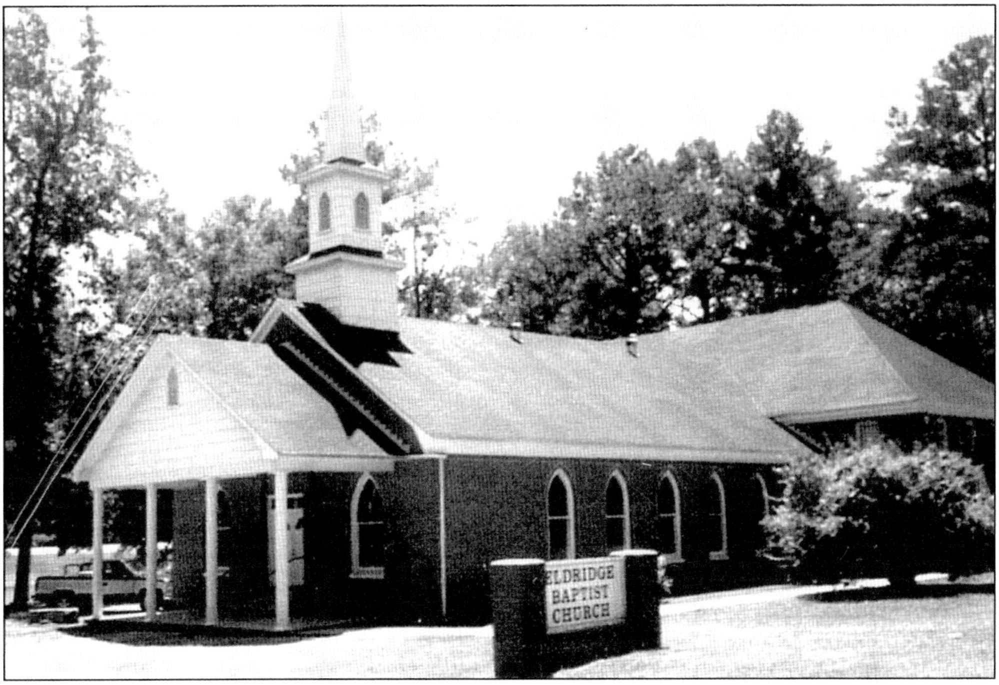

BAPTIST CHURCH, ELDRIDGE. The Eldridge Baptist Church was the first church in the history of Eldridge. The first building was constructed in 1870 on land donated by Esom Kelley, and the present church, seen above, was built in 1956. This church used the same stone steps and bell as the 1870 church, and the stained-glass windows were saved from the 1905–1906 structure.

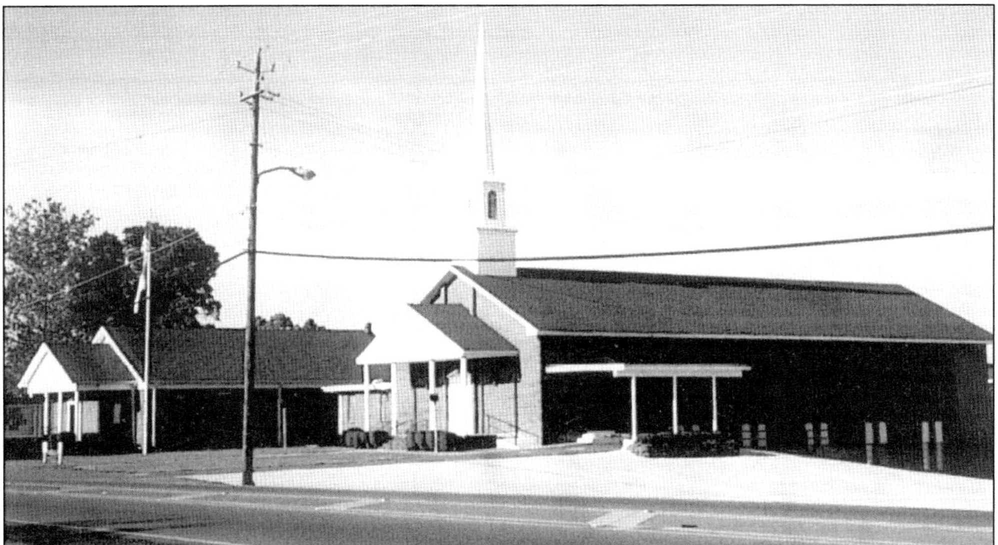

MOUNT VERNON BAPTIST CHURCH, CURRY. Located 10 miles northeast of Jasper at Curry, Mount Vernon Baptist Church was once part of the Blooming Grove Church and community. W.E. Williams donated two acres for a church at its present site on Curry Highway 157. The present building was constructed in 1942 and remodeled numerous times. In 1972, a new sanctuary was built, followed by a family life center in 1987.

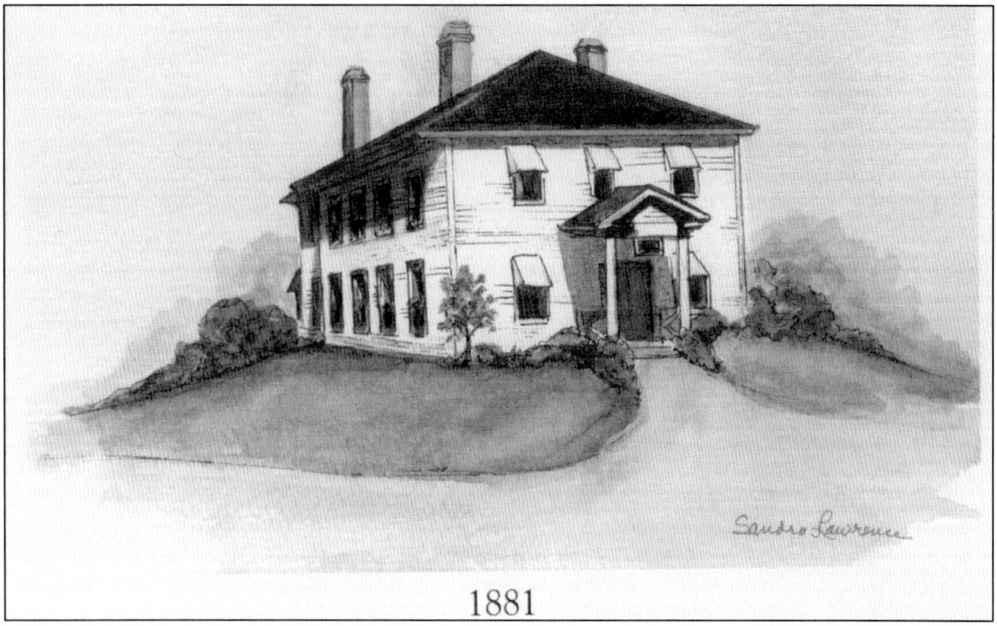

First Baptist Church, Jasper, 1881. This church was built on the west side of Fourth Avenue between Eighteenth and Nineteenth Streets, at a cost of $700. After meeting for three years in the county courthouse, the new, two-story wooden structure was completed in 1881. Rev. J.E. Cox was the first pastor, and the church was incorporated in 1898, which was extremely unusual for those early times.

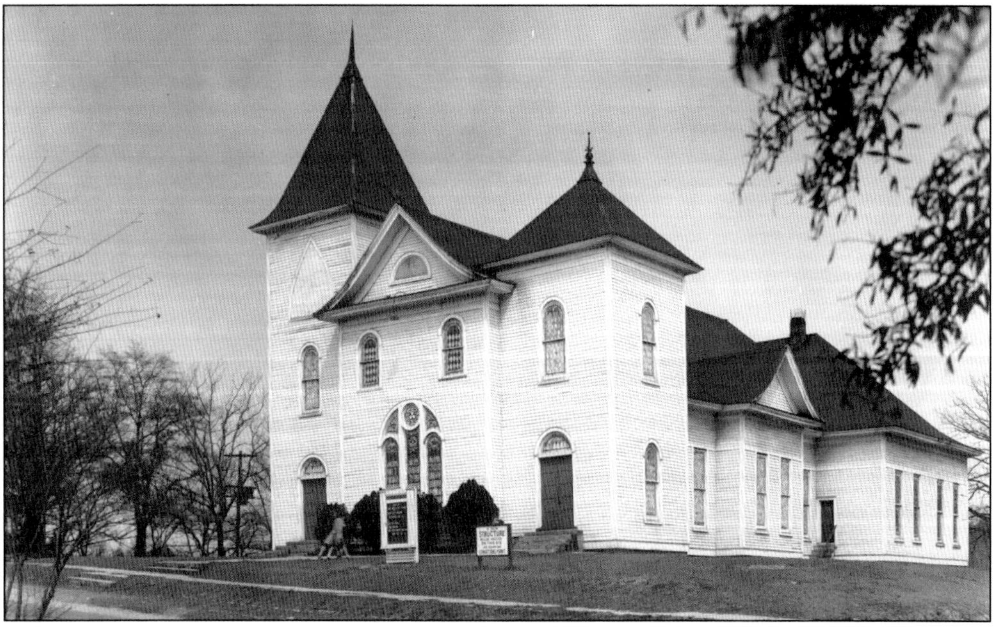

First Baptist Church, 1901. The second church built by First Baptist was this beautiful wooden-frame structure that covered most of Seventeenth Street between Third and Fourth Avenues. The entrance of the church faced Fourth Avenue and was built at a cost of $8,000, including the lot. Rev. James Longcrier was the first pastor at this new church building.

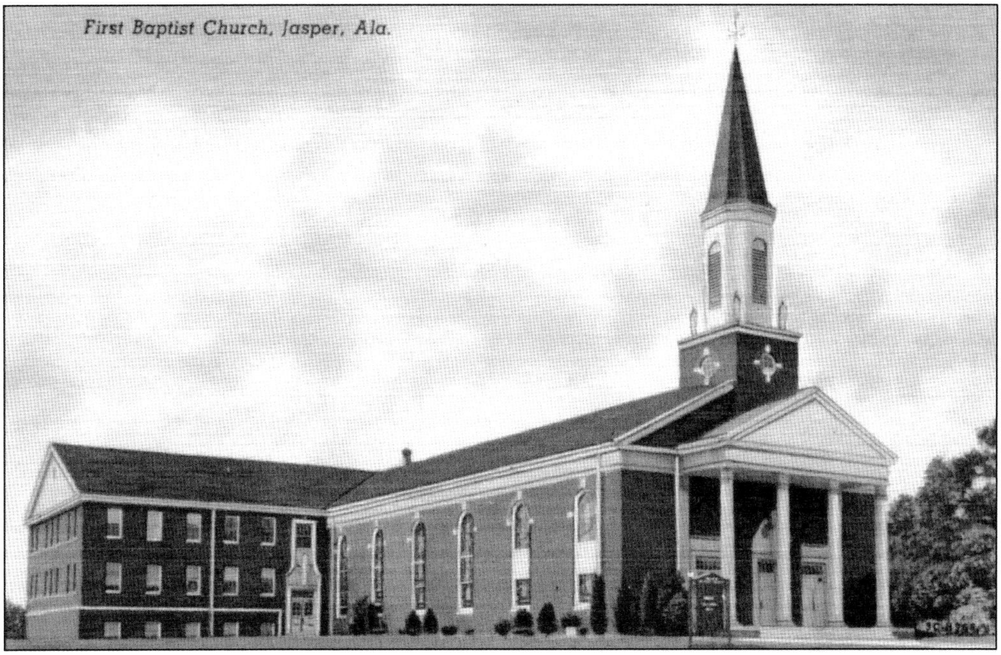

FIRST BAPTIST CHURCH, JASPER, 1950. From 1943 to 1946, the First Baptist Church membership raised over $95,000 for the construction of this building at 1604 Fourth Avenue, overlooking the city. On May 27, 1950, this church became occupied, and the move to the site was the third in the church's 72-year history. Dr. Waymon C. Reeves was the first pastor at this location.

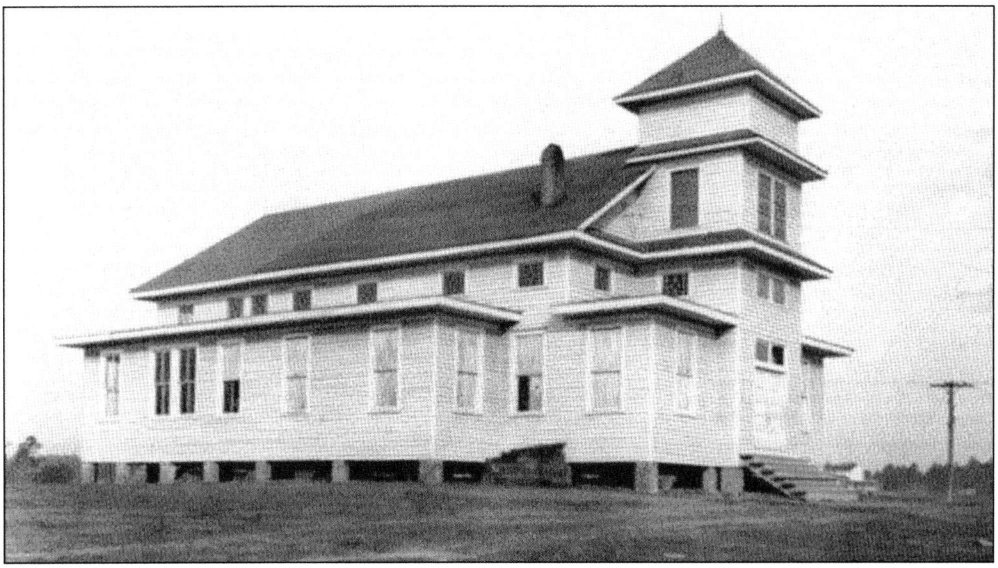

DEBARDELEBEN CAMP CHURCH, SIPSEY. Around 1913, this mining company built a church in Sipsey, causing a problem as to which denomination would hold services there—Baptist or Methodist. The respective denominations eventually alternated Sundays. Mrs. Rose Fies, worried that the children were being cheated, developed a Union Sunday School for all denominations to study the "one Bible" every Sunday.

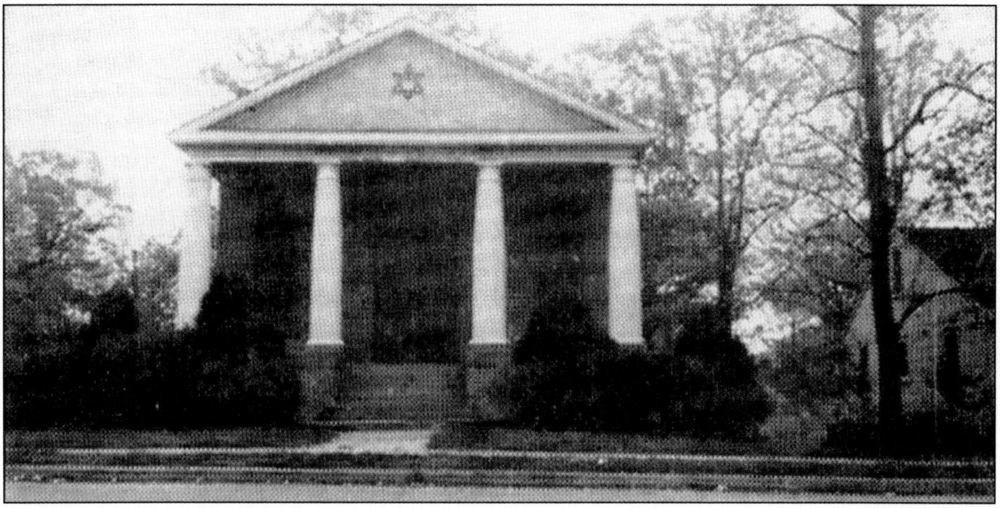

Temple Emanuel, Jasper. The Jewish citizens of Jasper purchased a lot on the southwest corner of Fifth Avenue and Fifteenth Street upon which to build a temple. The cornerstone was laid on Friday, October 12, 1922, and the building was completed and dedicated on June 3, 1923. Some family charter members were Green, May, Weinstein, Newmark, Shapiro, Newburger, Engle, Coplin, and Gilbert.

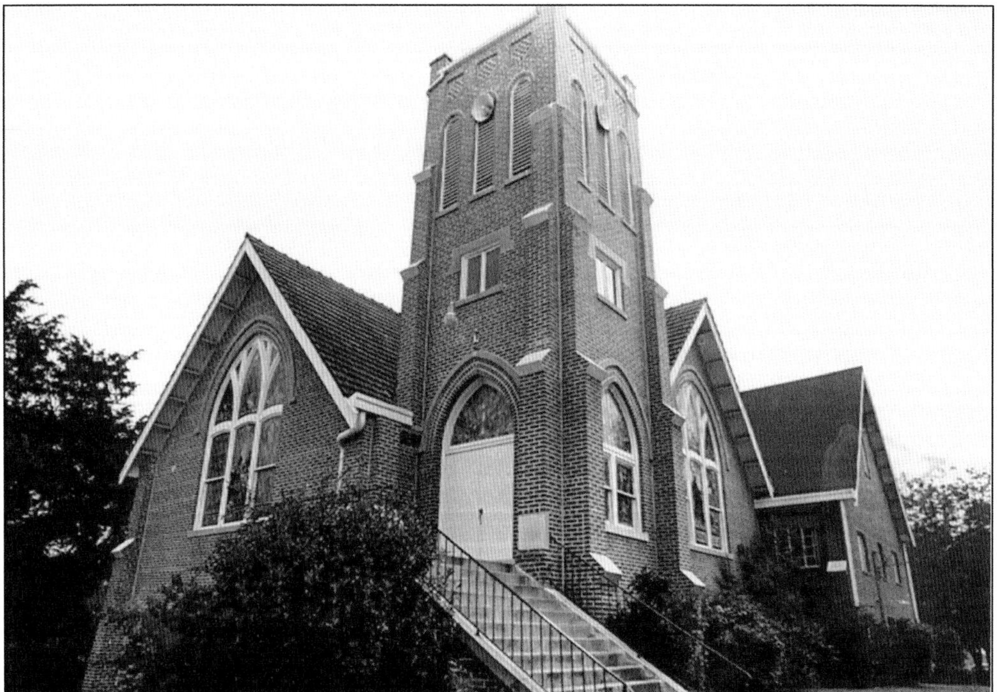

Long Memorial Methodist Church, Cordova. The Methodist Episcopal South in Cordova was organized in 1888. Judge F.A. Gamble was the leader in organizing this church. Capt. B.M. Long owned all of what was to become Cordova, and upon his death, his heirs built a new brick church named Long Memorial Church in honor of the "Father of Cordova." It was dedicated in 1912.

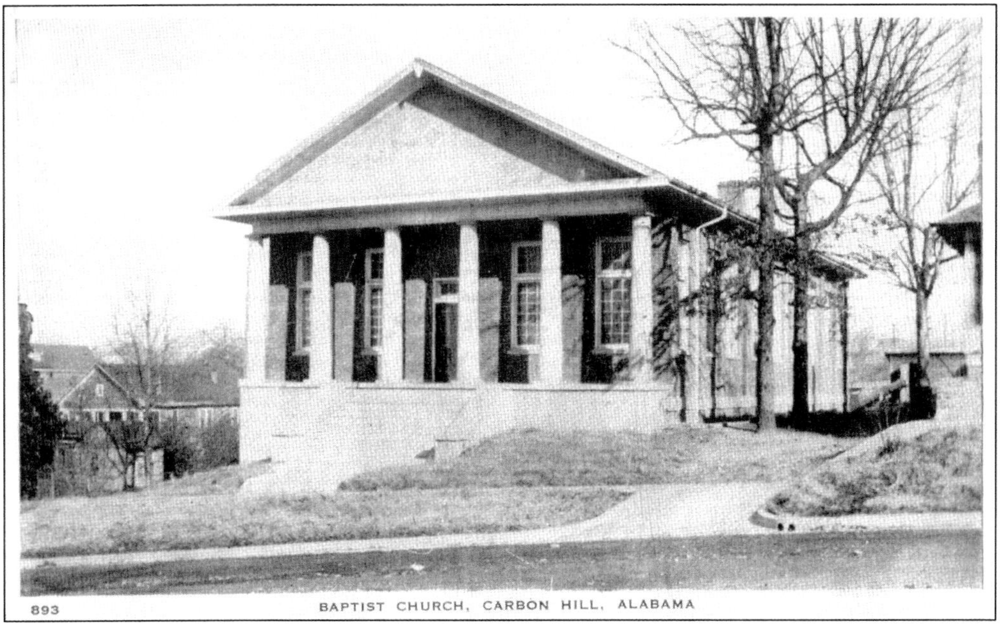

FIRST BAPTIST CHURCH, CARBON HILL, 1930. Constructed in 1926 for $30,000 under Pastor B.F. Atkins, this brick building replaced the one irreparably damaged by the 1917 cyclone. The church was originally organized in 1888, and the first pastor was a circuit riding preacher named Judge James Hilton. The present pastor is Rev. David Lowery.

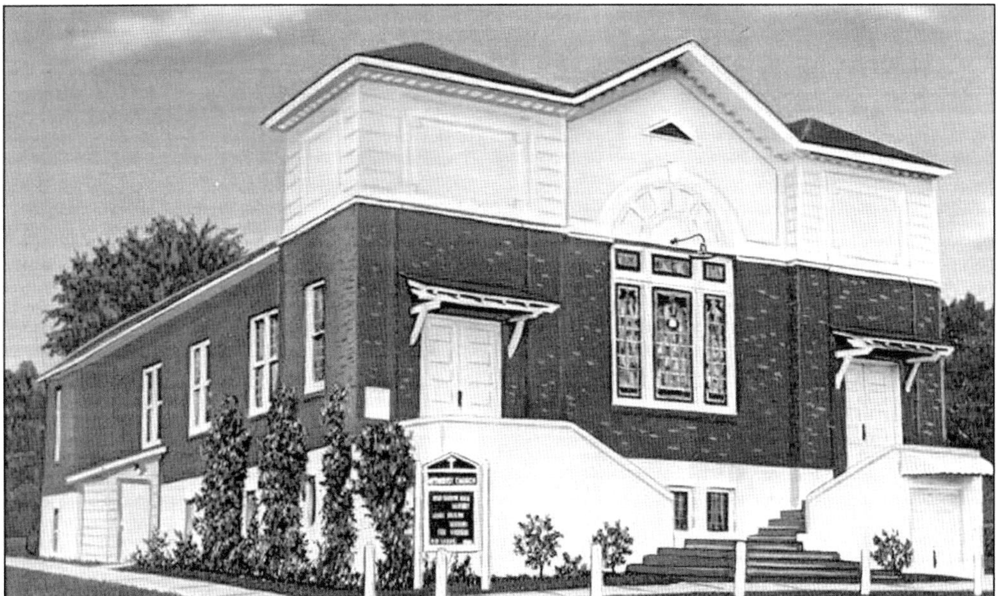

FIRST METHODIST CHURCH, CARBON HILL. The Methodist church was founded in 1888, and the first pastor was J.T. Wilkins. The members met in a house until the church building was completed in 1898. The cyclone of 1917 destroyed the church. The present building, shown above, was constructed in 1918, and its many antique stained-glass windows make it one of the most beautiful churches in Walker County.

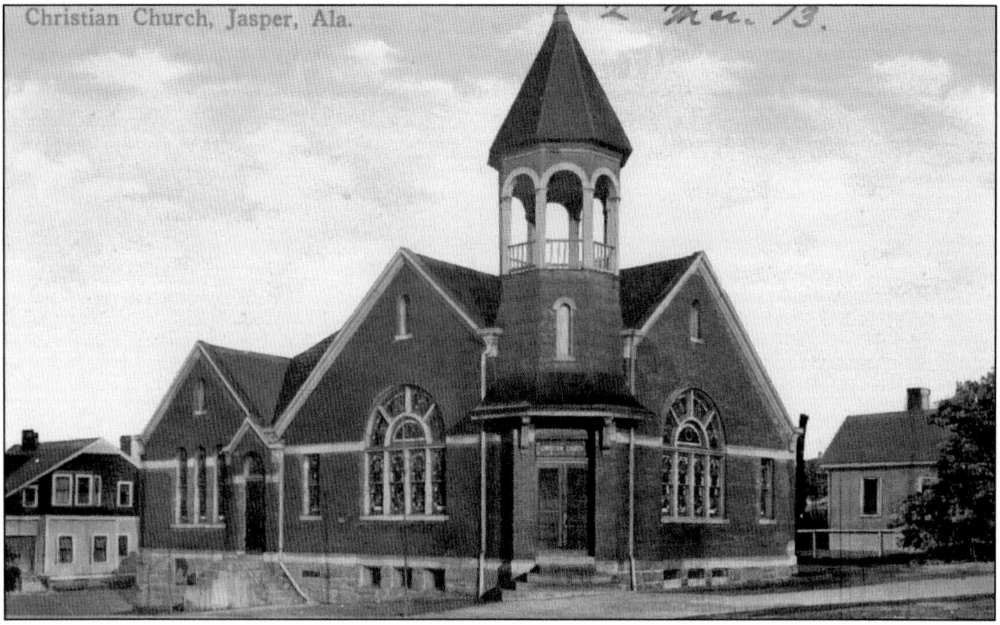

First Christian Church, Jasper. This church was organized in 1898 with 15 charter members. Until 1901, they met in a store in west Jasper, when they purchased the old Baptist church building on Fourth Avenue. In 1906, they constructed the beautiful building shown above, located on the northwest corner of Eighteenth Street and Fourth Avenue. This building was destroyed by fire on March 14, 1926.

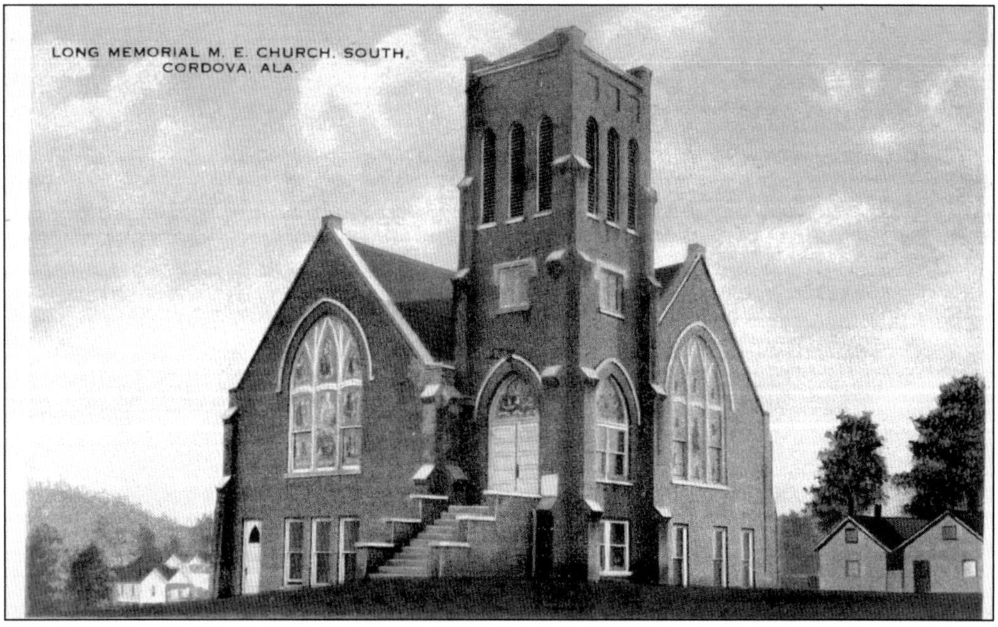

Long Memorial Church, Cordova, 1912. This beautiful Gothic Revival church is the most recognized structure in Cordova and one of the most recognized in the county. Capt. B.M. Long gave the land for the original building. The Northern Methodist and the Methodist Episcopal South merged to form the Long Memorial United Methodist Church in 1935.

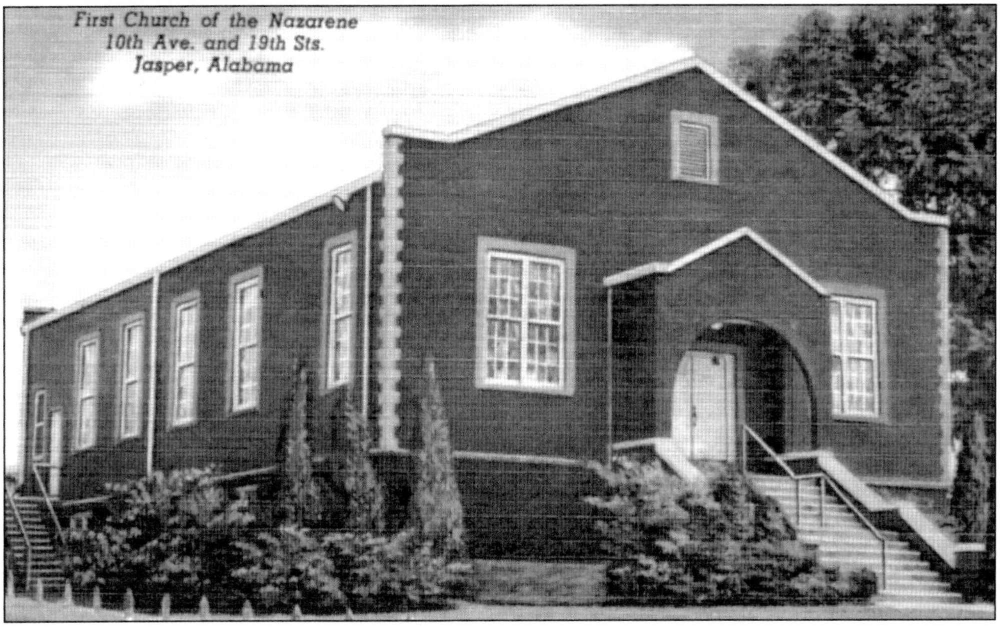

FIRST CHURCH OF THE NAZARENE, JASPER. This church, located on the southeast corner of Tenth Avenue and Nineteenth Street in west Jasper, tried a unique agricultural plan. It grew crops and raised livestock in 1928 to raise money for the church. Rev. Paul J. Stewart, who became pastor in 1954, wrote *My Beloved Vikings,* a history of Walker County High School athletics from 1920 through 1960.

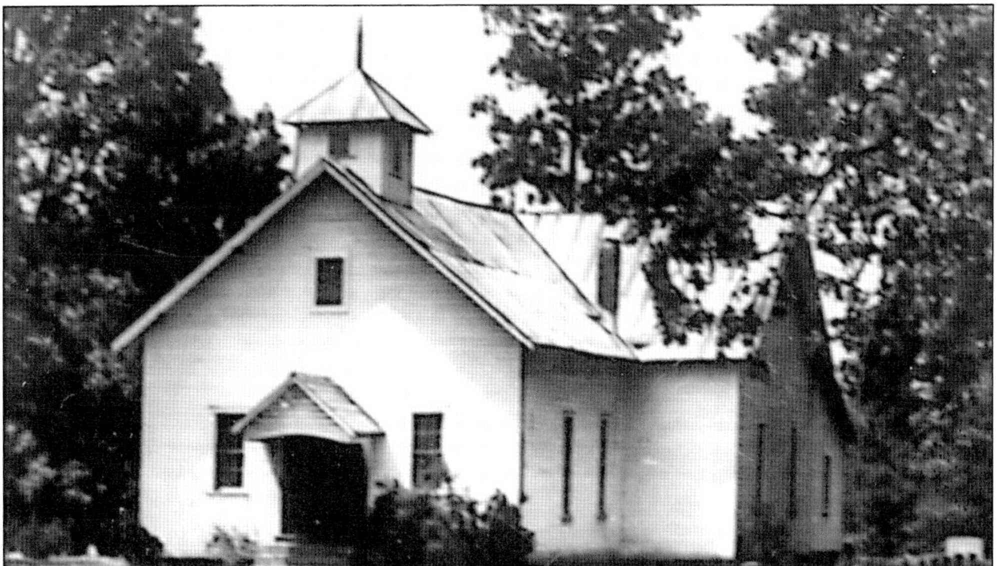

UNION CHAPEL METHODIST CHURCH. This church was founded by John Black, Sanford Argo, L.D. Gambell, John Mace Barton, and Samuel Black in 1859. It was built of logs with dirt floors. The name came from the fact that the pastors from different denominations would preach during the same service, hence the name "Union Chapel." This is the second building constructed on the site.

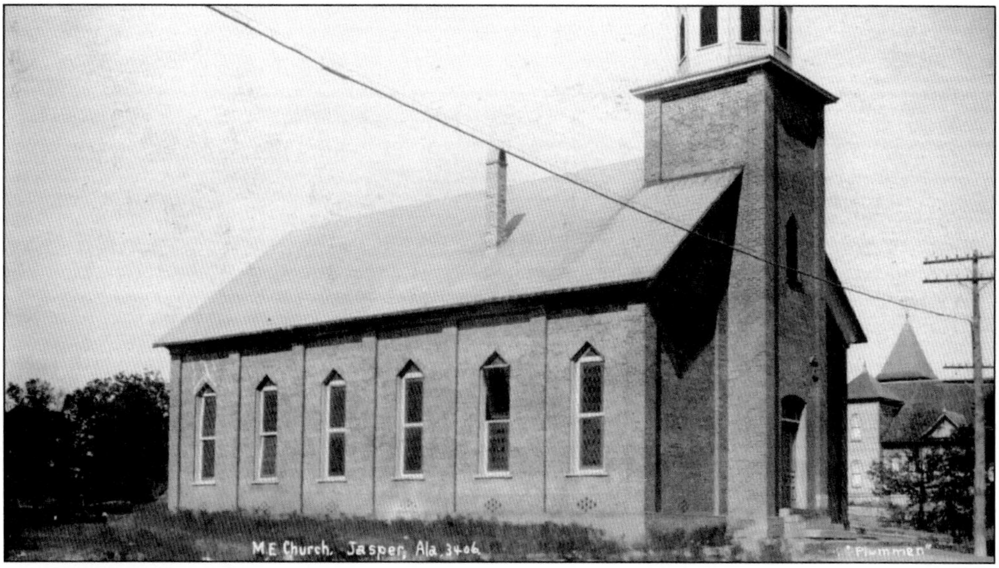

OLD METHODIST CHURCH, JASPER, 1908. In 1888, a new brick building was constructed to replace the wooden structure burned by raiders under Union Army general J.H. Wilson during the Civil War. This new church, above, would have a beautiful steeple topped by a belfry. Dr. Edward Gordon Musgrove gave the land for the church in 1833, making it Jasper's oldest church.

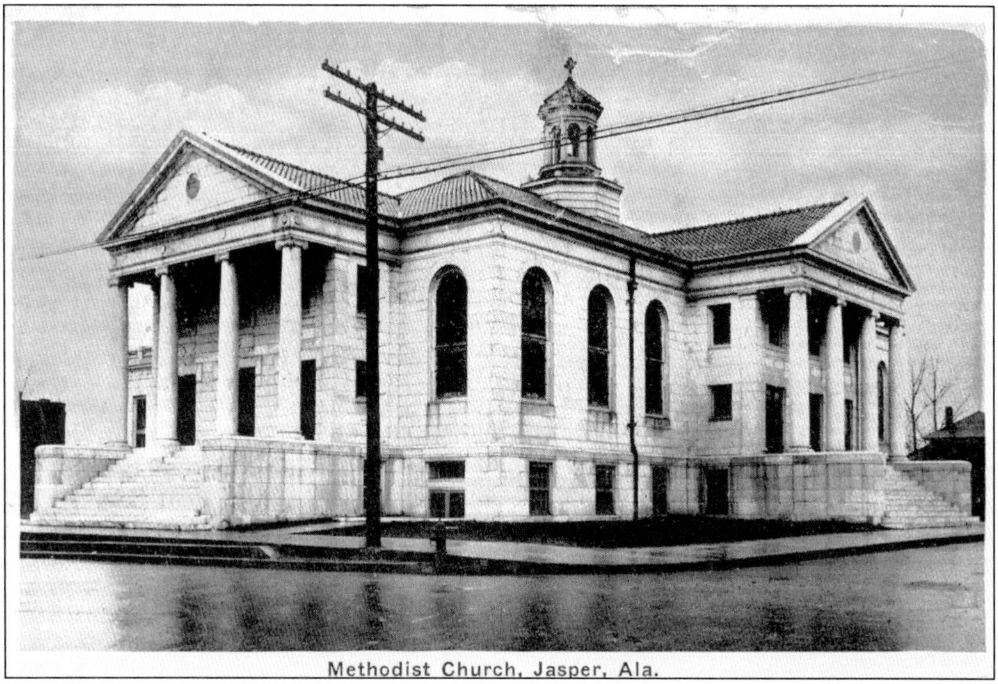

FIRST UNITED METHODIST CHURCH, JASPER. The building above was started in 1914 and dedicated on November 3, 1921. The grandson of Dr. Edward Musgrove, Lycurgus Breckenridge Musgrove, donated $2 for each $1 raised to build this Georgian white marble structure. It had columns made of one solid piece of marble. It is believed that Musgrove donated over $130,000.

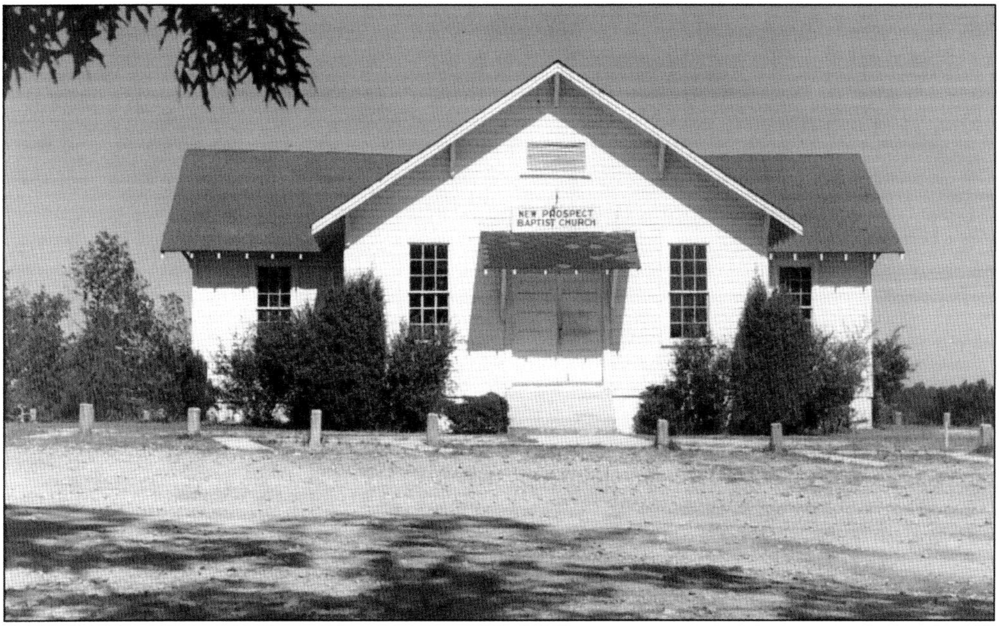

NEW PROSPECT BAPTIST CHURCH, 1920. The above church was built in 1918, and L.R. Wilson was the pastor at the time. Newton Hudson kept the two stoves on opposite sides of the church; he stoked them by walking back and forth in front of the pulpit during the service, surely somewhat of a distraction. This system was replaced in 1951 by a butane system at a cost of $706.

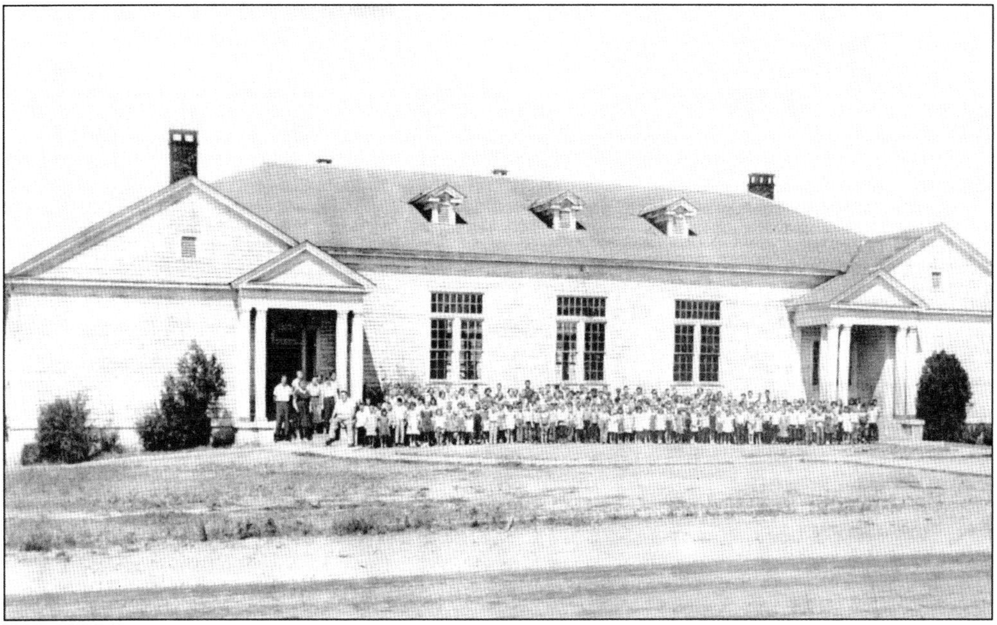

REDMILL SCHOOL, 1957. Redmill and Gamble Schools combined in 1937, and the above school was built with W.L. Brown as the first principal of the new school. This same year, the eighth and ninth grades from Saragossa began attending the Redmill School. The school closed in May of 1981 and was dismantled shortly thereafter. This school was at the present site of the Crossroads Church of Christ.

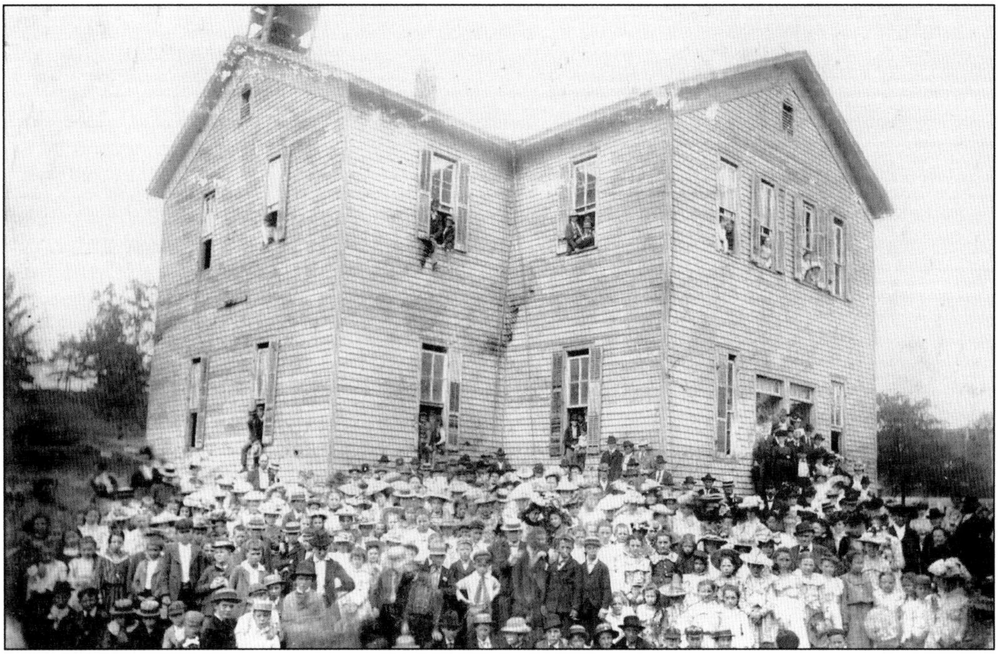

Old Academy, Jasper, c. 1890. The Academy was built in 1859, on what was to become Academy Hill. In 1879, the school was abandoned, but it reopened in 1886 by Prof. W.K. Brown, who also served as principal. The school burned in 1892, and classes were held in Tom Gray's home. Schools before this time were taught by traveling teachers or preachers, and the Bible was often the textbook.

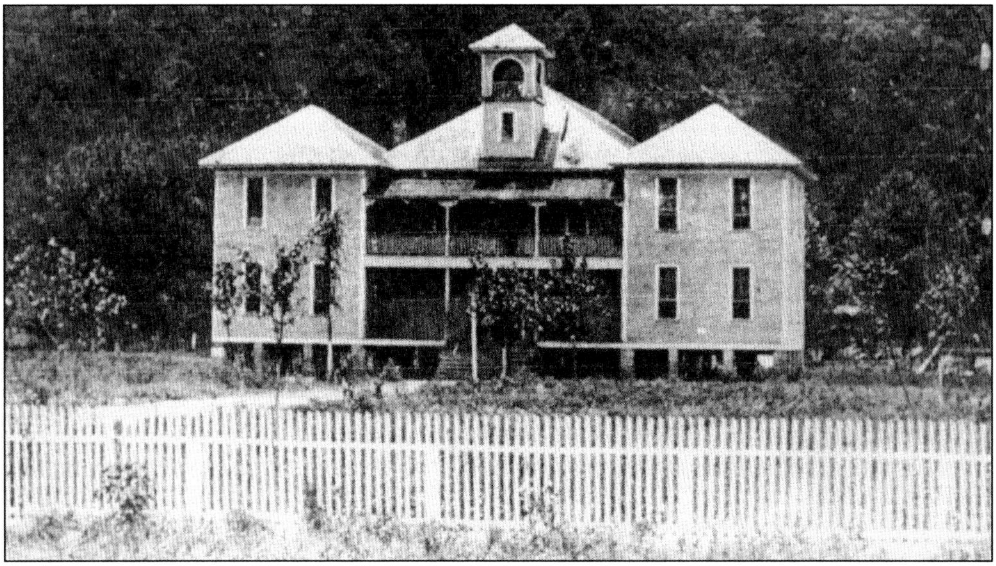

Walker County Training School, Patton. This beautiful old school building, which was for African-American children, was located at Patton near Oakman. The students, who came from all over the county, were housed at local homes. The school closed and was moved to the Frisco section of Jasper, and it kept the name Walker County Training School. In 1952, a new school was built in Coke Oven.

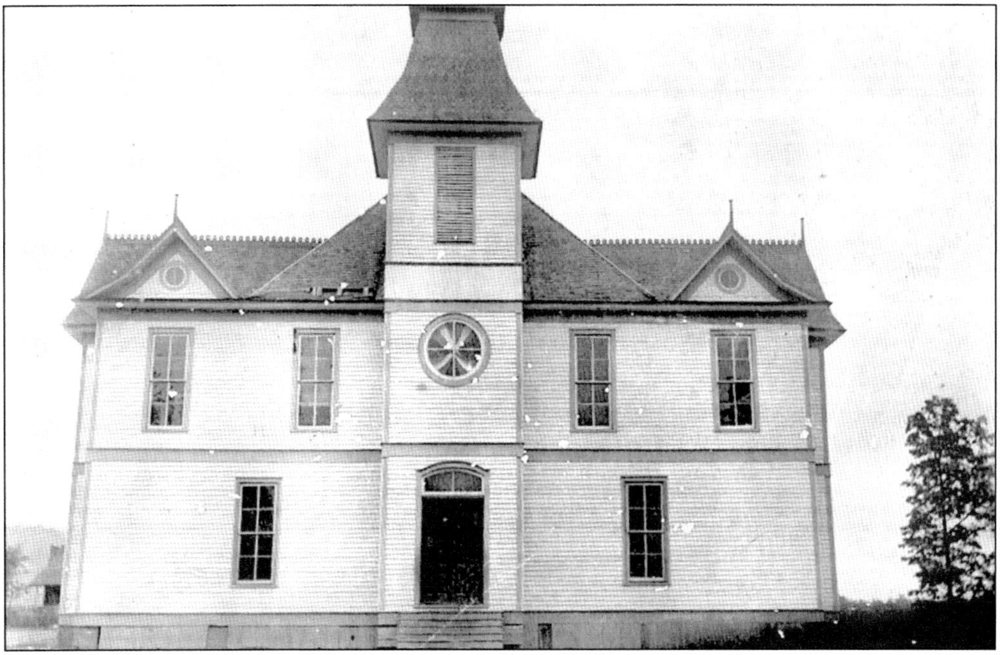

Day's Gap Boys and Girls School, Oakman. A school was built in Day's Gap around 1900 to educate the youth of the southern end of the county, and two of the first principals were Professor ? Reeves and Tom York. The school was a wood-frame building with a wood shake roof. The belfry contained a large bell that announced the beginning and ending of the school day.

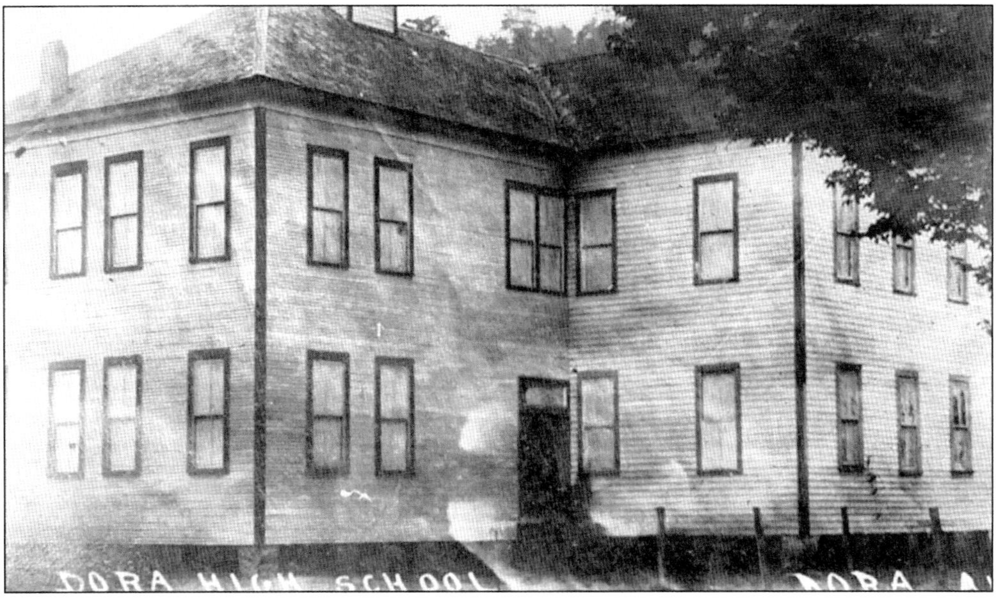

Dora Public School, 1903. The success of mining in Dora caused people to see a need for a new school, and in 1903, a new two-story frame building was constructed. The first principal was E.C. Palmer, and Dr. C.B. Jackson was a trustee and the driving force behind this new school. In 1921, the school building was replaced by the new 1921 "red brick school."

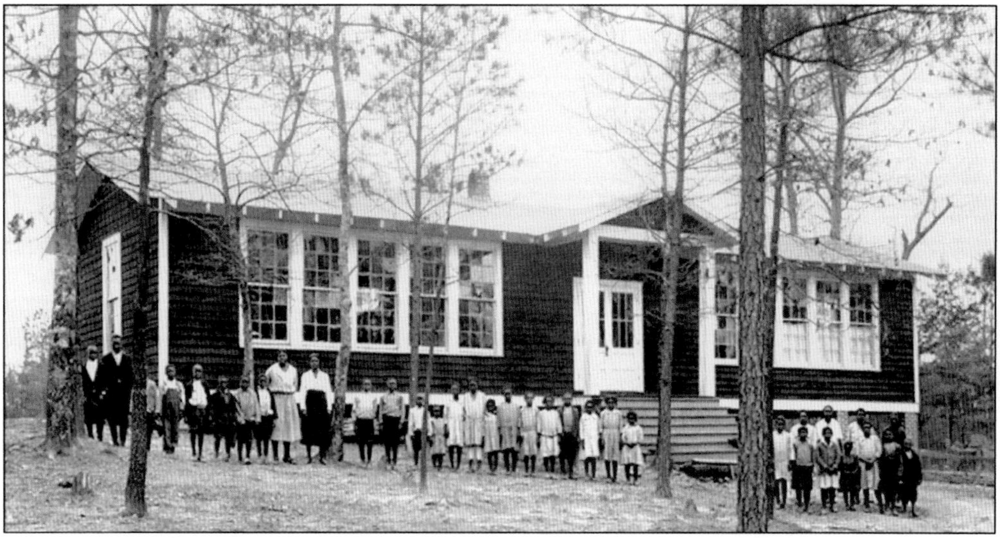

COLORED SCHOOL, EMPIRE. This school was built by the DeBardeleben Coal Company in 1923, after they purchased the Empire Coal Company. Robert W. Taylor was hired as the principal of the Sipsey and Empire Colored Schools, and he was one of the top educators, black or white, in the nation. Mr. Taylor was a Harvard graduate and a financial aide to Booker T. Washington.

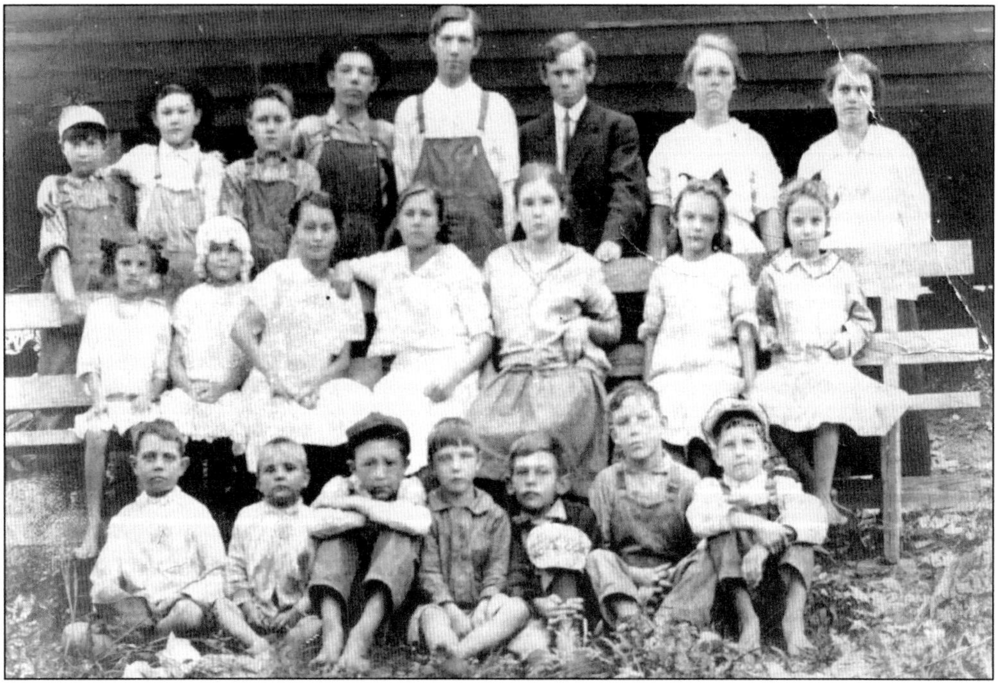

OLD BALTIMORE SCHOOL, 1915, CORDOVA. The old Baltimore School was a community school near Cordova. This picture was taken on November 18, 1915, in front of the wood-frame school building. The principal/teacher was Manley Barton (third from right, top row), who taught all grades in the one-room schoolhouse. Some names of families who attended are Coggins, Martin, Hunter, Hyche, Insor, and Putman.

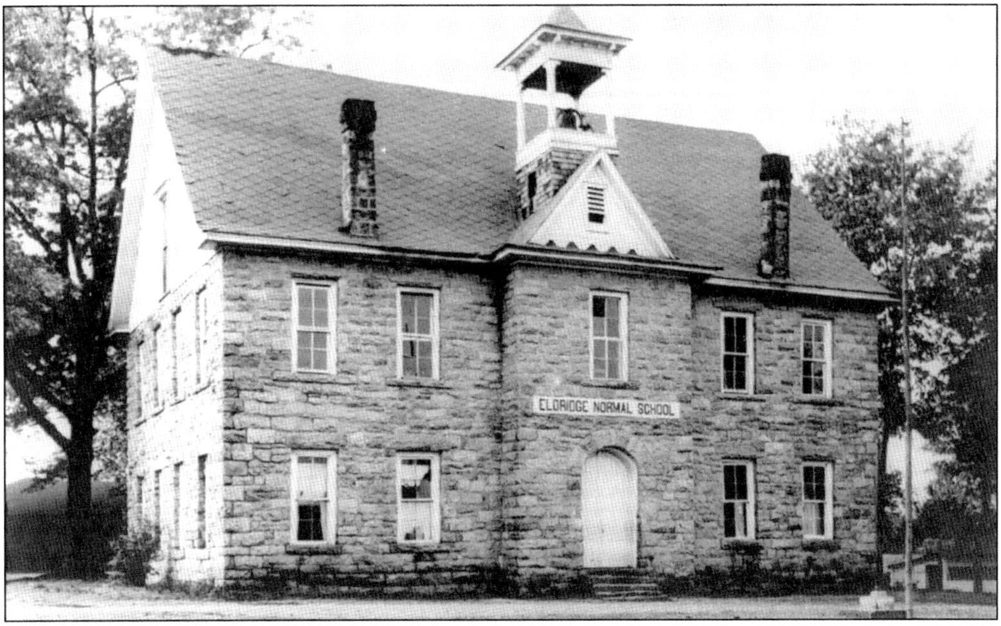

ELDRIDGE SCHOOL, 1897. With encouragement from teacher Robert Francis, a new school was initiated in 1890, and Easom Kelley and William Thorogood donated property for the building. Samuel Reed and his son William led the quarrying of the rock from the Thorogood Quarry, and the rock was then stacked at the site. The building was started in 1890 and finished in 1897. C.C. Kelley donated the bell that hung in the steeple.

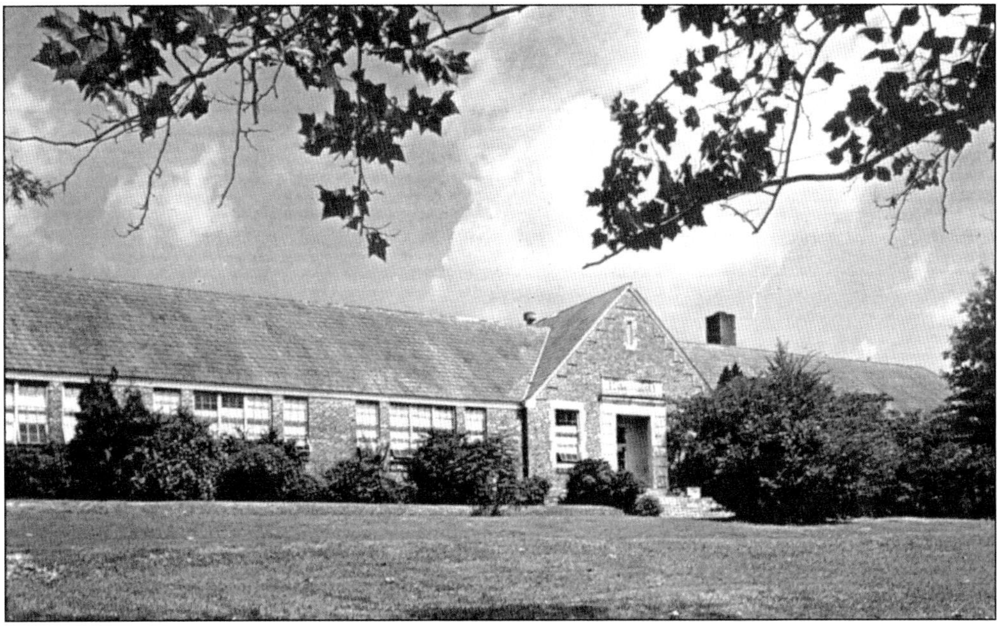

DORA HIGH SCHOOL, 1935. In 1935, a third school was built (shown above), and it served as the junior and senior high school. This building replaced the 1921 brick school, which then became Dora Elementary School. The first principal of the above facility was George Kilgore. Principals over the next 30 years were Amos Waldrop, Paul Hudson, and Glen Gant.

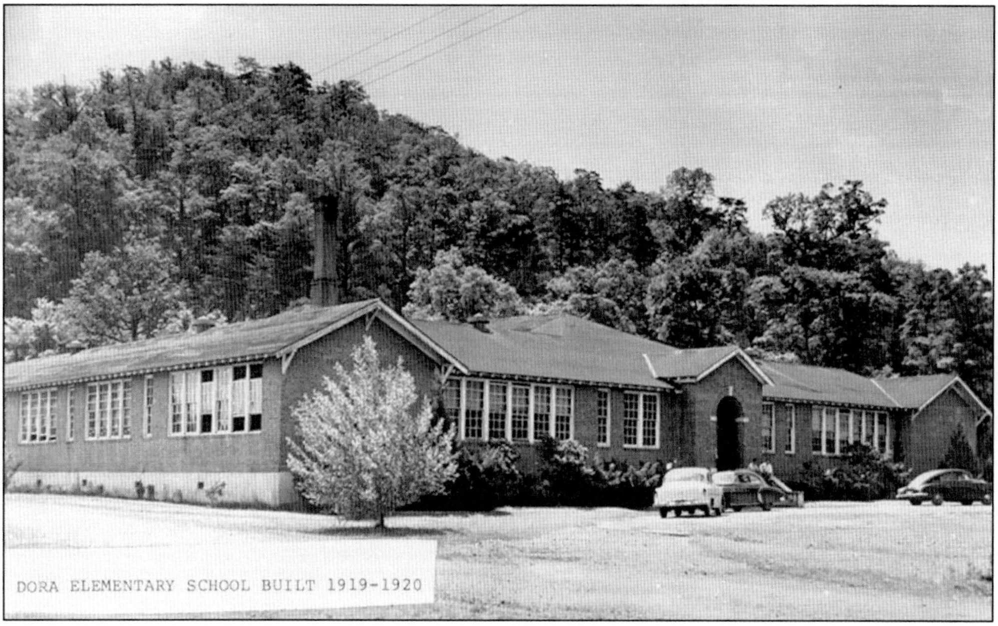

DORA ELEMENTARY SCHOOL, 1950. This building was completed in 1921 for $29,000 and served as the school for all grades, 1 through 12. When the new school was built in 1935, this one, which was located on School Street, became the Dora Elementary School. Principals of the elementary school over the years have been Mr. ? Sanford, Mr. ? Mitchell, Brack Putman, Dora Boyd, Ezra Evans, and Leonard Sartain.

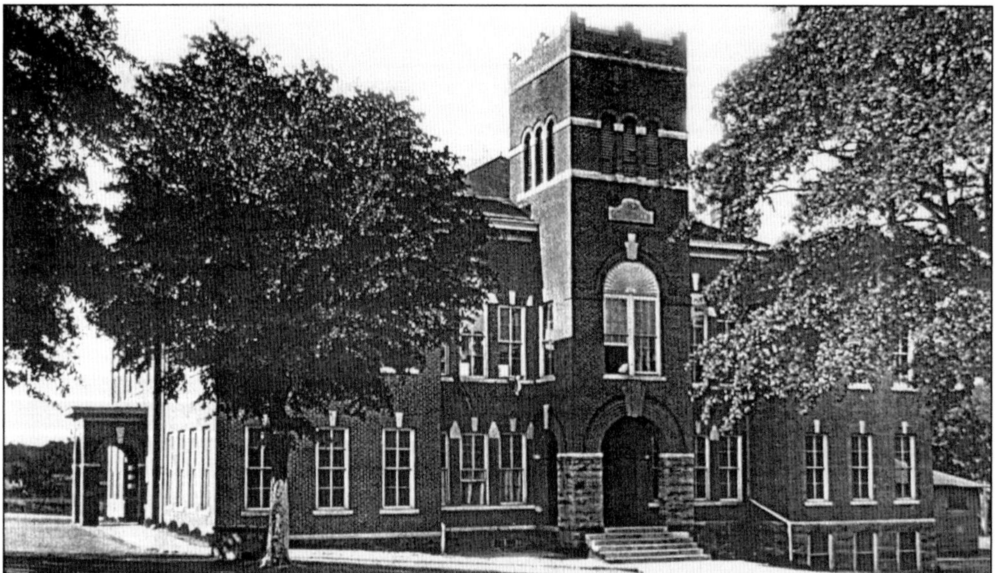

CENTRAL JUNIOR HIGH SCHOOL, *c.* 1949. This school was built in 1901 at a cost of $500,000. Shown here almost 50 years later is Central Junior High School, with the clock tower blown away in a storm. When the ninth grade moved to the high school, it became Jasper Middle School and finally Maddox Middle School, in honor of former Mayor Herman Maddox, who was a strong advocate of education.

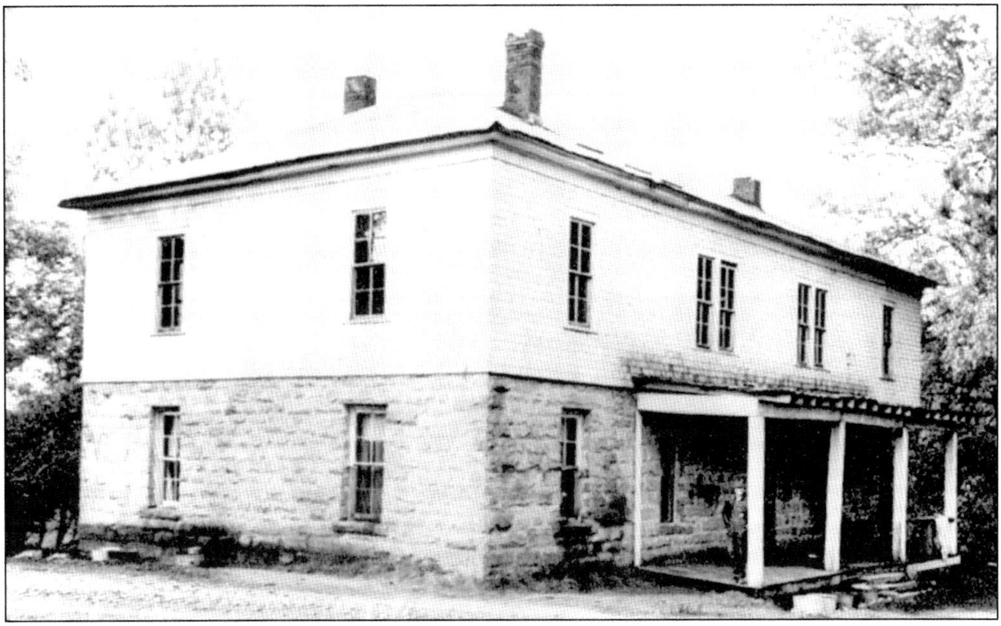

Eldridge Baptist Academy, Boys Dormitory. Located in the beautiful hill country of northwest Walker County lies the town of Eldridge. The Baptist Academy had been built on land that was previously a horseracing track. W.T. Colburn and Benjamin Kelley quarried the rock for the building. A large part of the construction was done with donated services and was completed in the fall of 1908.

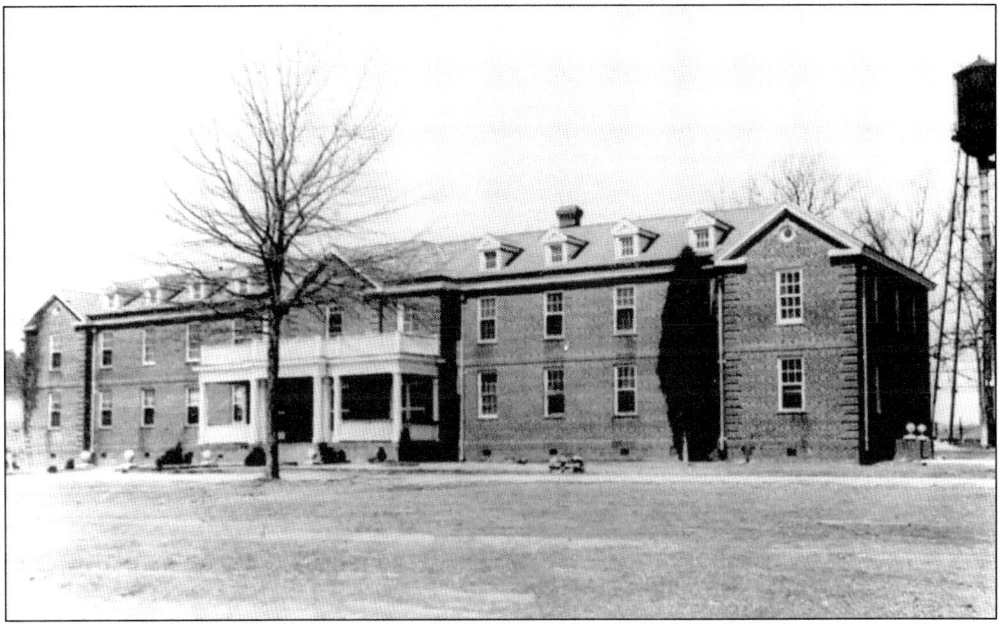

Eldridge Baptist Academy, Breckenridge Hall. After the girls' dormitory burned in the fall of 1925, a new brick structure was erected. This hall was named in honor of Breckenridge Musgrove of Jasper, who gave a substantial donation for the construction of the new building. All records of the school up to 1925 were lost in this fire.

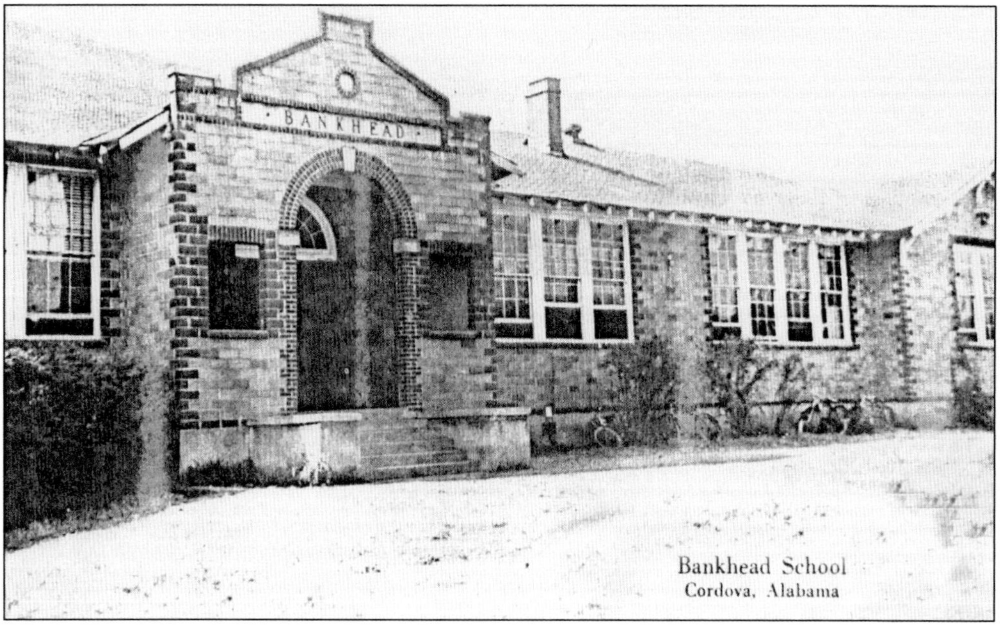

BANKHEAD HIGH SCHOOL, CORDOVA, 1925. The Bankhead High School was built in 1925 at a cost of $25,000 on land donated by Pope Long. It was named in honor of the late John Hollis Bankhead Sr. On September 21, 1976, the school building caught fire, and the wooden structure quickly burned to the ground. The only thing to survive the fire was a statue of the bust of Senator Bankhead.

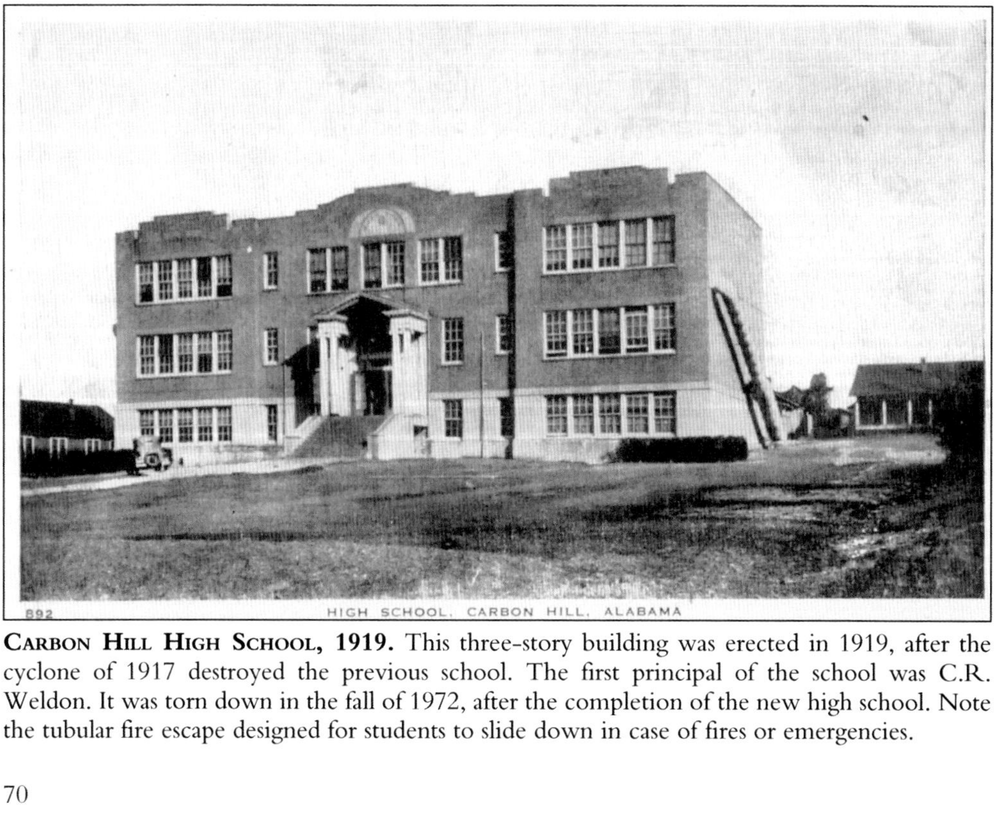

CARBON HILL HIGH SCHOOL, 1919. This three-story building was erected in 1919, after the cyclone of 1917 destroyed the previous school. The first principal of the school was C.R. Weldon. It was torn down in the fall of 1972, after the completion of the new high school. Note the tubular fire escape designed for students to slide down in case of fires or emergencies.

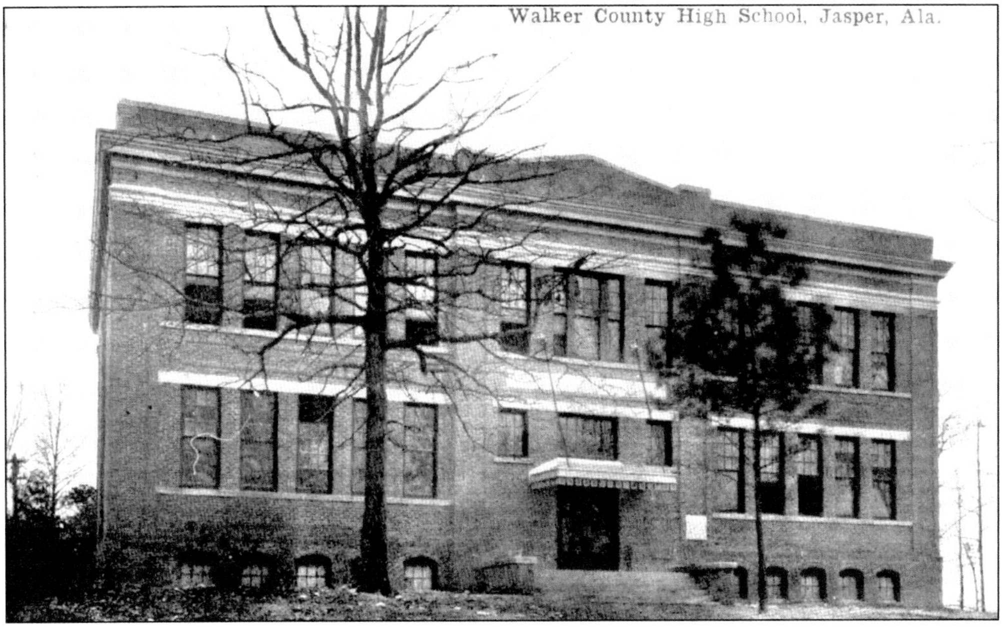

WALKER COUNTY HIGH SCHOOL, 1909. After the burning of the Academy, L.B. Musgrove donated five acres on Academy Hill to build the first Walker County High School. This handsome two-story building was totally destroyed by fire on January 28, 1916. Students were taught at the Thornhill residence for the remainder of the session. Daniel Harmon was the principal at the above school.

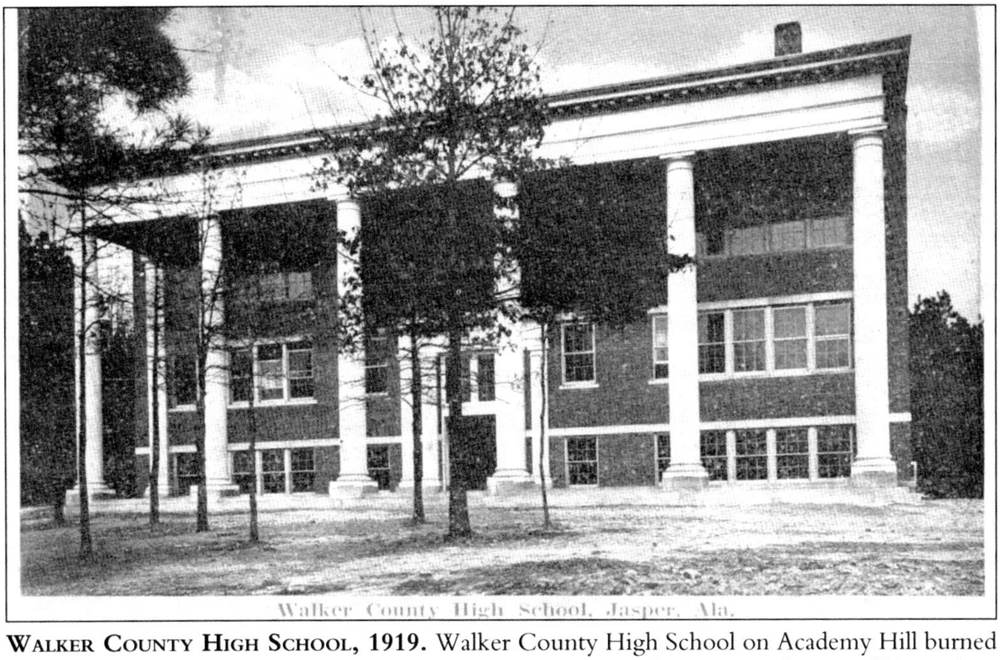

WALKER COUNTY HIGH SCHOOL, 1919. Walker County High School on Academy Hill burned in 1916, and a new school was needed. L.B. Musgrove donated 47 acres in honor of his mother, Elizabeth Cain Musgrove, for the new school. The citizens of Jasper donated land to add to the east Jasper site, where a three-story brick building was constructed at a cost of $40,000.

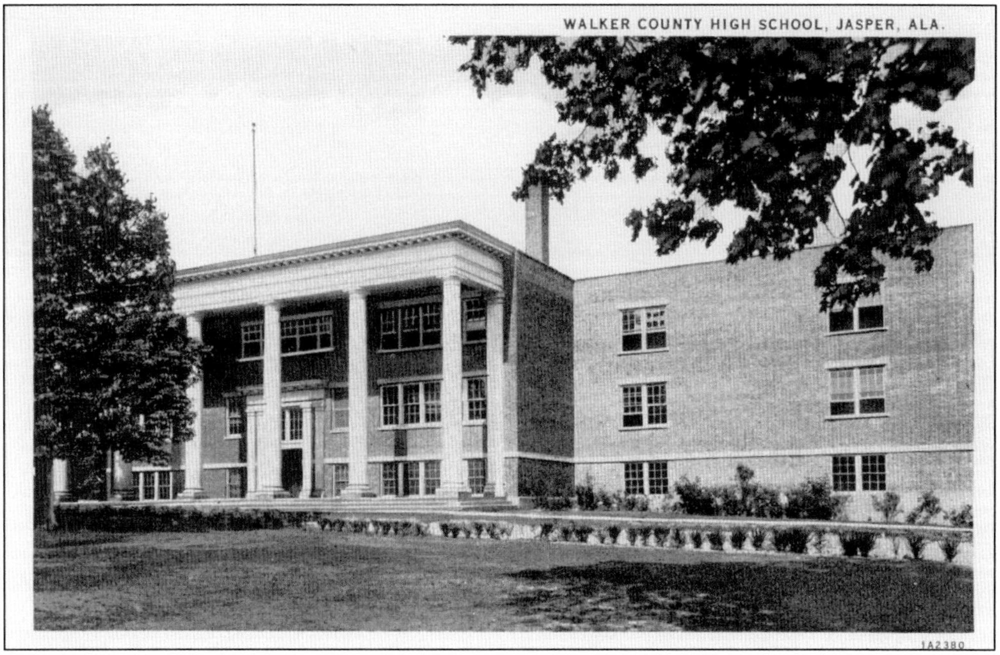

WALKER COUNTY HIGH SCHOOL, 1930. In 1929, Walker High School and the Jasper Junior High consolidated, and a wing was added to the school at a cost of $17,500. In 1930, the WPA made another addition, which consisted of a new auditorium, classrooms, library, cafeteria, and athletic dressing rooms. This gave Walker High the first indoor basketball facility in the county.

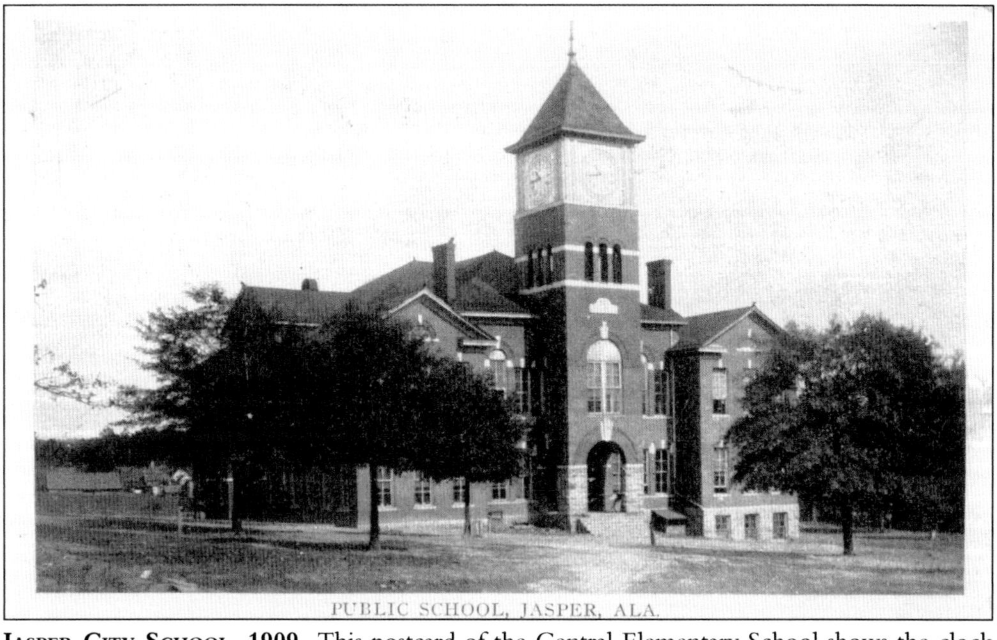

JASPER CITY SCHOOL, 1909. This postcard of the Central Elementary School shows the clock tower that was a landmark in Jasper for many years. The three-story brick building was originally constructed in 1901 for $50,000. This building kept with the success that Jasper was enjoying with economic growth in railroads, mining, lumber, cotton, and farming.

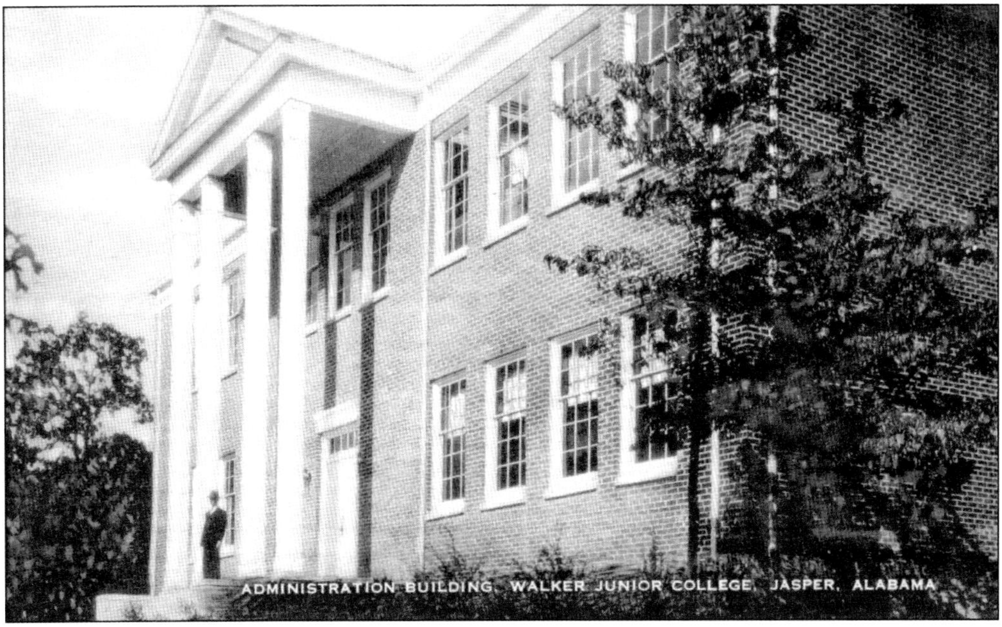

WALKER COLLEGE ADMINISTRATION BUILDING, 1941. Walker College technically began as Cheatham Conservatory with Mrs. R.L. Cheatham as president and Dr. Carl Jesse as the dean. The administration building, constructed in 1941 by the WPA, was the first building on the new college campus. Dr. Carl A.E. Jesse (shown above, standing between the columns) was appointed as the first president of Walker Junior College, serving as president until his death in 1955.

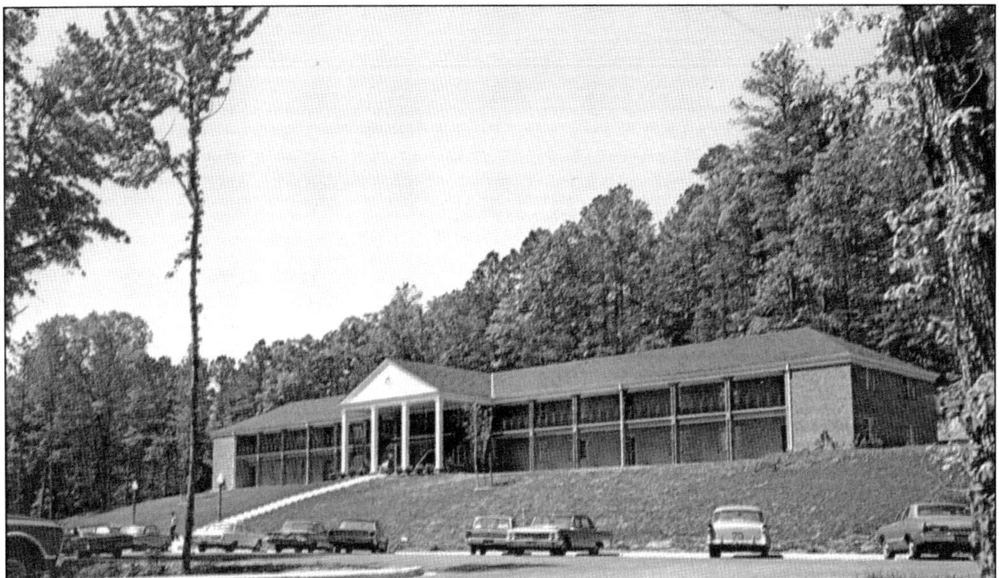

WALKER COLLEGE MEN'S DORMITORY, JASPER. The new Walker College dormitory for men was added in 1949 on this hill on the west side of campus. This dorm allowed male students from Jasper and surrounding areas to stay on campus rather than commute back and forth to school. It would not be until 10 years later, in 1959, when the ladies would get their dormitory, which was called Fair Hall.

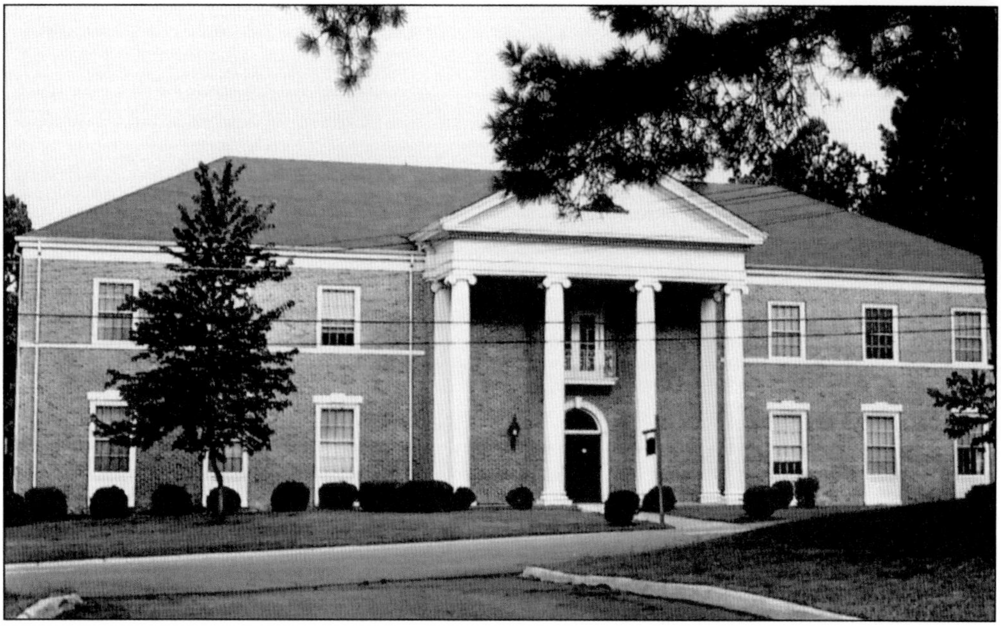

IRMA DILG NICHOLSON LIBRARY, 1971. The library at Walker College, built in 1971, was named in honor of Mrs. Nicholson, a donor and supporter of Walker College. The library houses over 30,000 titles and over 1,700 bound periodicals, and it subscribes to 185 periodicals and 50 microfilm titles annually.

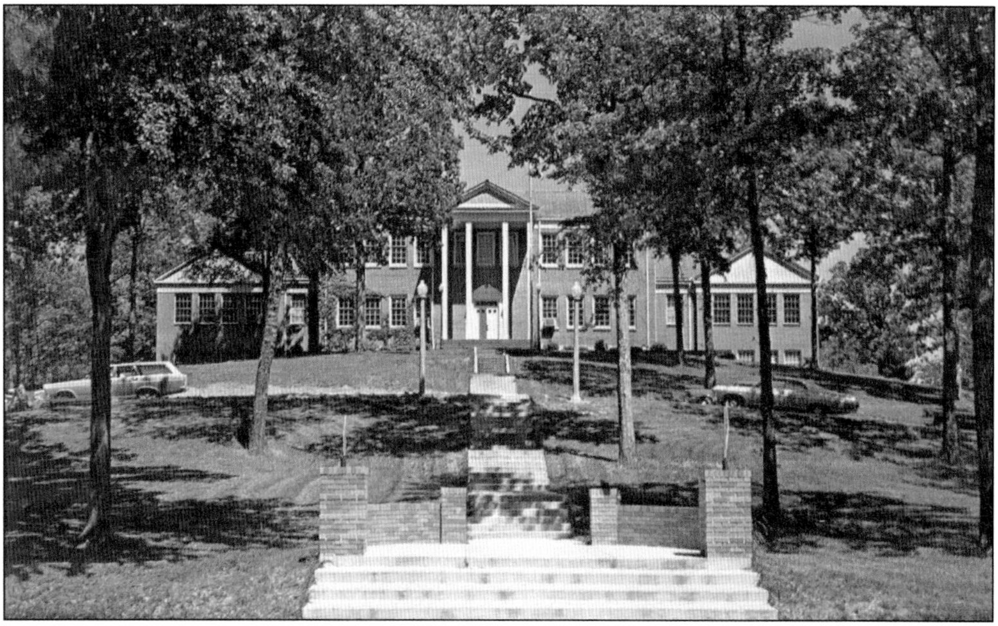

ADVISE HALL, WALKER COLLEGE. This building was originally situated atop a gently sloping hill, overlooking the wooded campus. In 1956, Walker Junior College started an extensive building program under the leadership of Dr. David Rowland. The buildings are in the Georgian style and well-placed on the 50-acre campus. It became a branch of Bevil State Community College in 1998.

Four

People and Homes

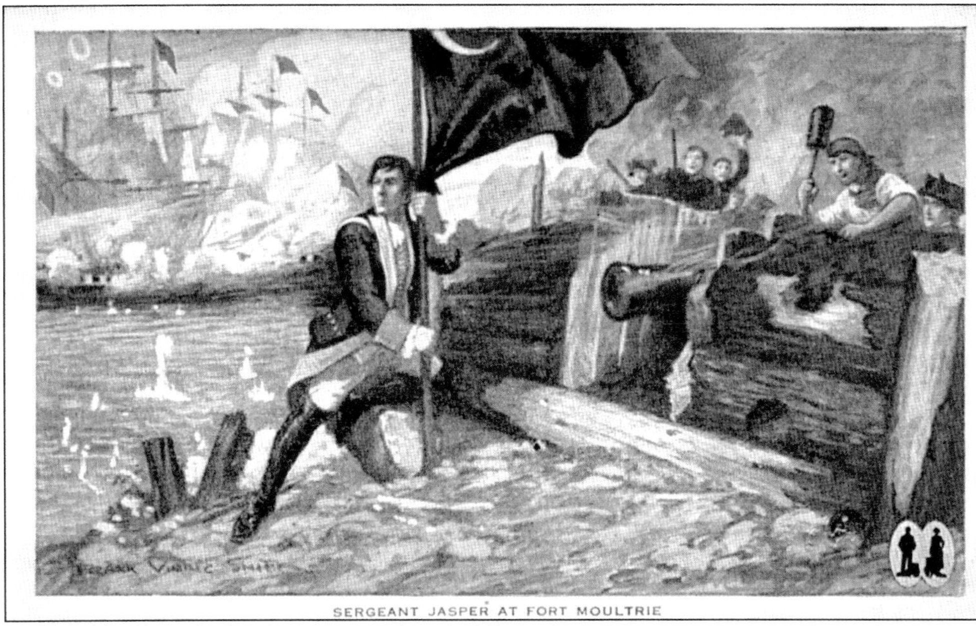

Sgt. William Jasper. Sergeant Jasper was a Revolutionary War hero who gained distinction for his valor at the Battle of Fort Moultrie after risking his life to save the new American battle flag. At the suggestion of Hugh Lollar, an early Walker County settler, the town of Jasper was named in honor of this war hero, and it became the seat of Walker County.

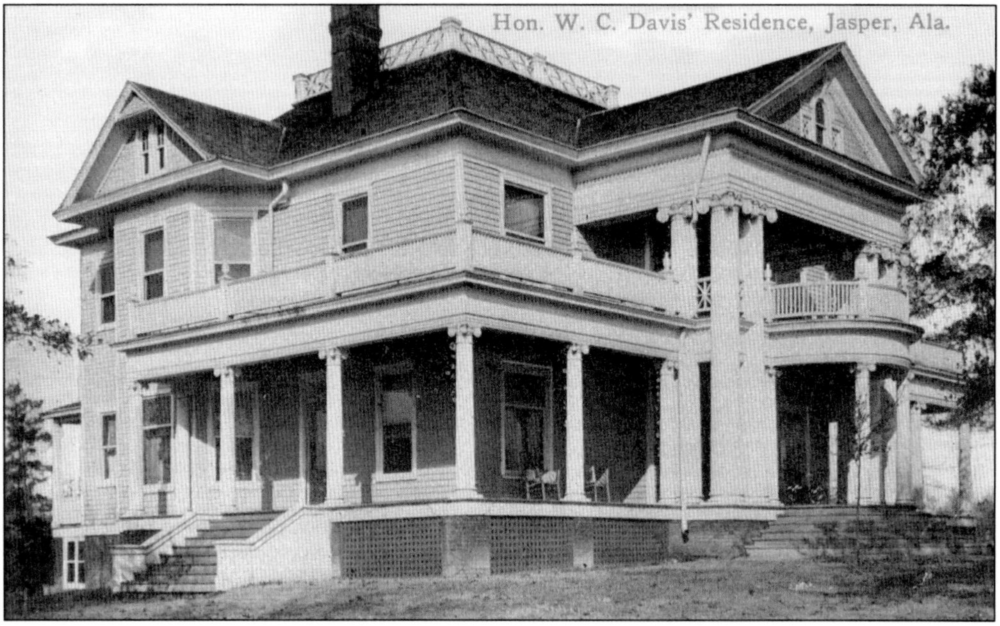

WILLIAM COLUMBUS DAVIS HOME, JASPER. The honorable William C. Davis built this house on Seventh Avenue in early 1899. It is a neo-classical revival, two-story frame house with six Ionic columns. Davis was elected lieutenant governor of Alabama in 1927 and was known for his prison reform program. He retired in 1931 and opened a law office in the First National Bank building.

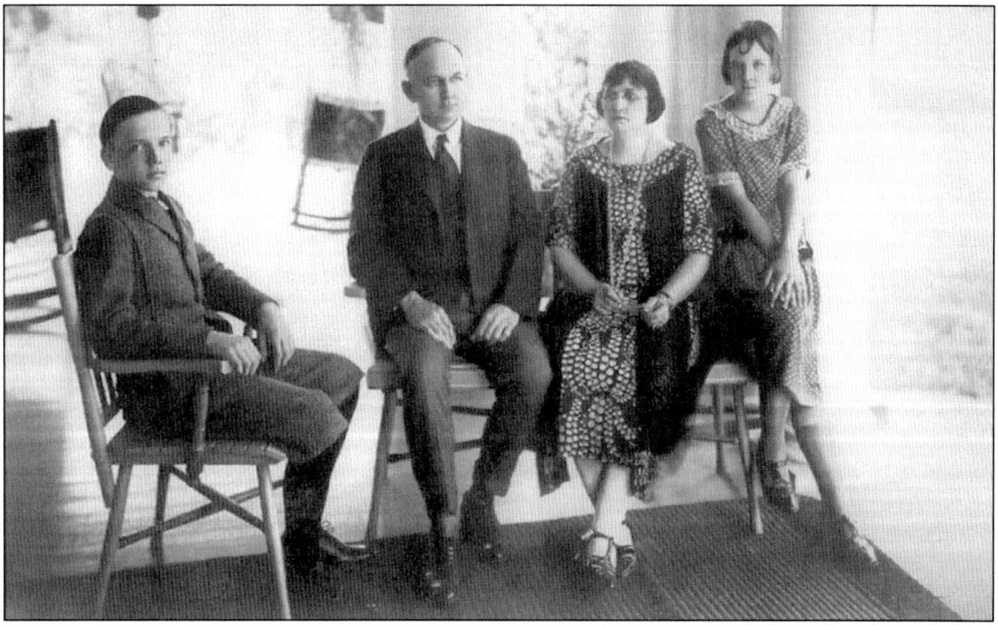

WILLIAM C. DAVIS FAMILY, JASPER. In the picture above, we see the family of W.C. Davis, a well-known Jasper politician and lawyer. He was elected to the state legislature in 1915 and then lieutenant governor in 1927. Pictured above, from left to right, are son W.C. Davis Jr., W.C. Davis Sr., wife Mard Elizabeth Gray, and daughter Elizabeth Gray Davis.

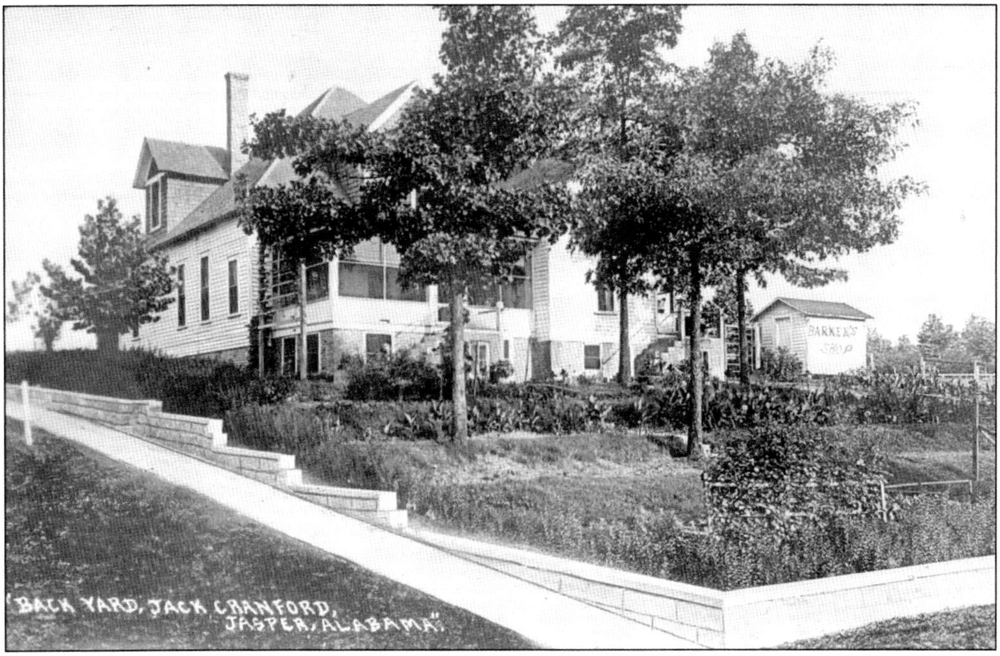

JOHN H. CRANFORD HOME, JASPER. This 19th-century, two-story white frame house with 23 Doric columns was built by John H. Cranford in 1899. The house was sold to John Hollis Bankhead Sr., founder of one of Alabama's most prominent political dynasties, which influenced American politics for more than half a century. The house previously named Forest Hill was renamed Sunset by Bankhead.

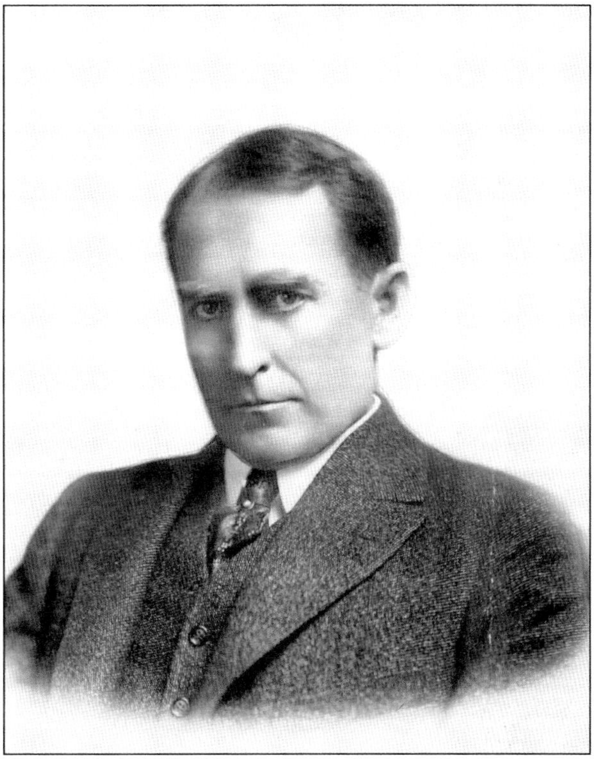

WILLIAM BROCKMAN BANKHEAD, JASPER. Senator Bankhead married Ada Eugenia Sledge and they had two daughters, Eugenia and the famous Tallulah. Bankhead became the speaker of the U.S. House of Representatives and held that position until his death in 1940. His funeral was the most celebrated event in Walker County's history and was attended by famous politicians and military leaders, as well as over 25,000 spectators.

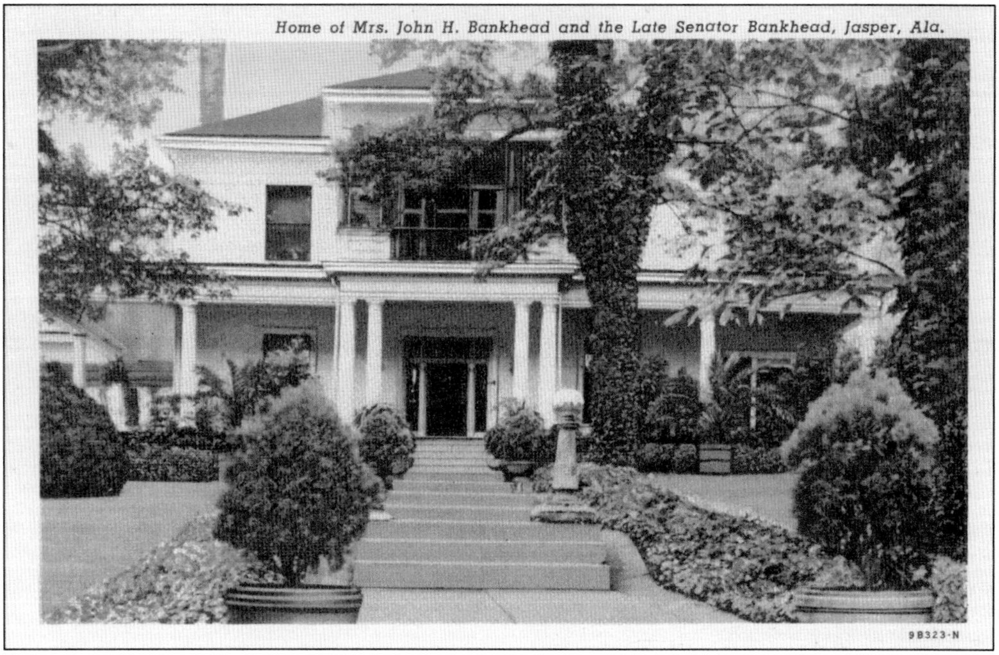

JOHN H. BANKHEAD HOME, JASPER. This 19th-century two-story home on Seventh Street was built by John H. Cranford in 1899 and sold to John Hollis Bankhead. The house was the home of many members of the legendary Bankhead family. Dr. Steve Johnson purchased the house from the Taggert family.

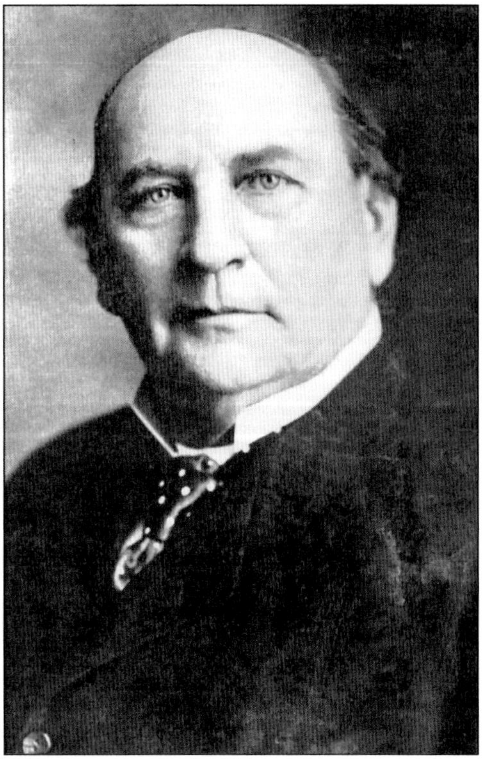

JOHN HOLLIS BANKHEAD SR., JASPER. Legendary politician John H. Bankhead enlisted as a private in the Confederate Army. Senator Bankhead was the last Confederate soldier to occupy a seat in the senate. He and his wife, Tallulah Brockman Bankhead, celebrated their golden wedding anniversary at Sunset in Jasper. He represented the citizens of Walker County from 1886 until his death in 1920.

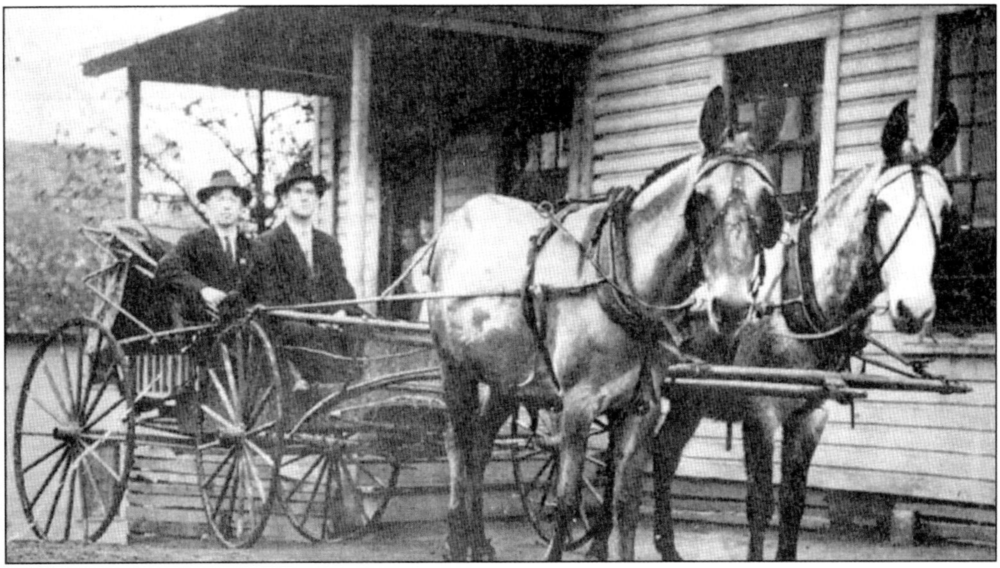

THE WHITE HOUSE, WALKER COUNTY. This one-and-a-half story 1855 house was the first of three houses built by Capt. Benjamin M. Long, the founder of the town of Cordova. The house's name came from the fact that it was the first house painted white, or any other color, in Walker County. Pictured above in the buggy, from left to right, are Noah Johnson and Will Skinner.

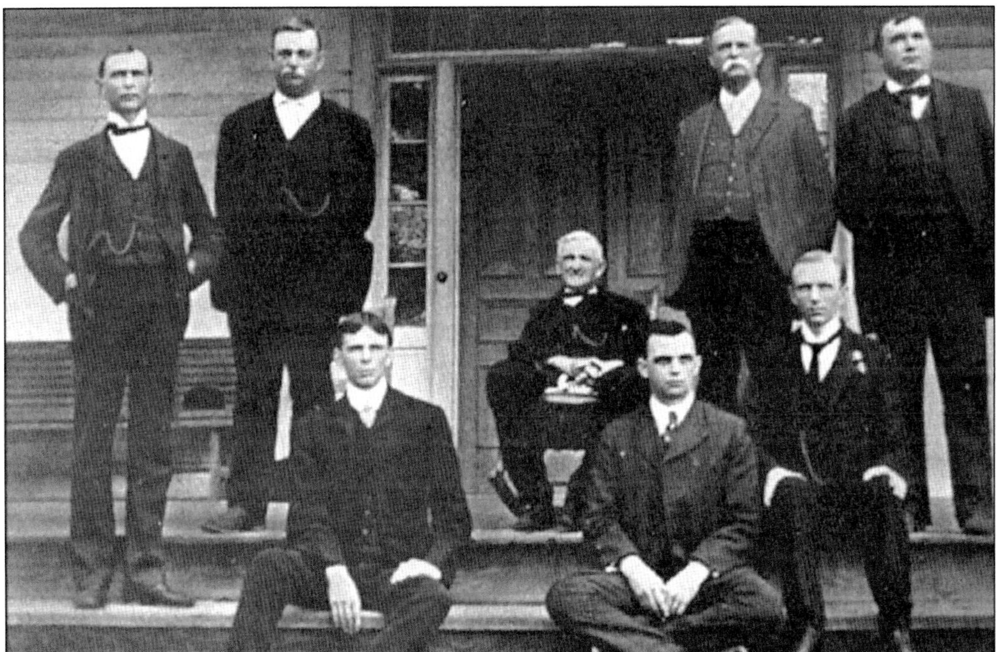

BENJAMIN M. LONG AND SONS, CORDOVA. Captain Long built the house shown above on Green Street in Cordova *c.* 1883. Pictured with him are the sons of Long and his wife Caroline Amanda. From left to right are Bill, John, Ed, Captain Long, Jess, Whitt, Pope, and Tom. Benjamin Long renamed the town of Dent "Cordova," after a town in Mexico in which he was wounded during the Mexican War.

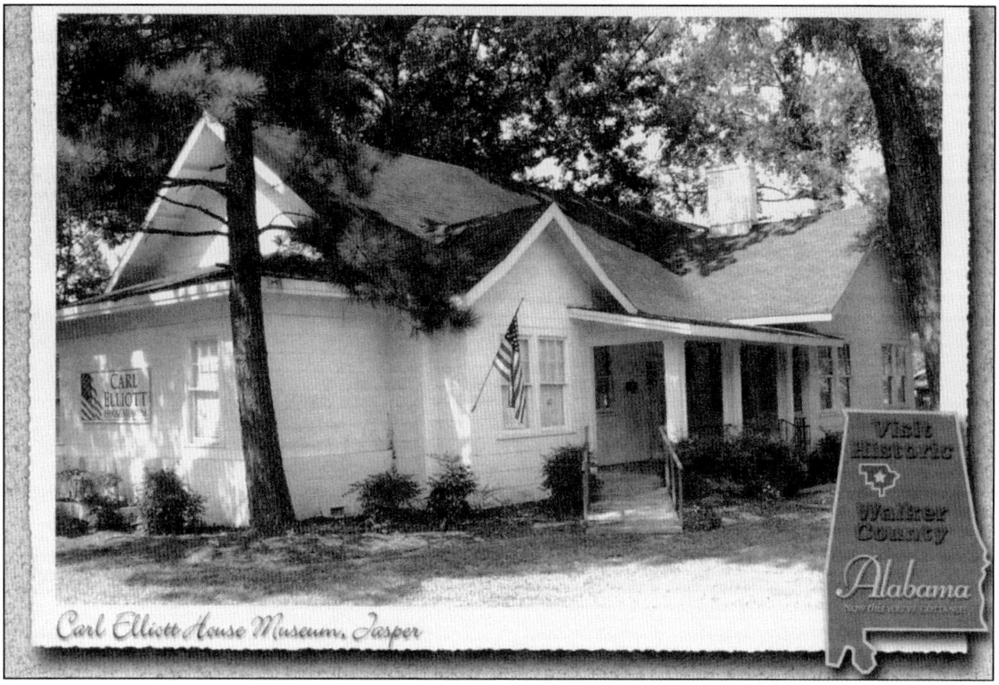

Carl Elliott Home and Museum, Jasper. Carl Elliott lived in this house and raised his family here in Jasper. He was a United States congressman from 1949 to 1965. Congressman Elliott was responsible for the National Defense Education Act, which helped to obtain low-cost loans for students. He was very involved as a civil rights advocate and received the first John F. Kennedy "Profile in Courage Award."

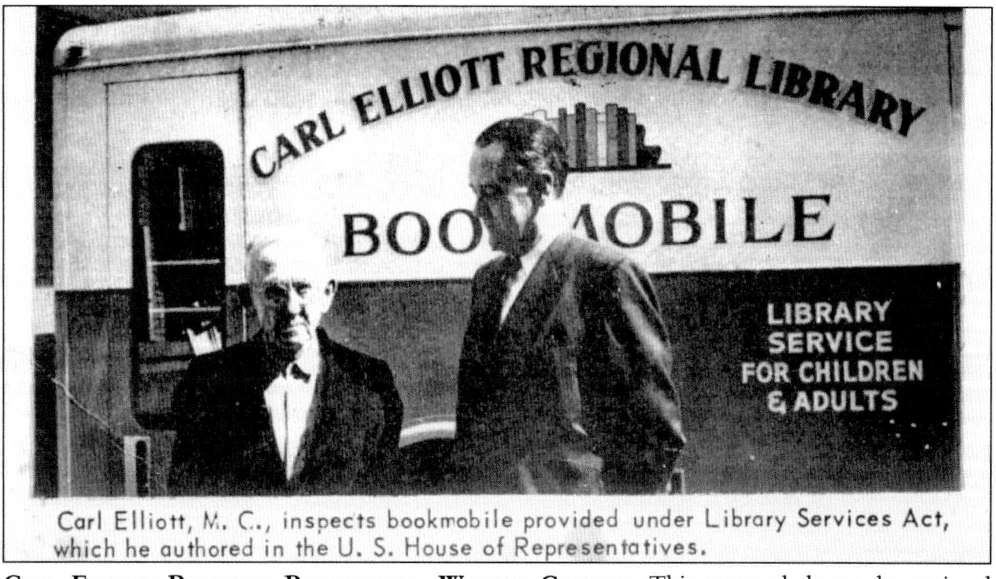

Carl Elliott Regional Bookmobile, Walker County. This postcard shows the regional bookmobile that Carl Elliott, right, helped to develop. As one of his two great accomplishments, the Library Services Act brought library services to rural America. The bookmobile brought books to all county schools where teachers would take their classes through it to check out books.

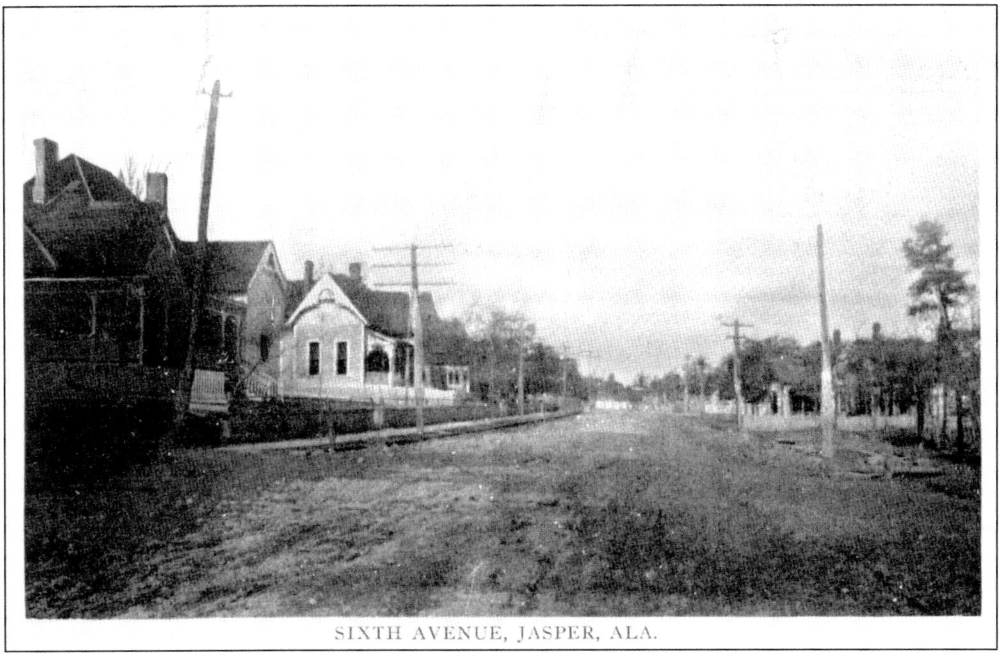

O'REAR, MASSEY, WILSON HOUSE, JASPER. In 1854, James O'Rear built his house on what is today Sixth Avenue and Thirteenth Street, making it possibly the oldest surviving home in Jasper. William Massey, one of Walker County's top photographers, produced many county postcards and was one owner of the house. Mark and Kay Wilson now own the house.

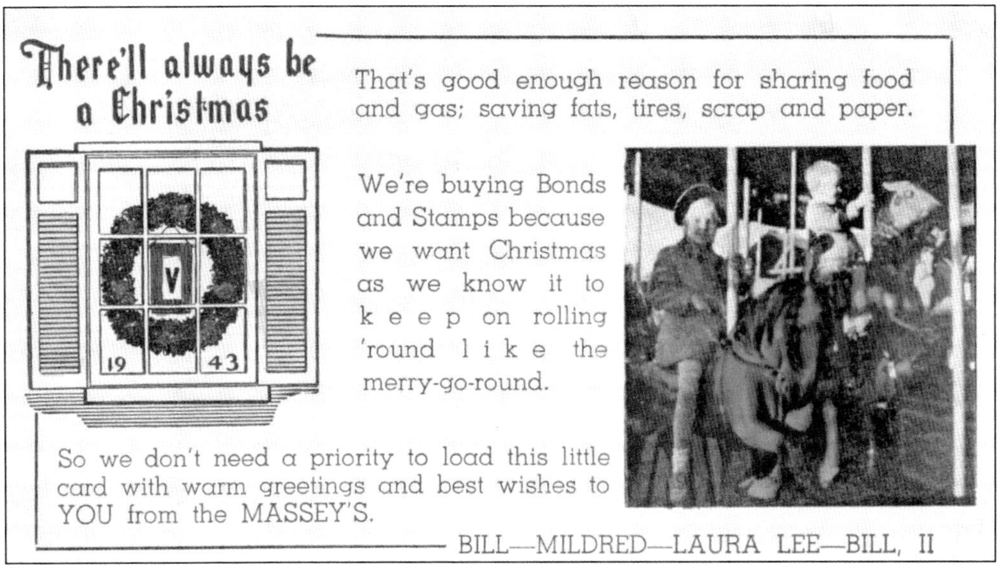

MASSEY FAMILY CHRISTMAS POSTCARD. This card, produced by photographer William Massey, shows his two children. From left to right are Laura Lee and Bill II. Notice both the "victory wreath" in the window with the year 1943 on it, as well as the promotion for buying war bonds for World War II. There is a strong message in this simple card: home, family, war bonds, victory, saving, and sharing.

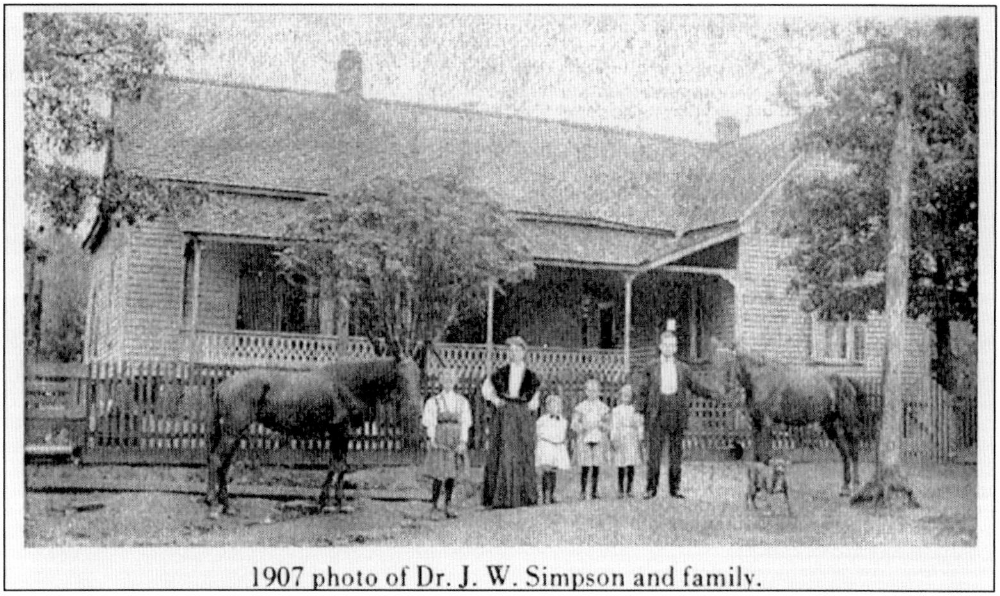

Dr. J.W. Simpson, Parrish. Dr. John Wesley Simpson, an early Parrish physician, appears in this 1907 card with his wife and their four daughters in front of their house. They are flanked by two beautiful Chestnut horses and the family dog. The town of Parrish was originally known as Hewitt-Jonesboro, then Hewitt, and finally Parrish.

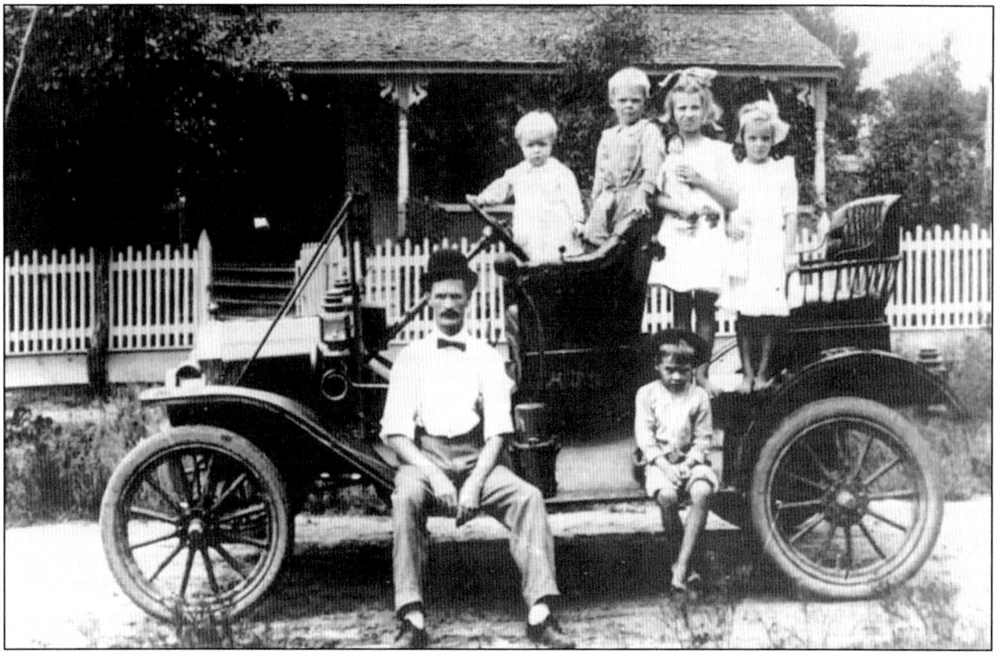

Dr. H.J. Sankey, Nauvoo, 1912. Dr. Sankey, most famous for his delivery of the Short quadruplets in 1940, is shown here on the running board of his 1912 Model T Ford. Pictured from left to right are Dr. Sankey, his son Howard "Boots" Sankey, his son Ben Sankey (a professional baseball player), Margie Holland (neighbor), and his daughter Francis Sankey. His Nauvoo home is in the background.

TALLULAH BANKHEAD, ACTRESS. The actress Tallulah was a liberated woman long before her time. She was a struggling actress, so when she turned 16, she borrowed $1,500, went to England, and took the London Stage by storm. She starred with Marlon Brando in *The Eagle has Two Heads*, and in Tennessee Williams's *A Streetcar Named Desire*. She also played the Black Widow in the television series *Batman*.

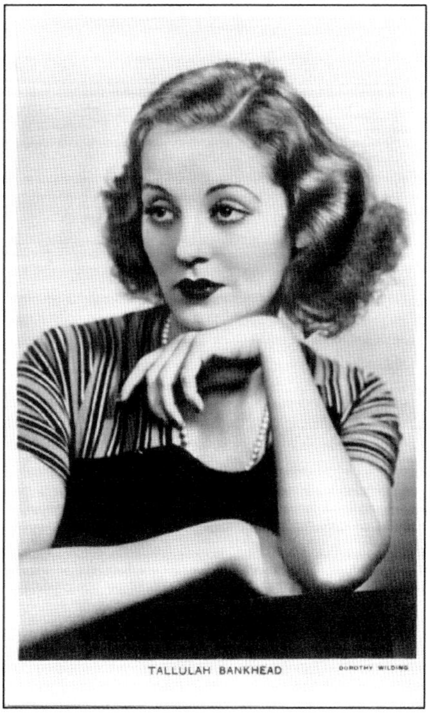

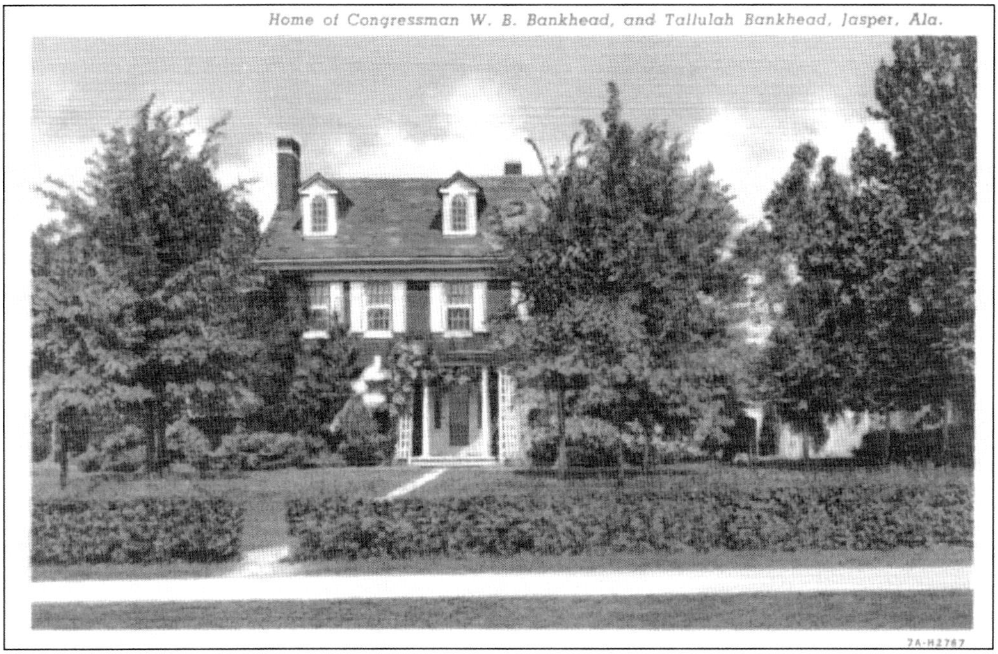

BANKHEAD HOME, JASPER. The William Brockman Bankhead home was built on Seventh Street between Eighth and Ninth Avenues. The house was the sometime home of both Tallulah and her father, Congressman Bankhead. Tallulah was best known for her deep baritone "dah-ling" and her racy quips. Her wedding to John Emery in 1937 was held in this house, which is now owned by Mrs. Clarence Gardner.

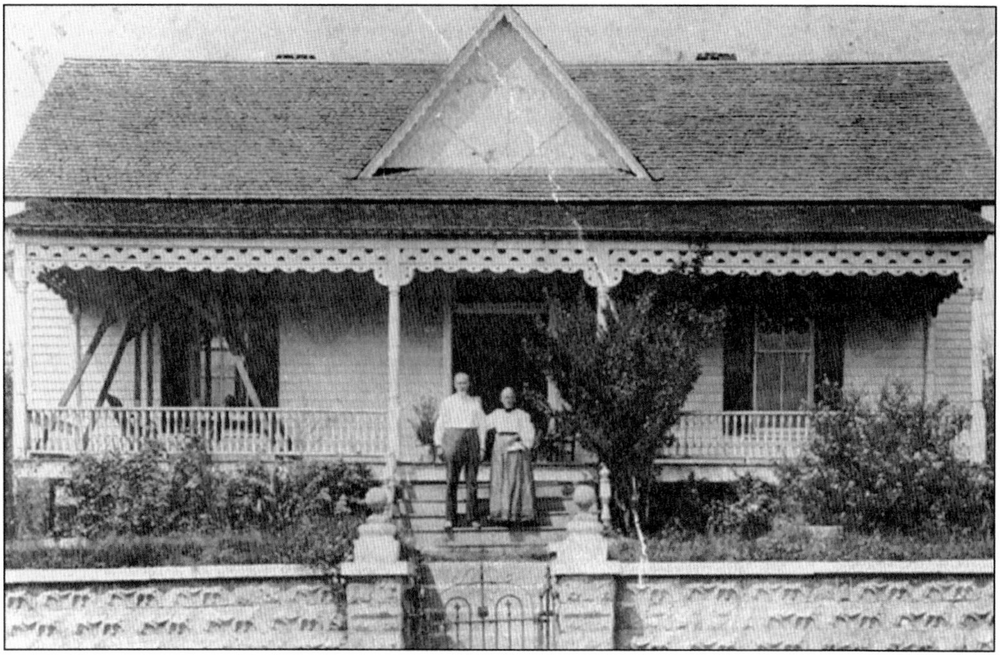

JOHN B. LOLLAR HOME. John Lollar was born on November 30, 1835, near Jasper. He married Elizabeth Taylor in 1857, and both are shown above. He was commissioned in the Confederacy as a lieutenant in Company G, 13th Alabama Regiment. He served Walker County as sheriff in 1880, postmaster in 1885, and clerk of the circuit court in 1886. He was the grandson of Hugh Lollar, who named the town of Jasper.

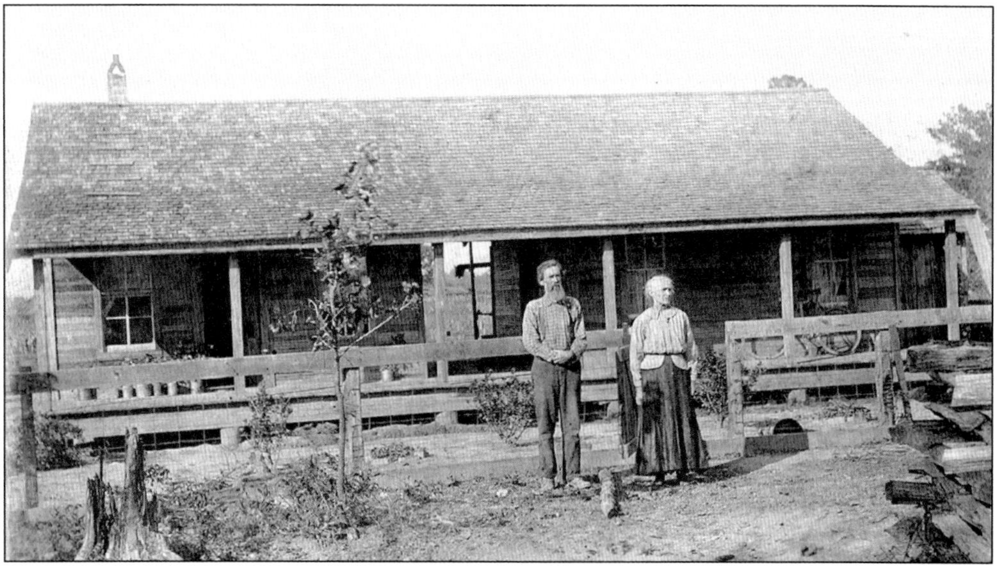

SOUTH LOWELL HOME. In the early 1900s, the home above was located in South Lowell, which was once the most progressive and fastest growing town in the county. The town was developed by Northern investors and was considered a Yankee town. While Jasper was dry, South Lowell had at least five saloons, and one night the drunks, angry at being arrested, burned the jail to the ground.

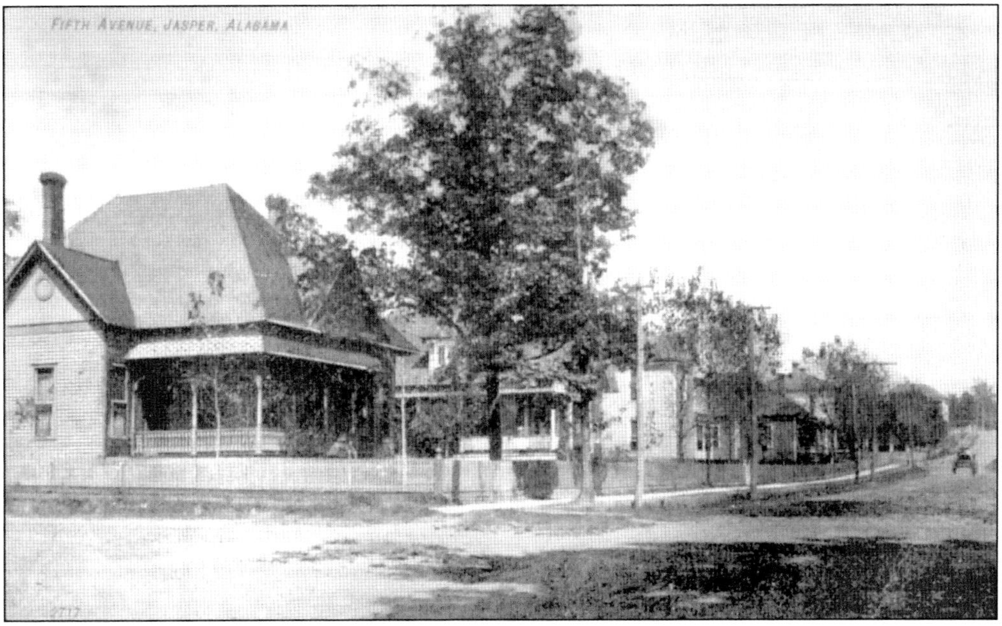

WEINSTEIN HOME, FIFTH AVENUE, 1910. This house is located at Fifth Avenue between Seventeenth and Eighteenth Streets near downtown Jasper. It was owned by Sylvia Shapiro Weinstein, who taught piano and gave speech lessons to many of the county youth. The house was then used for the offices of the Central Mining Company, and it has now been restored as the law office of Pat Gustin and Brian Royster.

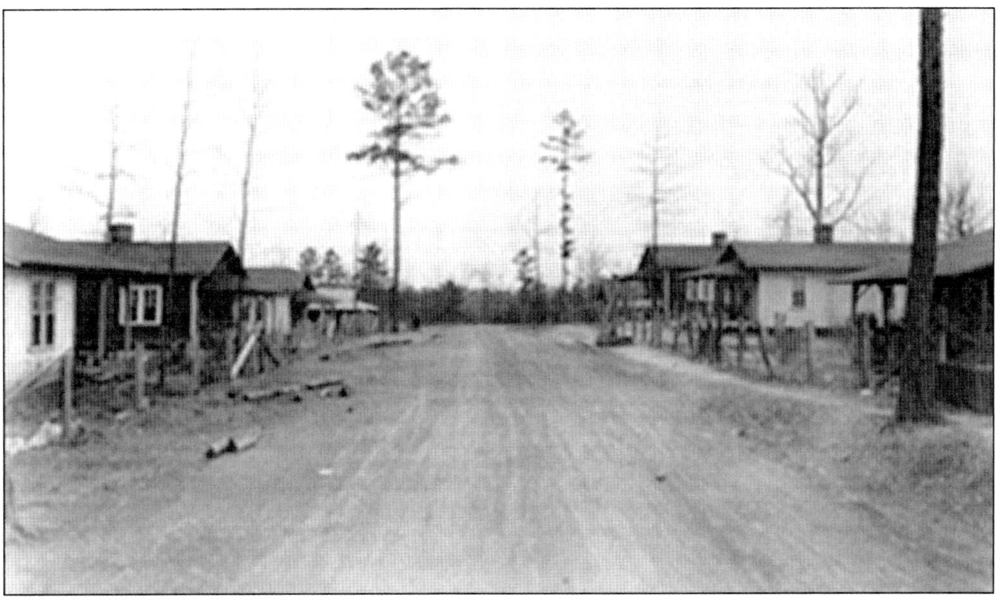

LEVINE STREET HOMES, PARRISH. A view of Levine Street in Hewitt (or, as we know it, Parrish) is shown above. This was a part of the company housing for the Railway Fuel Coal Company and was used by many of the 500 mine employees. From left to right above are Jeff Green's house, Frank Lee's house, Salter's house, and in the far background, Mayor Wilfred Cagle's house.

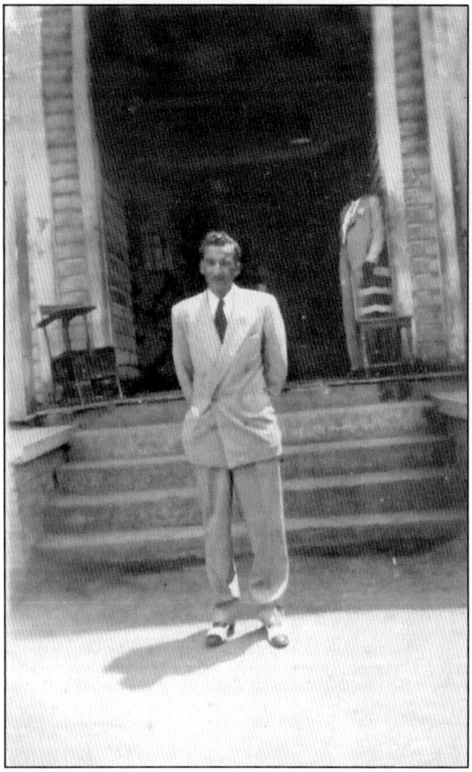

Clarence White, Educator. For 64 incredible years "Professor" White was involved in all areas of education, from teacher to administrative assistant. Here in 1948 he stands in front of the Walker County Training School. He lived through the Civil Rights Movement with a dignity that few people on either side could exhibit. He was the first president of the Black Athletic Association.

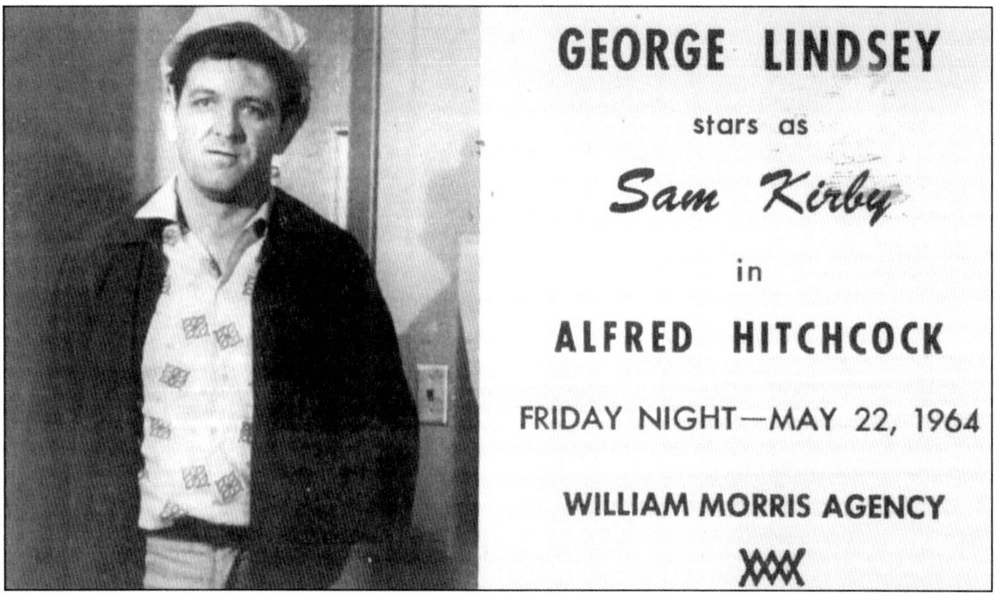

George "Goober" Lindsey, Actor. Best known as Goober on the *Andy Griffith Show*, George "Goober" Lindsey is one of Walker County's most famous and best-loved sons. He is shown here in his debut as a dramatic actor on the *Alfred Hitchcock Show*. George graduated in 1946 from Walker County High School, where he won a football scholarship to Florence State College.

Eric "Butterbean" Esch, Boxer. At 5 feet, 11 inches and 350 pounds, "Butterbean" was considered the "king of the four rounder" and is Walker County's most famous professional boxer and personality. His record of 63-3-2 with 48 knockouts is outstanding. He lost his most famous fight, against former heavyweight champion Larry Holmes, in a close decision.

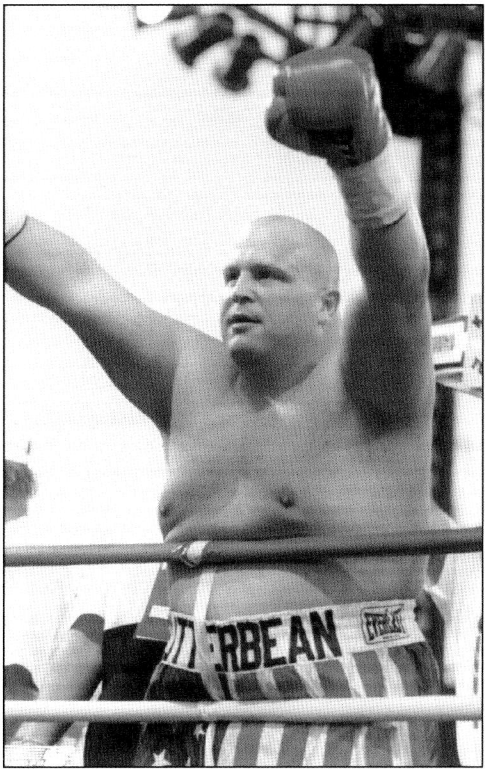

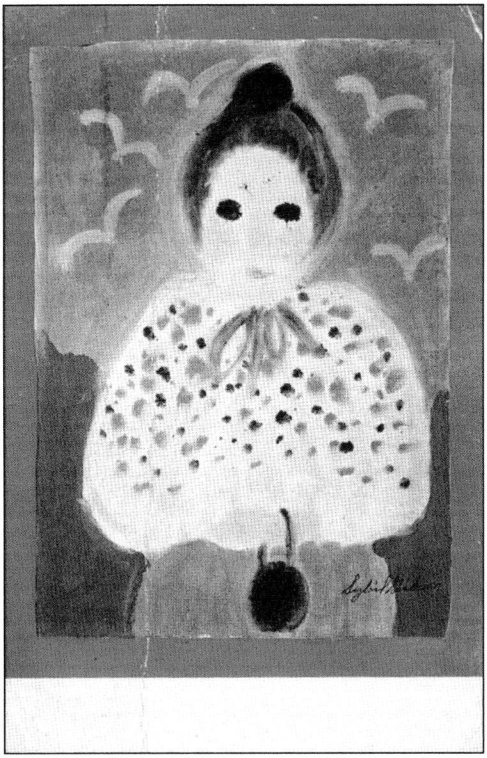

Sybil Gibson, Folk Artist. A Dora native born in 1908, Sybil Gibson started painting at the age of 55 using wet grocery bags and cardboard as her pallet. Examples of her work are on exhibit at the Fayette Art Museum. She was an eccentric artist who threw much of her work away. She was much more popular in Florida and California than she was here in her home state of Alabama.

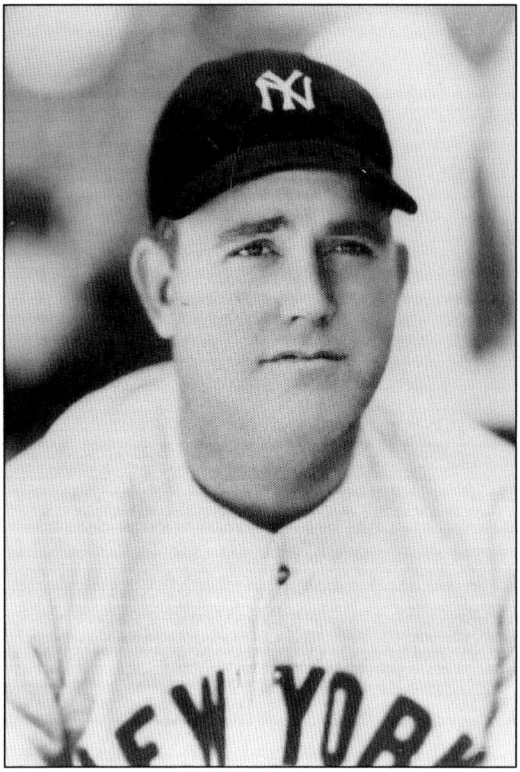

IVY PAUL ANDREWS, PROFESSIONAL BASEBALL. A right-handed pitcher, Ivy Paul Andrews was a Dora native who started his career with the New York Yankees in 1931. The legendary Babe Ruth and Lou Gehrig were his teammates, as was Joe DiMaggio later in Andrews's career. He played eight years in the majors and pitched in the 1937 World Series with the Cleveland Indians. He managed the Birmingham Barons in 1947.

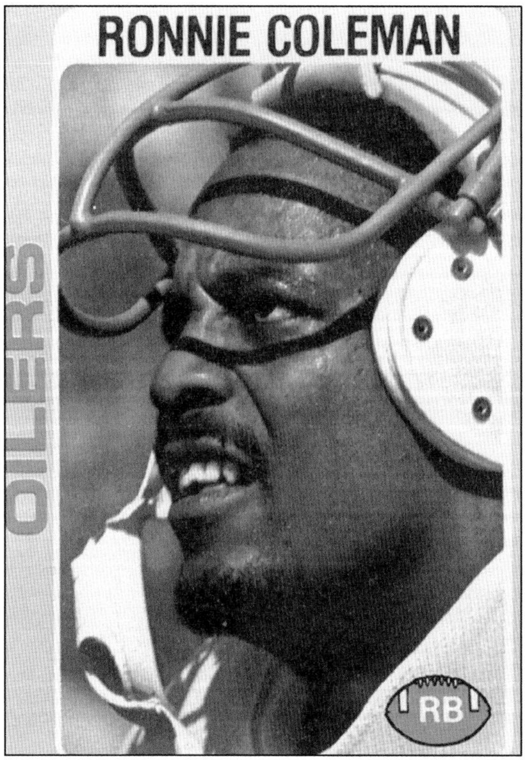

RONNIE COLEMAN, PROFESSIONAL FOOTBALL. Jasper native Ronnie Coleman received a scholarship to play football at Alabama A&M. He was drafted in 1974 by the Houston Oilers, where he was a teammate of the legendary Earl Campbell. He led the team two successive years in rushing and played through the 1981 season. He is the associate pastor of St. Agnes Baptist Church in Houston.

DATES TO REMEMBER
(Including new Monday holidays voted by Congress)

1985		1986	
Tue.	Jan. 1	Wed.	Jan. 1
Tue.	Feb. 12	Wed.	Feb. 12
Mon.	**Feb. 18**	**Mon.**	**Feb. 17**
Wed.	Feb. 20	Wed.	Feb. 12
Sun.	Mar. 17	Mon.	Mar. 17
Fri.	Apr. 5	Fri.	Mar. 28
Sun.	Apr. 7	Sun.	Mar. 30
Sun.	May 12	Sun.	May 11
Mon.	**May 27**	**Mon.**	**May 26**
Fri.	June 14	Sat.	June 14
Sun.	June 16	Sun.	June 15
Thur.	July 4	Fri.	July 4
Mon.	Sept. 2	Mon.	Sept. 1
Tue.	Sept. 17	Sun.	Oct. 5
Mon.	**Oct. 14**	**Mon.**	**Oct. 13**
Tue.	Nov. 5	Tue.	Nov. 4
Mon.	Nov. 11	Tue.	Nov. 11
Thur.	Nov. 28	Thur.	Nov. 27
Wed.	Dec. 25	Thur.	Dec. 25

New Monday holidays, each creating a three-day weekend, are in boldface.

* Fly Your Flag   [1] Begins at sundown previous day.

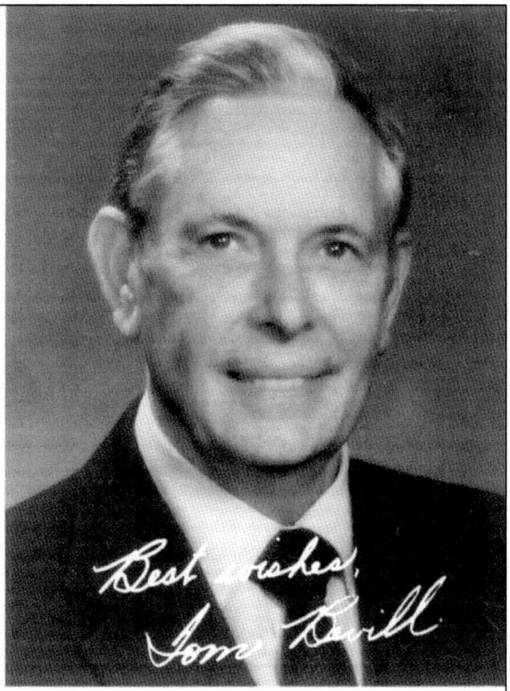

YOUR CONGRESSMAN

CONGRESSMAN TOM BEVIL, TOWNLEY. Tom Bevil served the people of Alabama from 1959 to 1993, and perhaps his biggest achievement has been the Tenn-Tom Waterway. The visitors center was named in his honor. He was a 1939 graduate of Walker County High School and received his law degree from the University of Alabama. He was a retired lieutenant colonel in the United States Army.

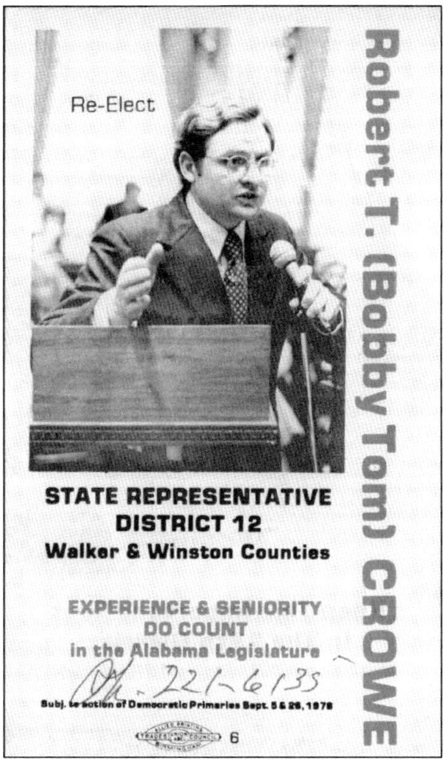

ROBERT T. CROWE, TOWNLEY. Jasper native Bobby Tom Crowe was elected to the state legislature for the 12th district, which encompasses Walker and Winston Counties. He was the Speaker Pro Tem of the Alabama House of Representatives, the second-most powerful position in the house. He served the people of the county for eight years and is now retired.

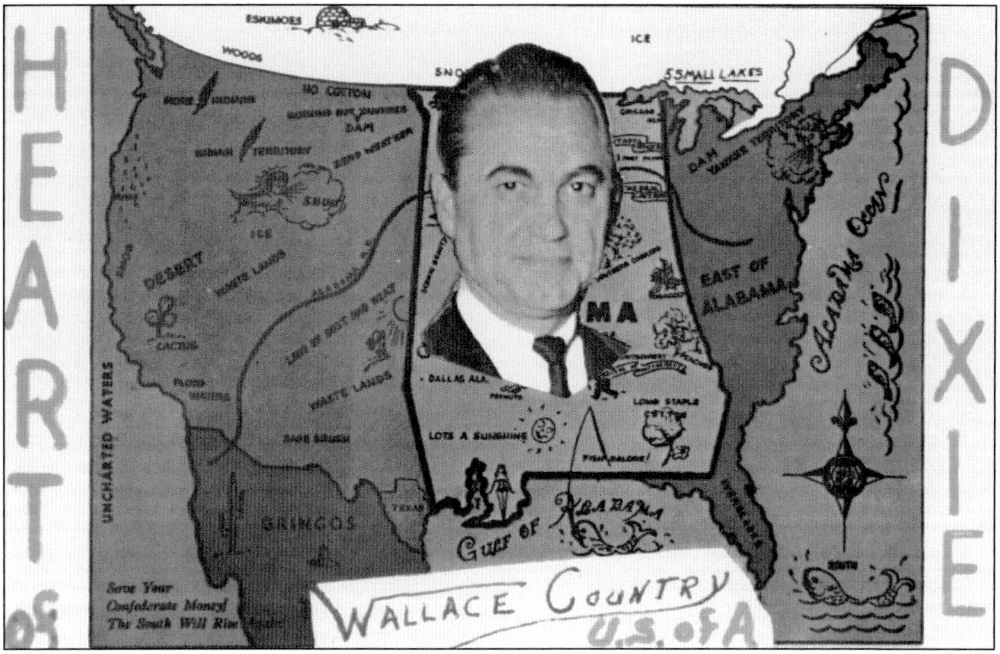

George C. Wallace, Governor. This four-time governor of Alabama and two-time candidate for the president of the United States had deep ties to Walker County. His third wife, Lisa Taylor Wallace, was a native of Jasper. His run for the presidency was cut short by an attempted assassination that left him crippled for the rest of his life.

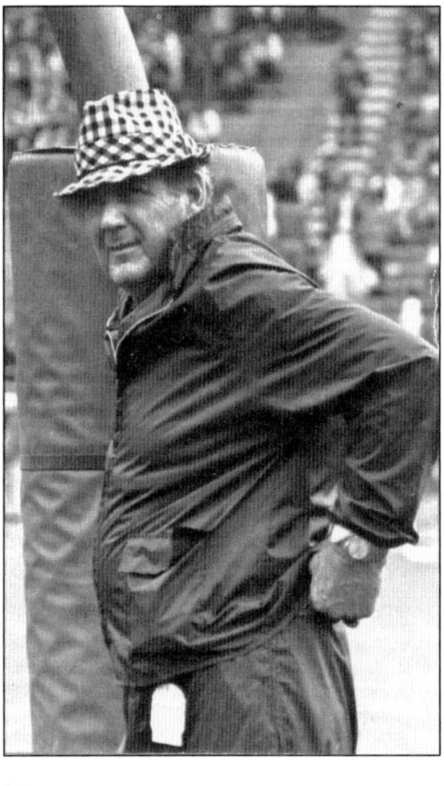

Paul "Bear" Bryant, Coach. Coach Bryant may well have been the most respected and recognized man in Alabama. Everyone felt as if they knew him personally, and his first public speaking engagement was at the Walker County High School Quarterback Club meeting. One of his first recruits as the head coach at Alabama was Walker's Billy Richardson.

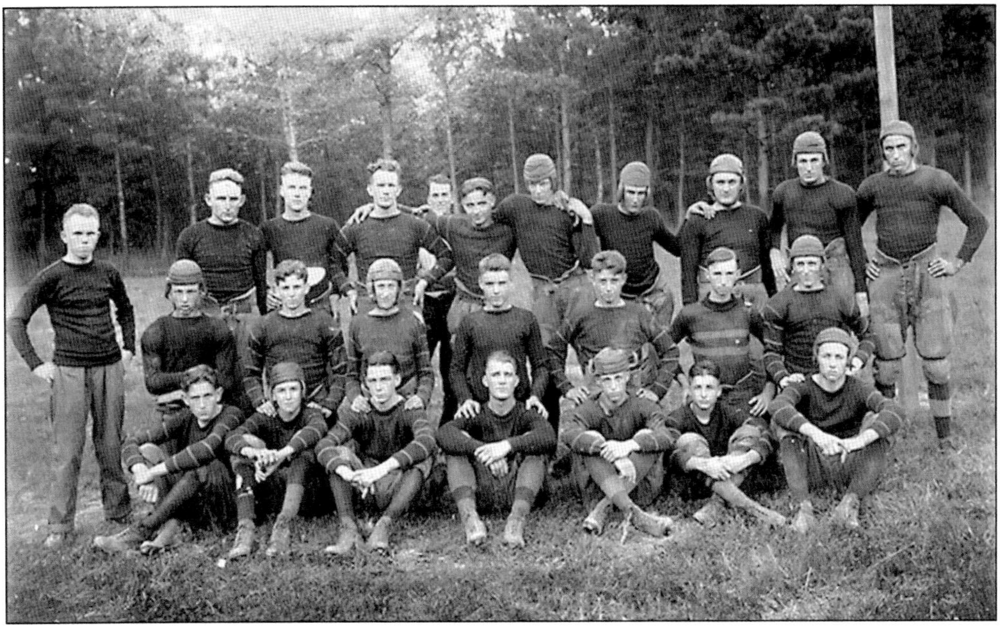

State Champions, 1921. The Walker County Vikings went undefeated in 1921, allowing only 13 points the entire season. Ten players from this team played college football, and two went on to professional careers. The coach of the 1921 team was F.E. Christopher. Bruce Jones played on a state championship, a national championship, and a world championship team; he was also captain of each team.

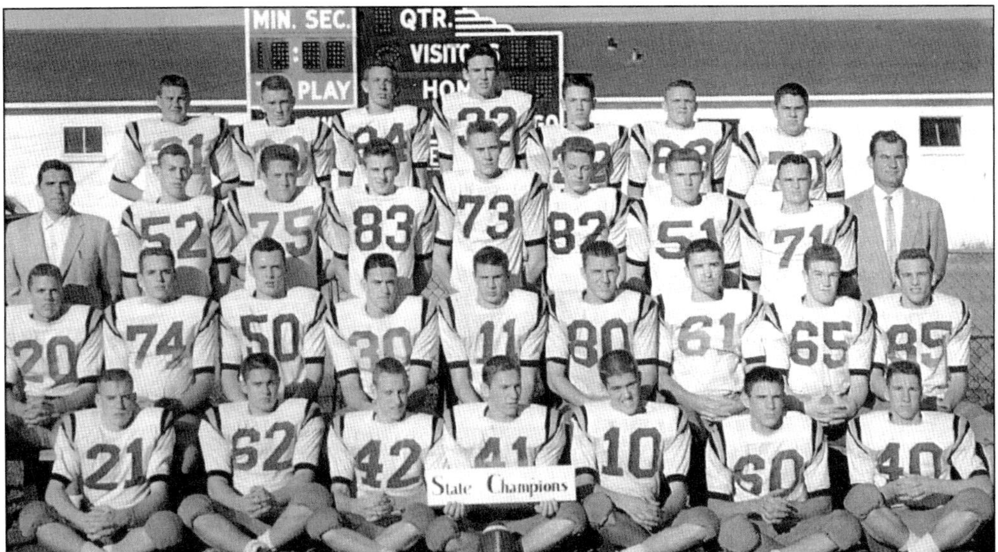

State Champions, 1957. The Walker County Vikings were, for the second time, Alabama state champions in 1957, ending the season undefeated and untied. Their record was a perfect 10–0 with 7 shutouts, and the team gave up only 20 points for the season. The coaches were D. Joe Gambrell and Jack Caldwell, and the principal was Geddes Self. Captains were Charles Sparks and Bill Richardson.

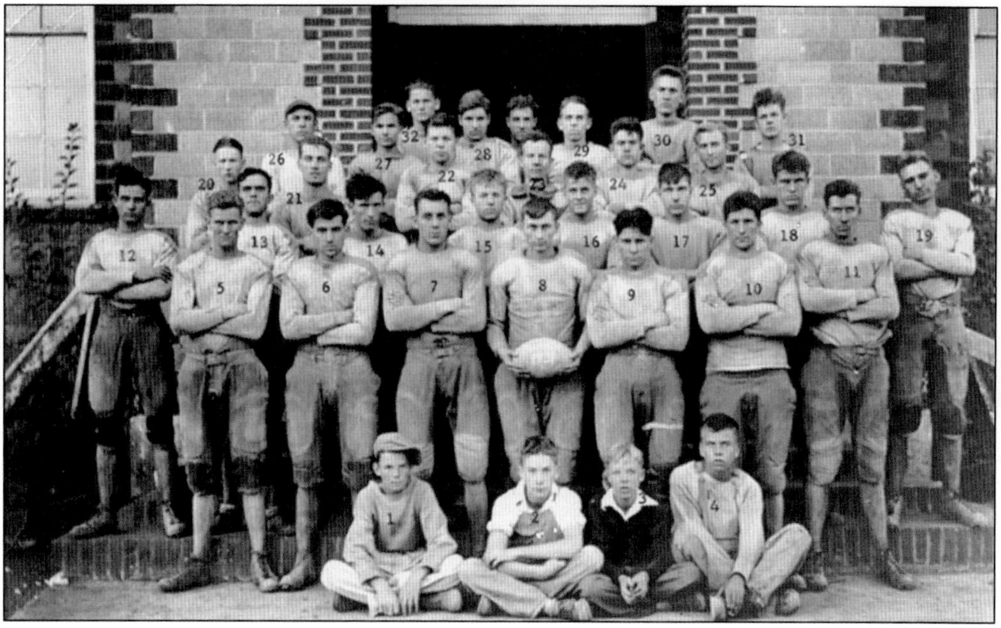

PARRISH HIGH SCHOOL FOOTBALL TEAM, 1931. This is an early Parrish football team, and we have not been able to determine their record. Some members of the team were Alton Kellum, who later became mayor of Carbon Hill; Judson Bailey, who was the center and captain of the team; Rile Blackwood, who became a successful insurance executive in Walker County; and Clay Knight (not pictured), the coach.

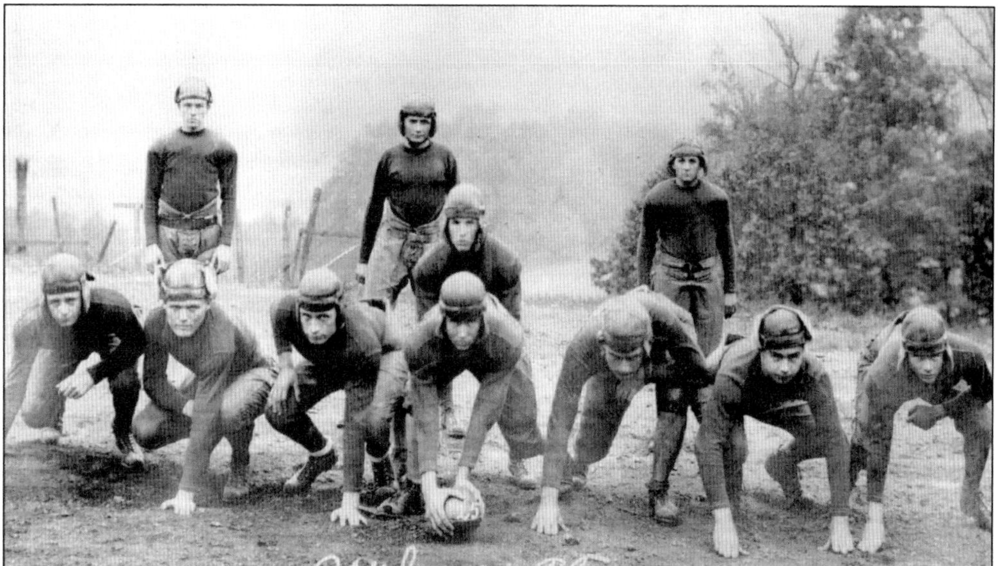

BANKHEAD FOOTBALL TEAM, 1925. This 1925 Bankhead team was the first football team in the history of Cordova. The starters pictured are Willard Haynes (center), Joe Root (right guard), Frank Ballenger (left guard), Acie Thacker (right tackle), Huey Underwood (left tackle), Herbert Rush (right end), Lewis Capps (left end), Elmore Cooper (quarterback), Phil Jones (full back), Ed Hood (right halfback), and Monroe Aaron (left halfback). They are lined up by position.

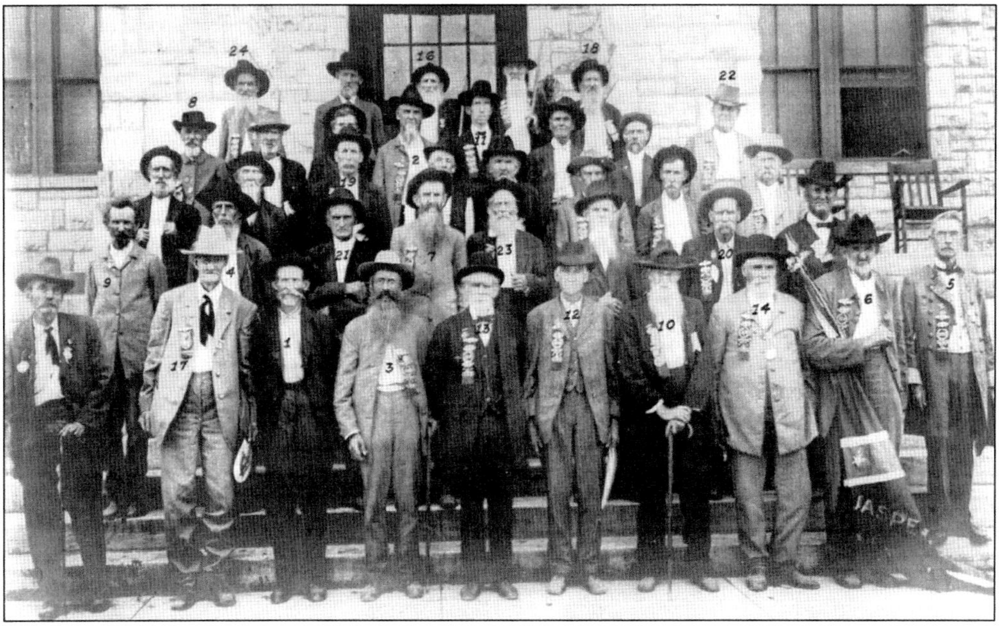

Confederate Civil War Veterans. The surviving Civil War veterans are pictured on the steps of the Walker County Courthouse as they gather for the last-known photograph of these Southern heroes. They gave their lives and limbs for a cause in which they deeply believed. Notice the Old Jasper flag at the bottom right of the picture. These men are the ancestors of many prominent Walker County families.

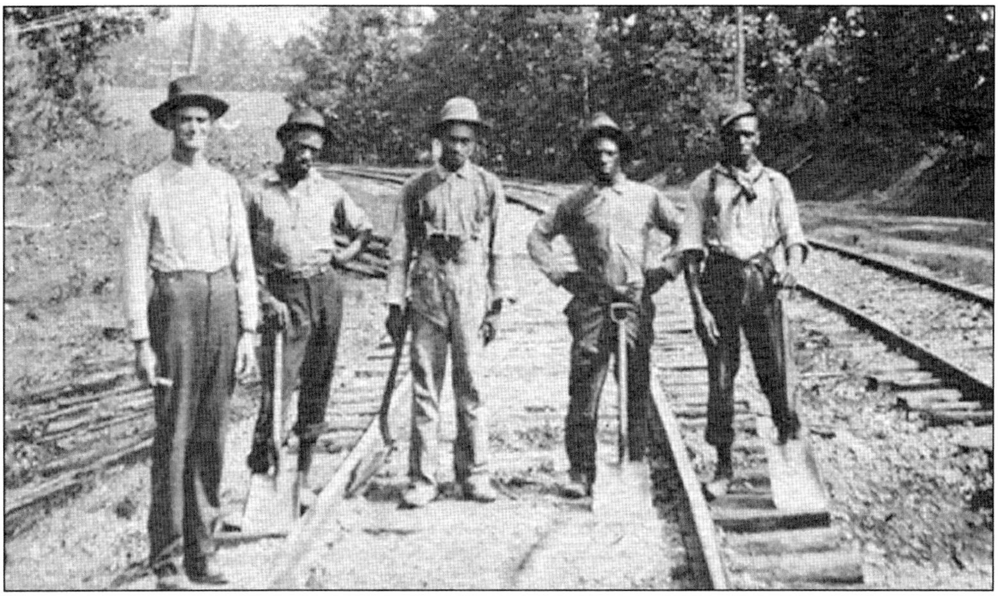

Southern Railway Section Crew, Parrish. Shown above in 1912 near Parrish is a section crew of the Southern Railroad Company. These crews would clear the tracks, replace the ties, lay rails, and keep the right of way safe. On the far left is L.V. Covin, section foreman, and next to him is Will Jones, identified by his granddaughter Essie Malone. The other workers are unidentified.

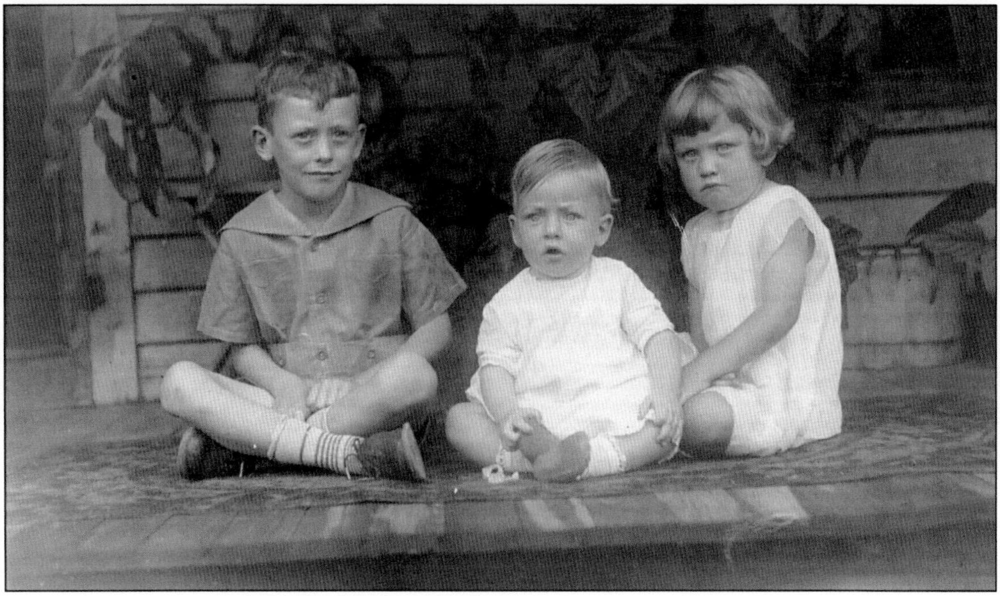

The Black Family, Cordova. Professional photographers would come through the county taking photos, which they would turn into postcards that could be kept or sent to friends or relatives, thus preserving family histories. From left to right are the children of J. Spencer and Ruth Sides Black in 1924: James Ray, Gorman Jackson, and Hilda Pernie Black Brown.

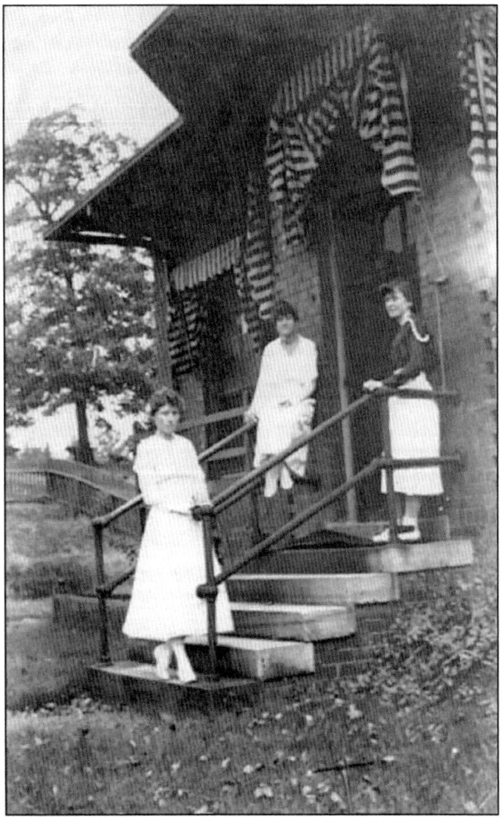

Indian Head Mill Office, Cordova. Another example of the work of professional photographers is shown at the workplace. Some of these images survive as postcards and some survive as photographs, but both preserve our heritage. Pictured outside of Walker County's largest employer, Indian Head Mill, are (from left to right) Ida Sides, Rosa Smith, and Ruth Sides Black.

SONGER FAMILY POSTCARDS, JASPER. This 1912 card has preserved this family image for future generations. It shows, from left to right, Clarence and Elton Songer, the sons of Robert and Scottie Songer. Clarence is the father of Bill Songer, the renowned fast-pitch softball pitcher, and Bob Songer, longtime superintendent of the Jasper City school system.

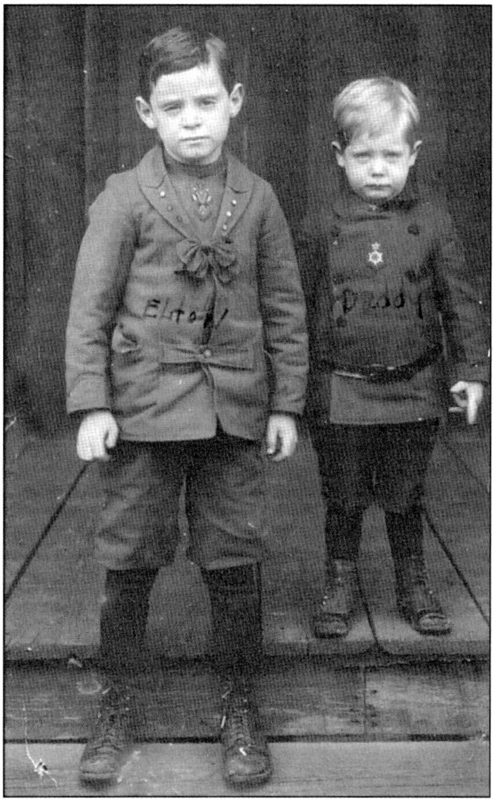

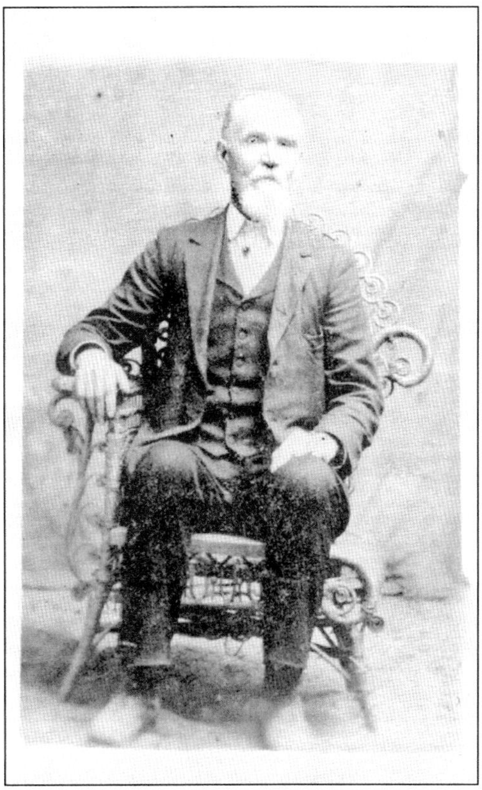

JAMES RUTLEDGE, C. 1915. James came to Walker County from Kentucky in a wagon at the age of two. His father, Edward, was a founder of the Pleasant Grove Baptist Church. James was a Confederate veteran of the Civil War, serving in Company E, 28th Alabama Infantry, and he served for the entire duration of the war. He died in 1918 and is buried in the Sides Cemetery.

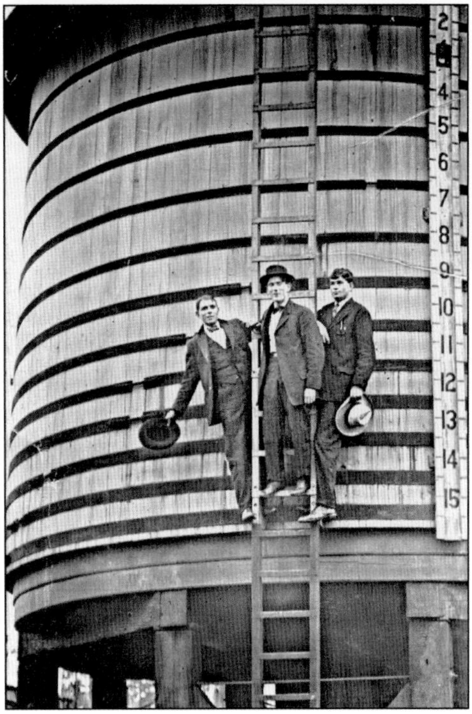

West Jasper Water Tower, *c.* 1910. The water tower that stood looking over Jasper was located northeast of the intersection of Williams and Josephine Streets until it was torn down. This tower was on the hill above the old Coca-Cola plant, off Elliott Boulevard. Pictured clinging to the side of the water tower are, from left to right, Alan Naramore, Moses Hyche, and Ezra Naramore.

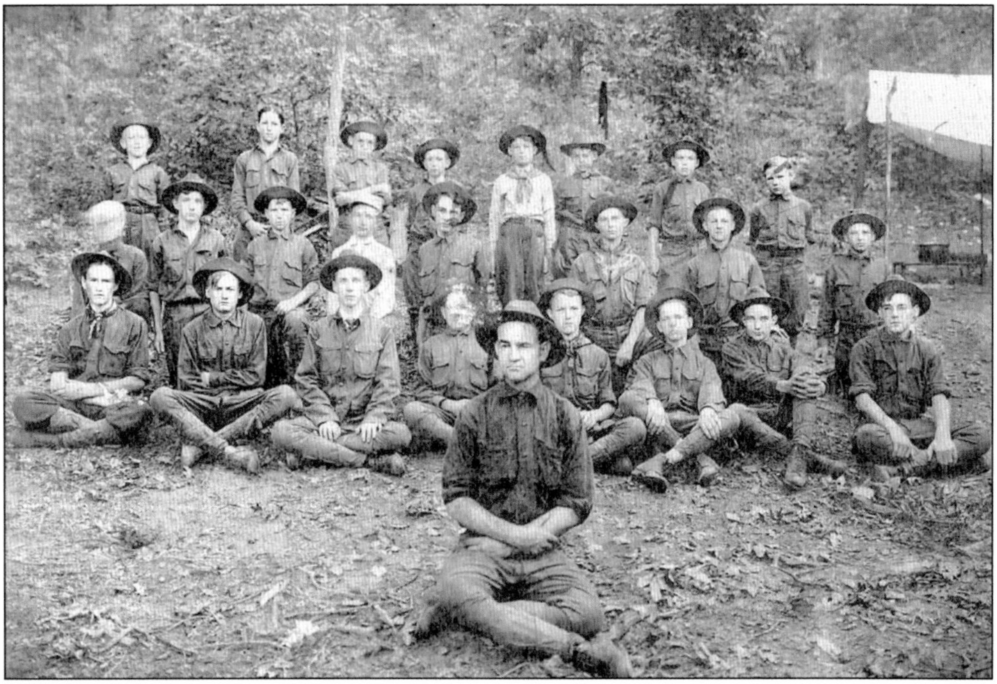

Boy Scouts, Blackwater Creek. Scoutmaster Rev. M.J. McLean was a Methodist minister who gave his time and energy to the young boys of Walker County. Here they are shown on a camping trip on the Blackwater. It is thought to be near where Camp O'Rear is located today. The only person identified is Reverend McLean, front and center.

Five

Recreation

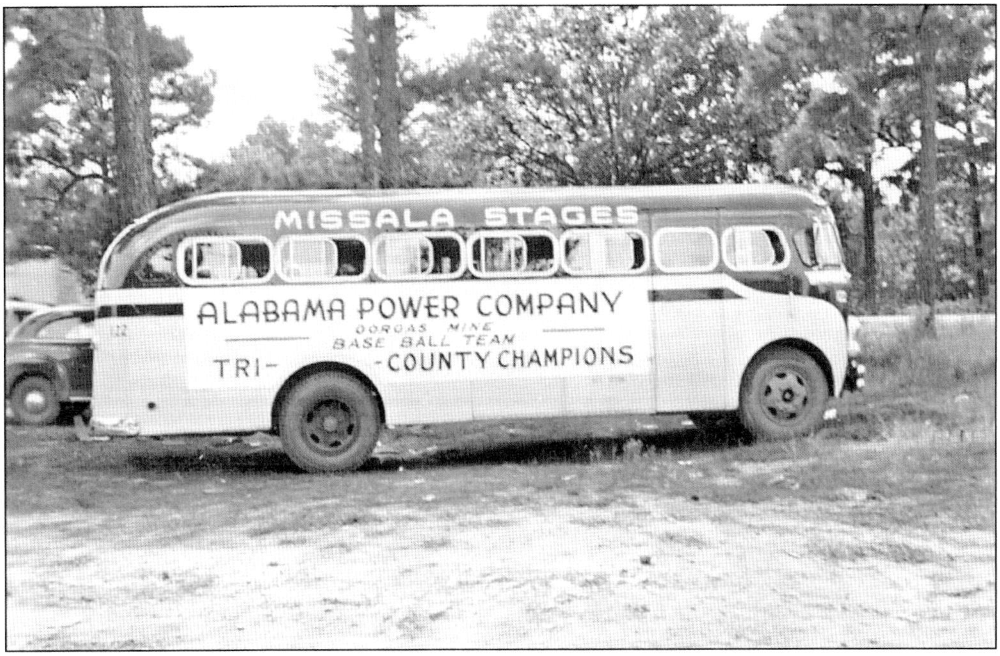

Missala Bus Lines. In the above image are three of Walker County's famous institutions: the Missala Bus Line, the Alabama Power Company, and baseball. Missala, owned by J.H. Deason, provided free bus service from the courthouse to the city park. The bus terminal was located on 20th Street. Alabama Power was one of the county's largest employers, and baseball, of course, is an American tradition.

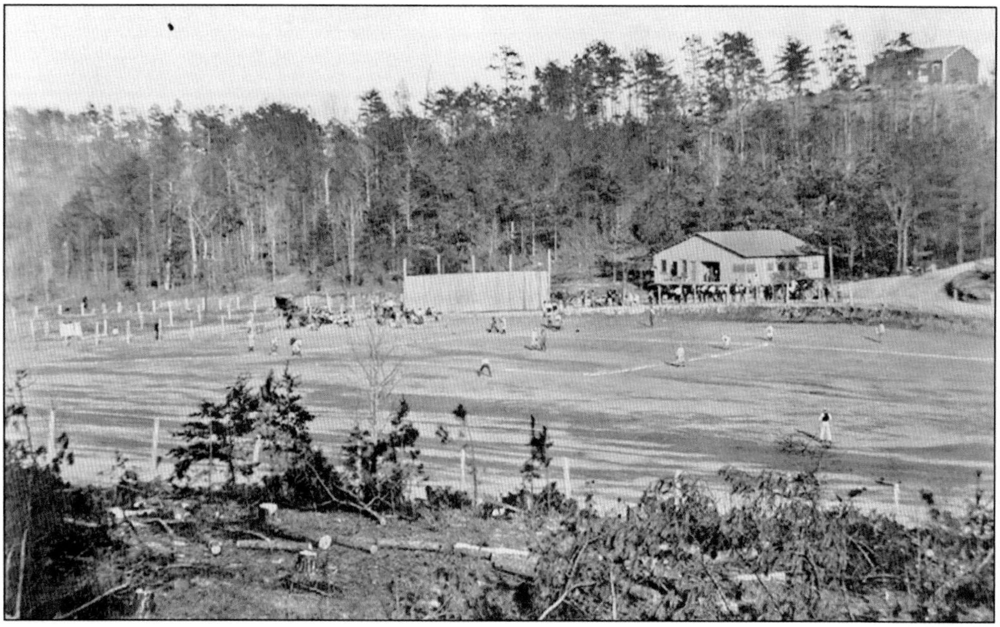

Mining Company, Baseball Game. Shown here is a view that was seen at every mining camp across Walker County, the company baseball game. Companies often recruited employees for their baseball skills and not necessarily for their skill as miners. These teams and players became the pride of that community, and in times where there was not much to celebrate, these games took on enormous importance.

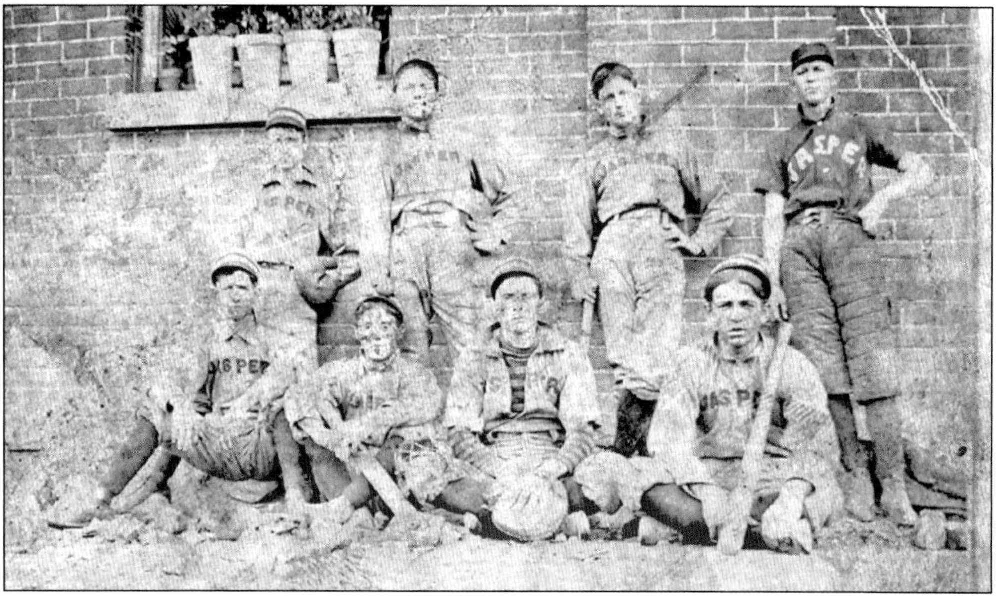

The Jasper Baseball Team, 1901. Many of the men who played on the community baseball team, like those shown above, became the heroes of that area. Saturday and Sunday afternoons became important times in the lives of the company towns, for this was the time of the baseball game. The pride exhibited in the company was in direct relationship to the success of the baseball team.

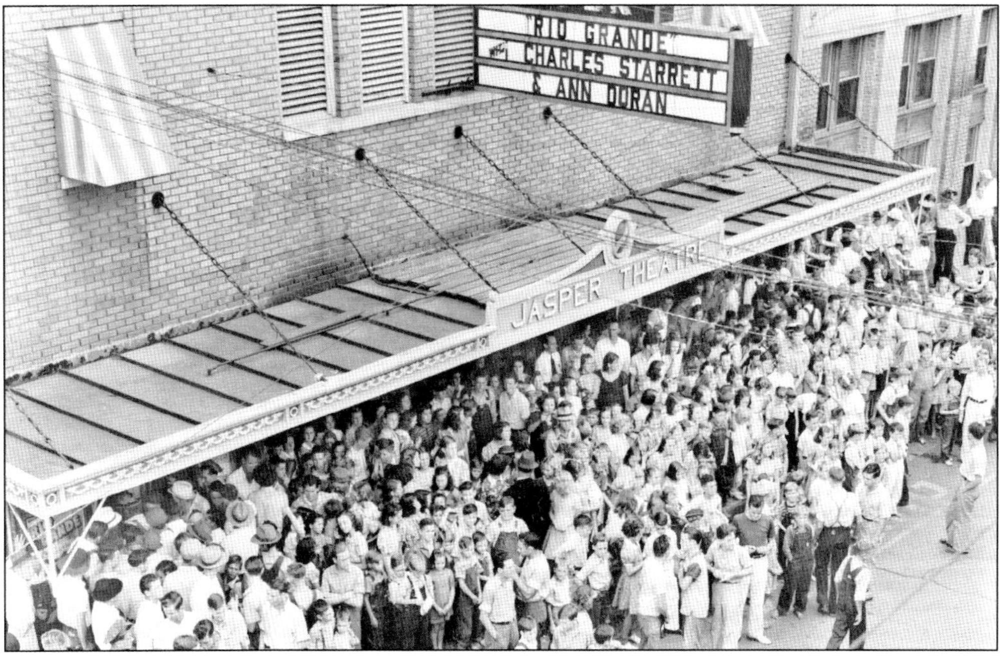

SATURDAY MORNING MOVIE THEATRE, POPEYE CLUB. Saturday morning was an important time in the lives of the area youth if they attended the "Popeye Club," which was started in 1936 by John Johnson, the owner of the Jasper Theatre. For 15¢, children could attend the movie, get refreshments, and either lose themselves in a western with Hoot Gibson or defend the *Planet of Peril* with Flash Gordon.

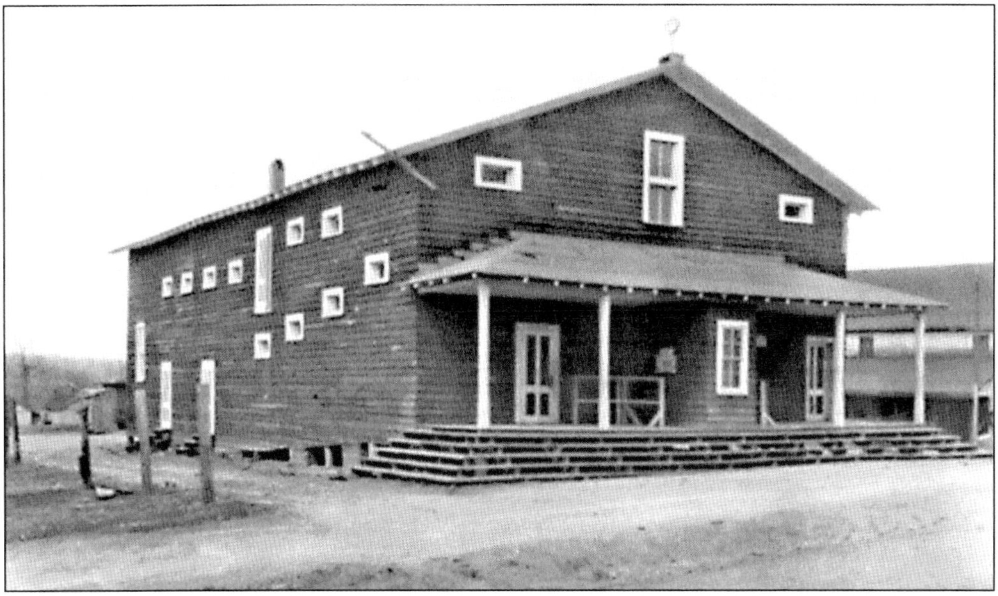

AUDITORIUM AND MOVIE HOUSE, EMPIRE. Just as Parrish, Dora, Carbon Hill, Cordova, and Jasper had their movie theaters, each mining camp had its own movie house. For a short time, these children could enter the fantasy world of movies, where they could become Hopalong Cassidy, Lash Larue, or the damsel in distress to be saved by these heroes.

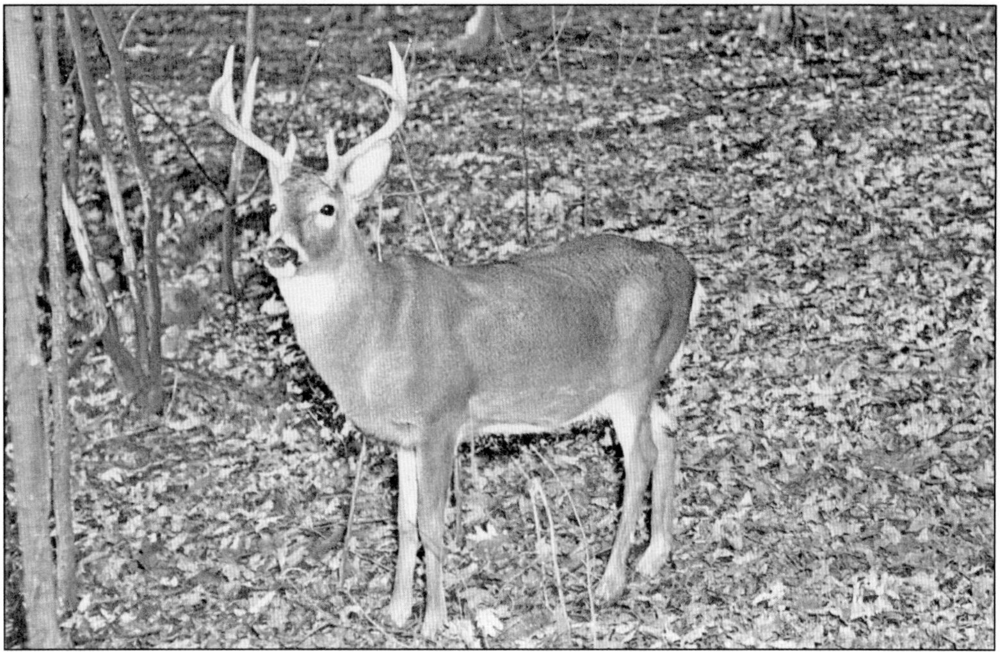

Deer Hunting. Each fall, a fever hits Walker County that compares to football fever: the opening of deer season. Husbands, wives, sons, and daughters take to the woods to test skills that were necessary for the survival of their ancestors in the pursuit of game. Alabama has one of the healthiest populations of deer in the nation, and venison is a prized addition to the Walker County diet.

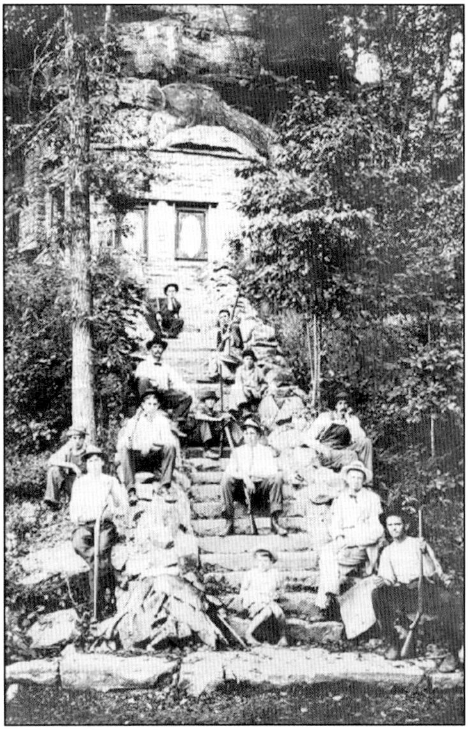

Last Wolf Hunt, Blackwater. The Rock House of Rufus O'Rear on Blackwater Creek, shown at left, is thought to be the location of the last wolf hunt in Walker County. Notice the wolves piled at the bottom of the steps and the age range of the hunters. Rufus O'Rear is pictured at the top left on the steps; he donated his 80-acre Camp O'Rear to the Boy Scouts of America.

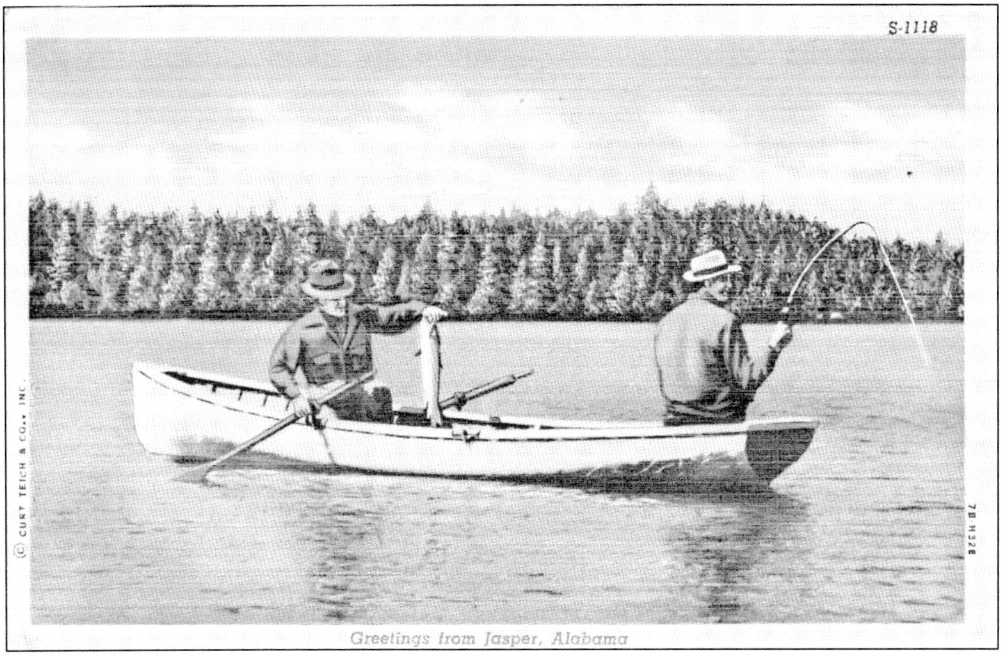

FISHING. Fishing is, and always has been, an important type of recreation, as well as a way of supplementing the family food supply. Walker County has always been rich in creeks and rivers. Now with the addition of Smith Lake, it has become one of the top bass fishing lakes in America, with several world-record fish caught from its cool, clear, deep waters.

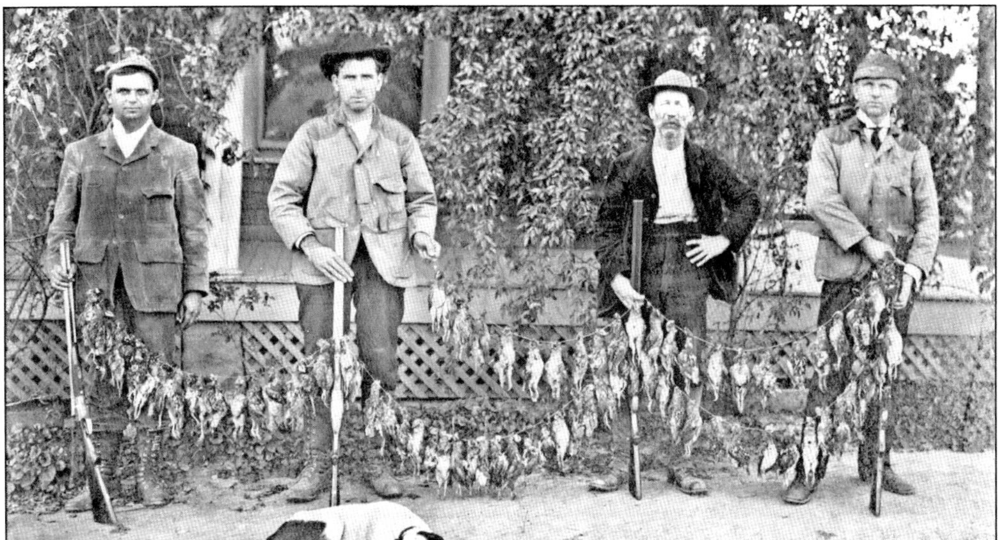

QUAIL HUNT, WHITE HOUSE, CORDOVA. Quail hunting was one of the favorite sports of the early Walker County residents, requiring great shooting skill. Pictured above from left to right are Jesse Long, unidentified, Jacob A. Jones (holding an L.C. Smith 12-gauge shotgun), and Pope Long. They are standing in front of the White House, one of the three houses built in Walker County by B.M. Long.

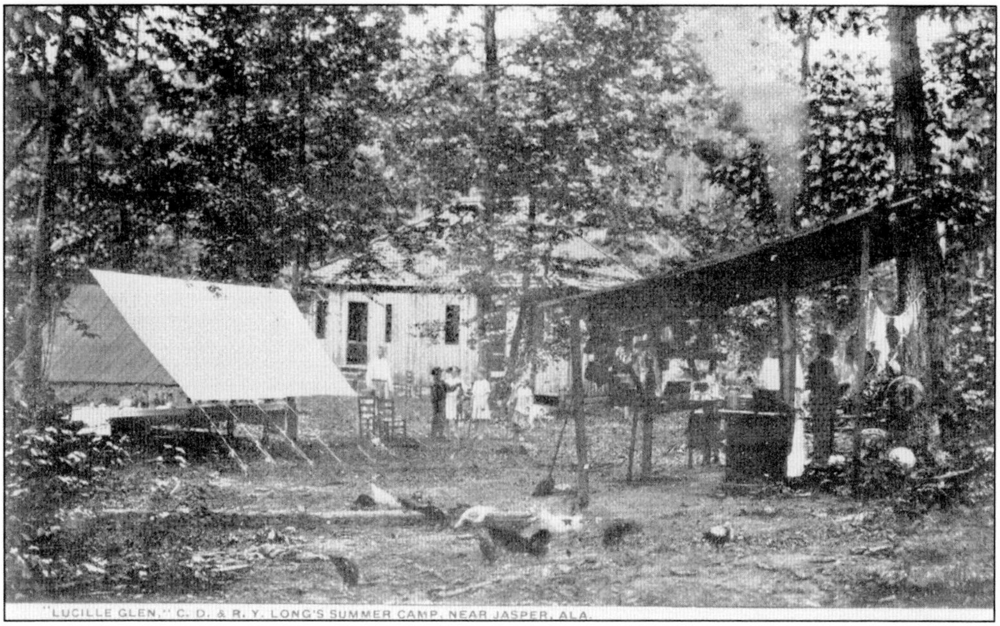

R.Y. LONG CAMP, CLEAR CREEK. R.Y. Long was a Jasper businessman in the 1900s who developed a summer camp on Clear Creek named Lucille Glen. He catered to the well-to-do hunters, hikers, fishermen, and outdoorsmen who wanted to experience all aspects of the wilderness. Long also produced many postcards in the early 1900s of his own business and other related enterprises.

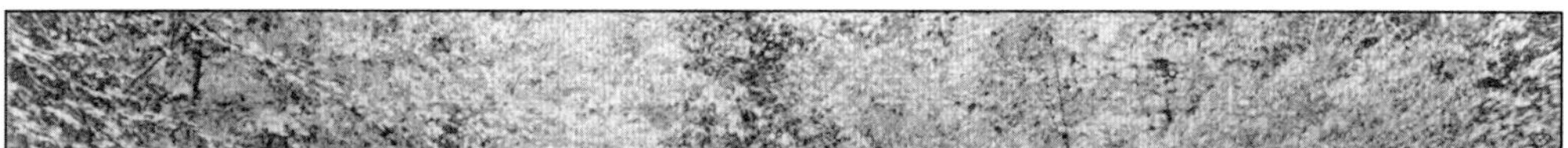

LUCILLE GLEN, FLY FISHING. As much a lifestyle as it is a sport, fly fishing was especially attractive to the upper class. This scene shows an old man fly-fishing on a small stream at Clear Creek, near what would later become the 200,000-acre Bankhead National Forest. At this time it was a part of the Lucille Glen summer camp. R.Y. Long produced this postcard in 1909.

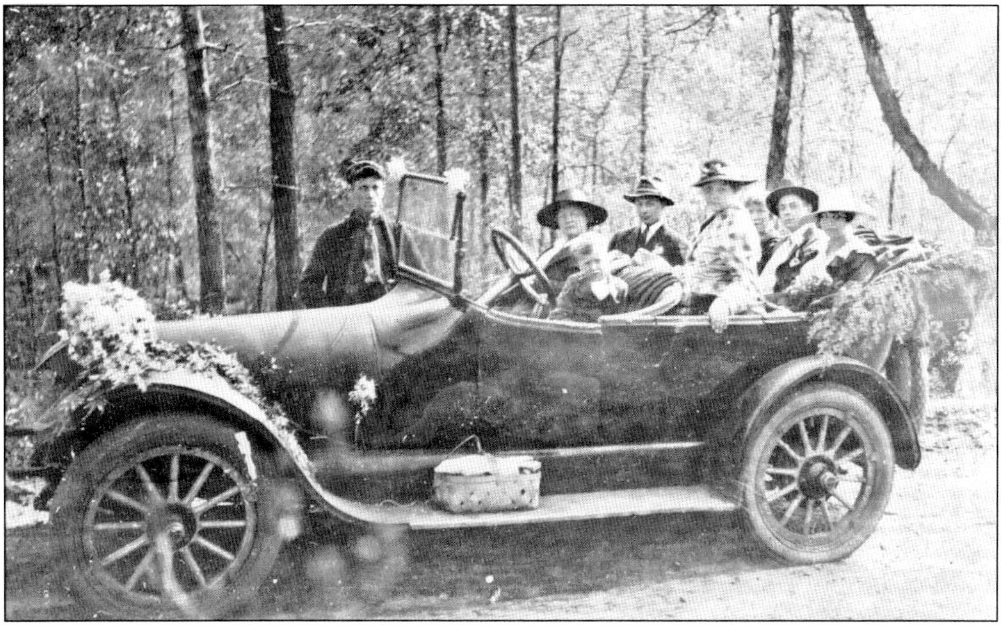

Touring in Bankhead Forest. A favorite recreational activity of the 1920s was driving into the national forest for a Sunday picnic. Pictured above in the front seat are Vanna Mathis and Coleman Mathis, wife and son of photographer Charlie Mathis, and in the back seat, from left to right, are Ethel Gibson, Bernie Gibson, Clara Steadman, and (barely visible) Ida Sides. The other two men are unidentified.

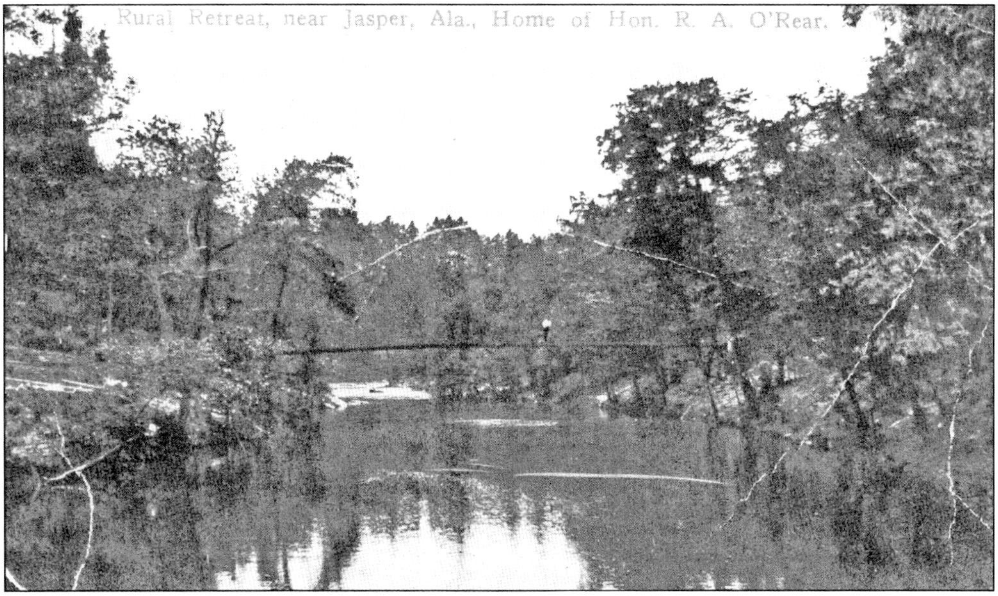

Camp O'Rear, Blackwater Creek. Rufus O'Rear donated this 80-acre site to the Boy Scouts of America in 1924. He had previously built a two-room rock house, a banquet hall, a dance hall, a swinging bridge (seen in the background of this postcard), and a tunnel, used to bring hydroelectric power to the property. The creek, which passes through the property, provides swimming, canoeing, and rafting activities.

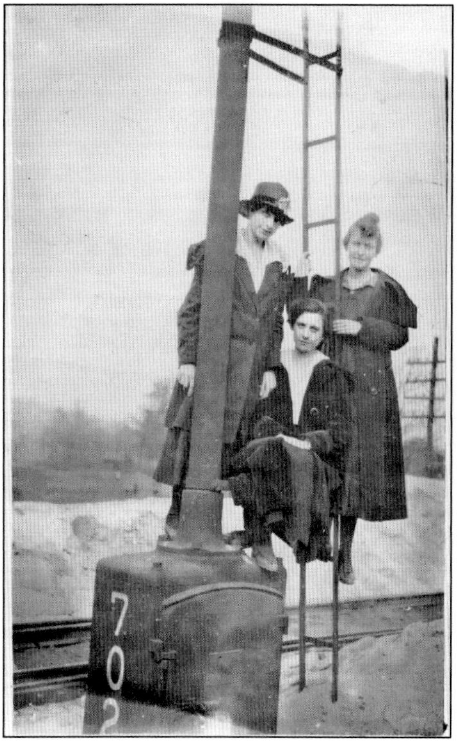

SUNDAY STROLL, CORDOVA. From left to right, Magaline Steadman, Sarah Davidson Kirkpatrick, and Ruth Sides Black are taking a break from their Sunday stroll down the railroad track to the river bridge in Cordova. There were no paved roads and no sidewalks, so the best place to walk when the roads were muddy was the railroad tracks, which were covered with gravel.

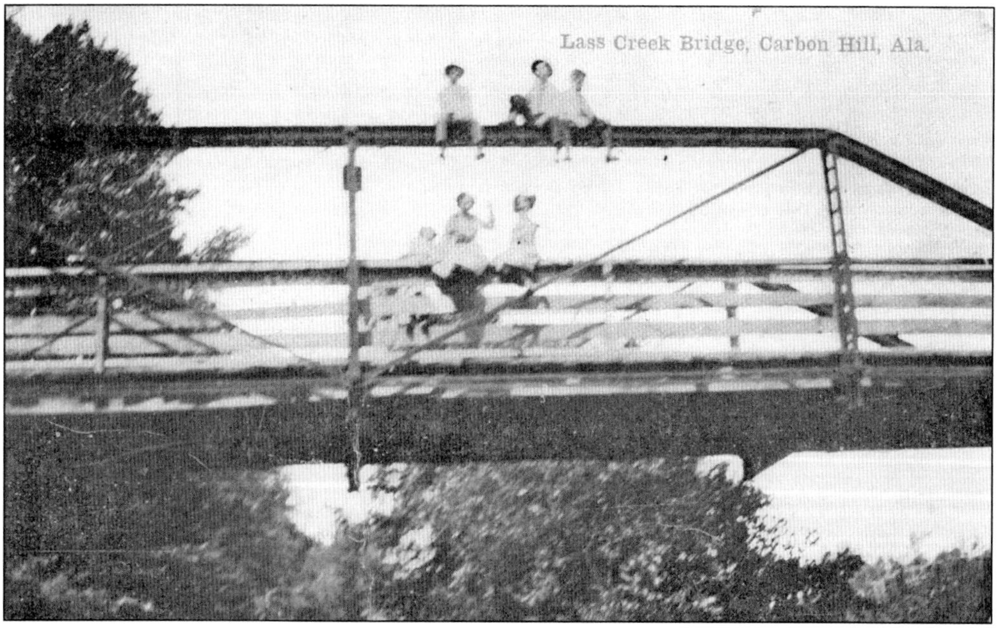

SUNDAY OUTING, CARBON HILL. On the western end of the county is the location of another favorite Sunday activity, walking to the Lost Creek Bridge. These young people are enjoying the exhilaration of sitting on the rails or climbing on the superstructure of the bridge. After church on Sundays, many residents walked the three miles from Carbon Hill to the bridge to enjoy the view available there.

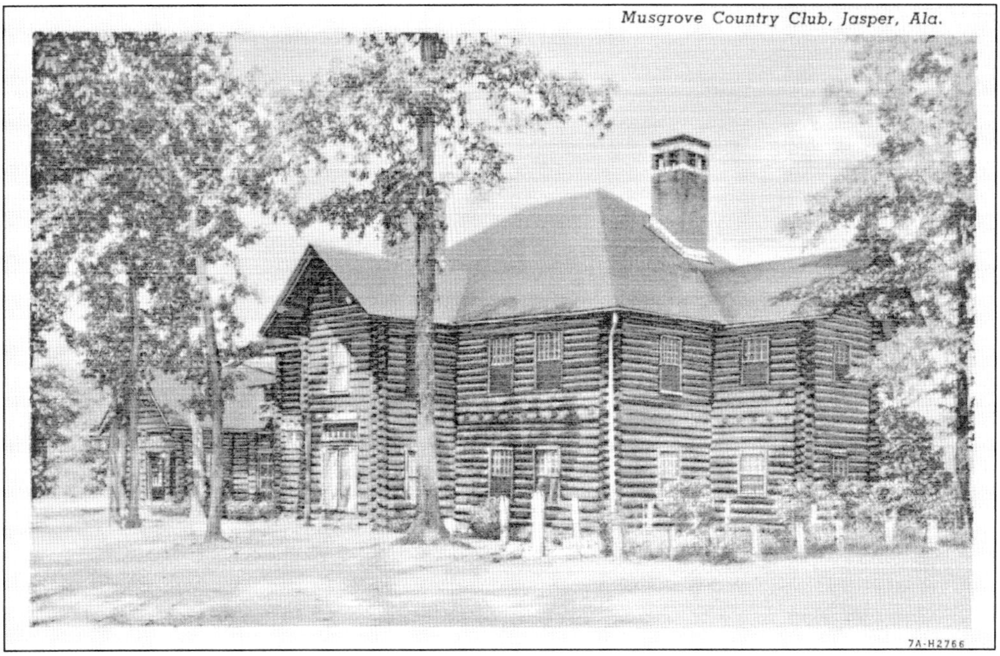

Musgrove Golf and Country Club, Manchester. This original log building completed in 1924 by Col. L.B. Musgrove was used to entertain his business associates and friends. The clubhouse on the 228-acre estate was built of 556 logs cut from the property. Musgrove lost his fortune in the stock market crash and sold his private club to 45 Walker County citizens who formed the Musgrove Country Club.

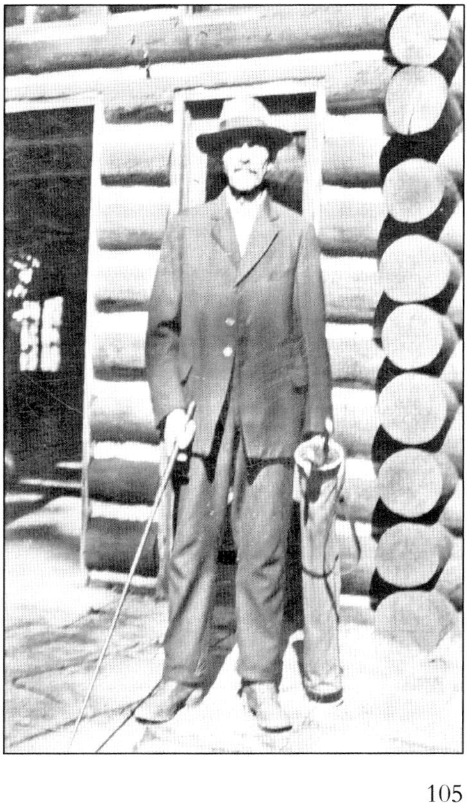

Musgrove Summer Home, *c.* 1925. Pictured at right is the builder of the Musgrove Summer Home, which later became the Musgrove Country Club. Thomas P. Scruggs is shown here with his golf clubs, and he has probably just finished a round with owner L.B. Musgrove. Scruggs also ran the Camak Mill just west of the clubhouse. Notice the number of clubs—two in his bag and the one in his hand.

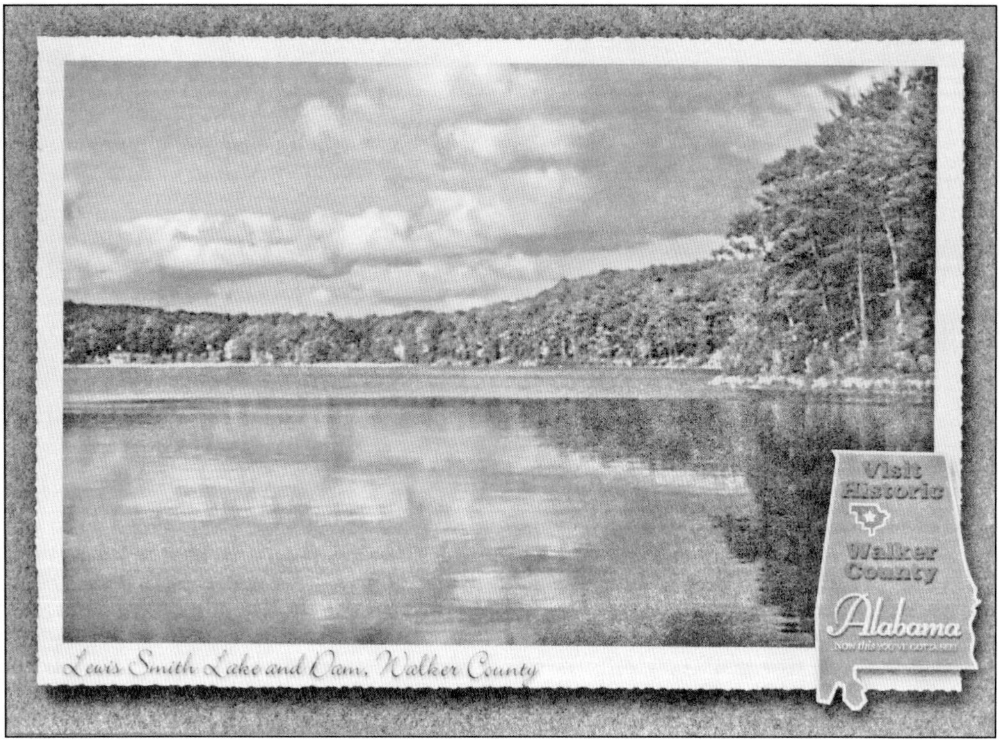

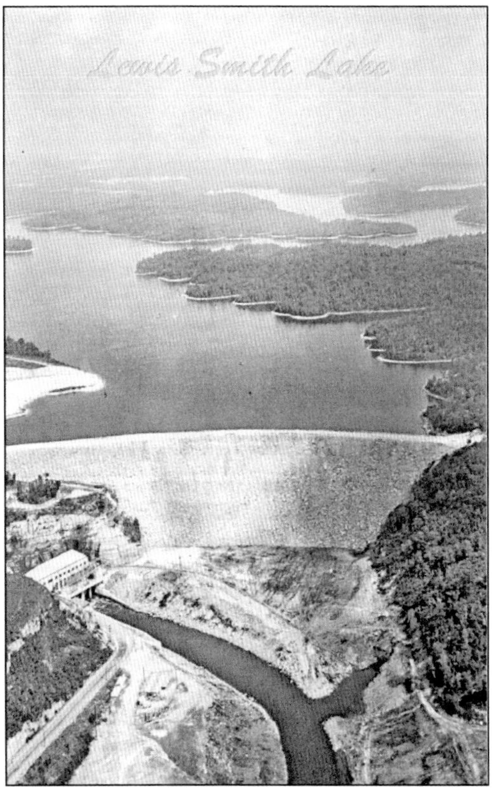

LEWIS SMITH LAKE, CURRY. Smith Lake's 21,200 acres of water is one of the deepest and cleanest lakes in the country. It was created in 1961, when the Sipsey fork of the Black Warrior River was dammed. Her 500 miles of shoreline make it a recreational paradise. Five world-record fish have been caught out of the more than 300-foot-deep lake.

LEWIS SMITH LAKE DAM, CURRY. Between Jasper and Cullman stands Alabama Power's Smith Lake dam. The earthen dam is 2,200 feet wide and 300 feet high and backs up over 21,000 acres of water. The dam has a 194.7 million-kilowatt-per-hour power storage and draws over 40,000 visitors per year. The creation of the deep, clear lake with 500 miles of shoreline has produced a bass-fishing paradise.

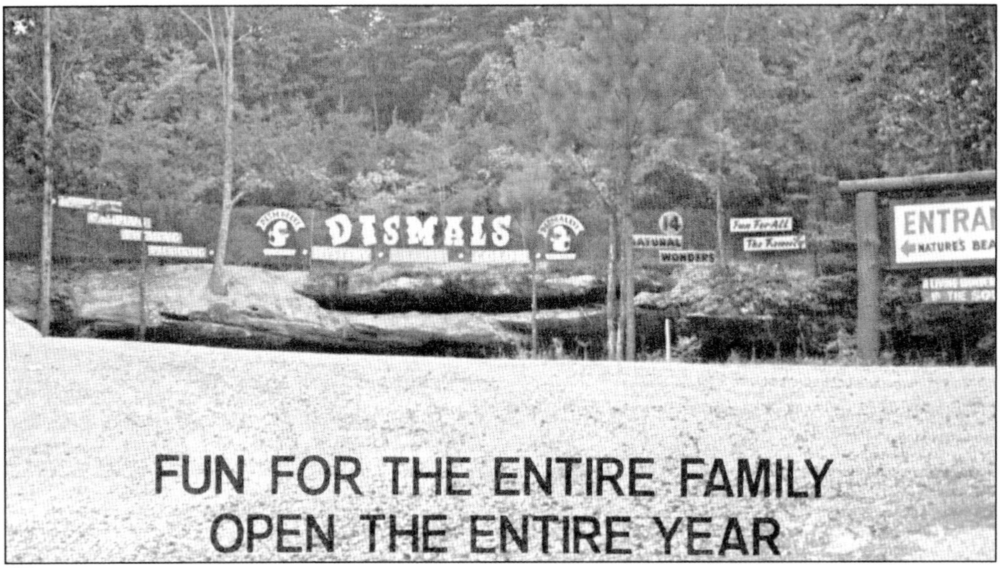

DISMAL CAVERNS. North of Walker County lies a natural wonderland called the Dismals. Numerous caves, natural bridges, rock formations, beautiful waterfalls, and a variety of mosses, ferns, wildflowers, and trees are truly enchanting, but what sets the Dismals apart are the dismalites (*Arachnocampa luminosa*), better known as glow-worms. They are found in only two places on the earth: here and in New Zealand.

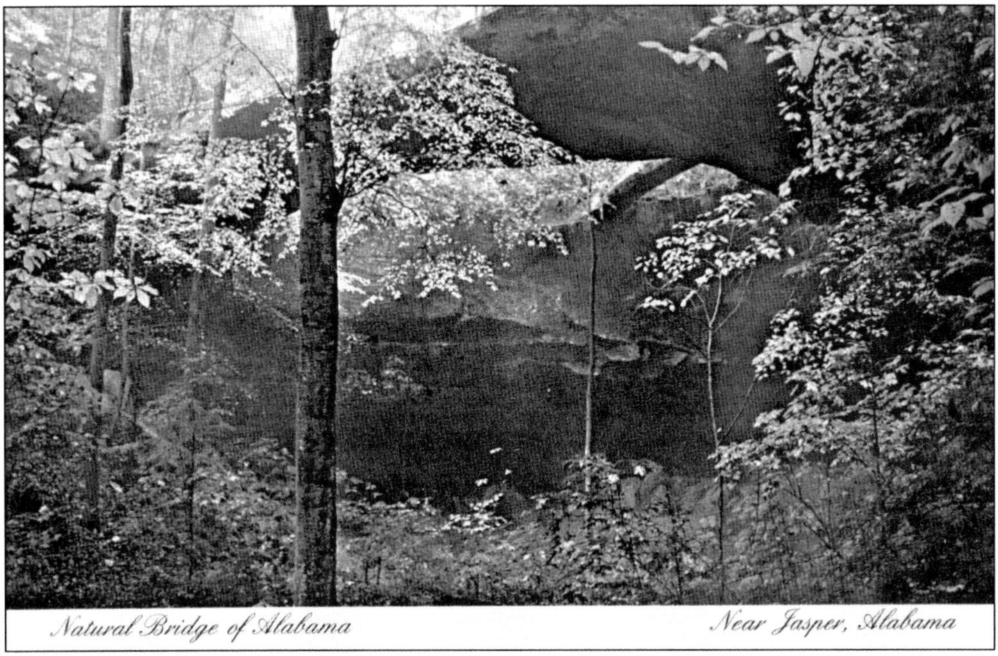

NATURAL BRIDGE. Located 25 miles north of Jasper lies the longest natural bridge east of the Rockies. Spanning 148 feet and standing over 60 feet high, it was formed millions of years ago by water erosion. The bridge itself is made of sandstone and iron ore. The park, which opened to the public in 1954, has hiking trails through a natural setting with nothing to distract from her natural beauty.

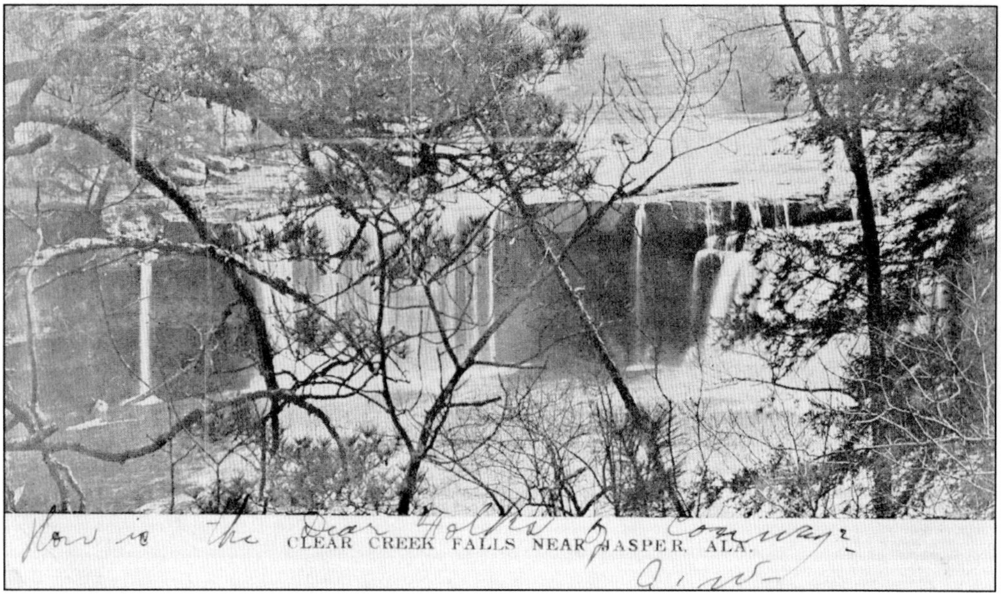

Clear Creek Falls, Fall City. One of the most recognizable spots in the area is the Clear Creek Falls. Jesse Livingston discovered them in 1812, and he then returned two years later and built a cabin near the falls. The upper falls measured 43 feet while the lower falls were 37 feet high, and the area was one of the favorite recreational spots for county residents. The falls disappeared below Smith Lake in 1961.

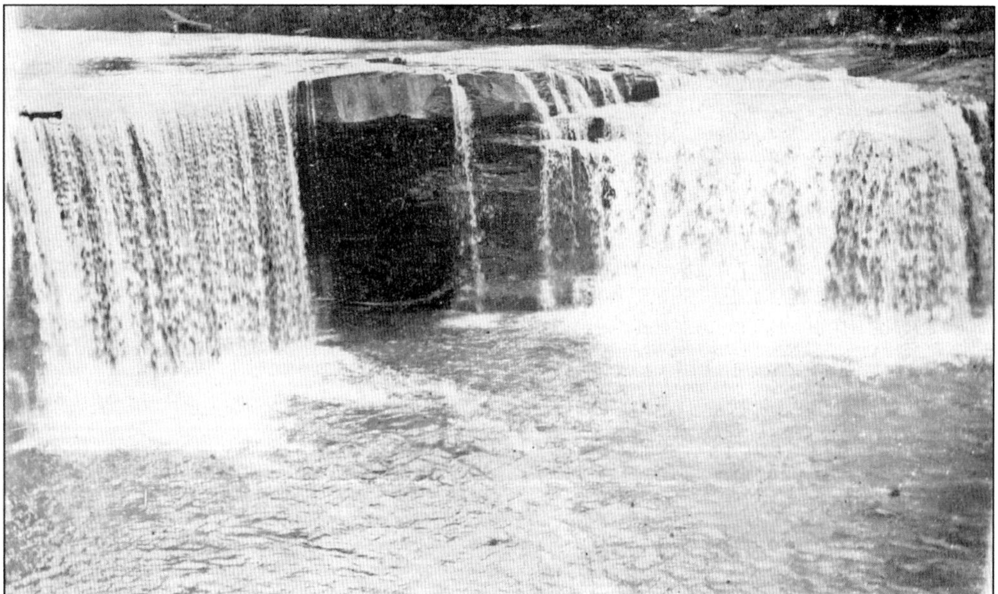

Clear Creek Falls, Counterfeiters. One of the legends of the falls says that counterfeiters used the cave beneath the falls to make their fake money. The leader of this activity, a certain Mr. ? Davis, was caught and hung in Tuscaloosa; a second one, Smith Randolph, was sentenced to hang. However, he escaped the noose by giving evidence that allowed them to capture the rest of the gang hiding beneath the falls.

BIG TREE, BANKHEAD FOREST. Located near the Sipsey Recreational Area in Bankhead National Forest is the largest known yellow poplar tree in Alabama. The giant poplar measures 80 inches in diameter and is 150 feet tall. It is located at the bottom of a beautiful waterfall in the 180,000-acre national forest. This tree has been a hiking destination for generations of scouts and outdoorsmen.

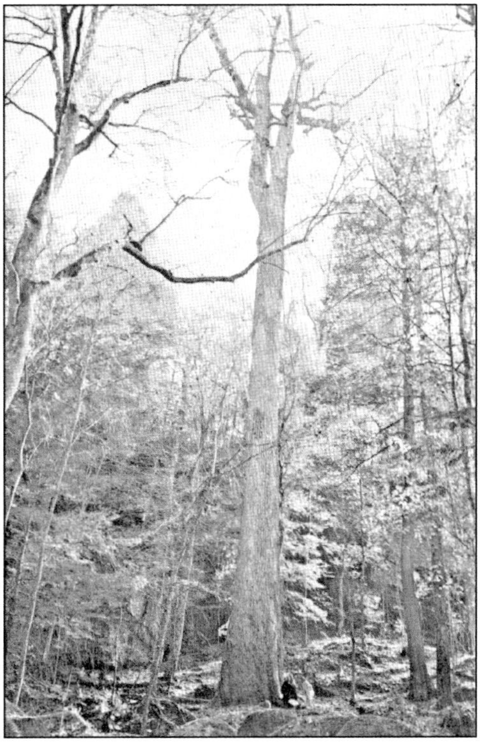

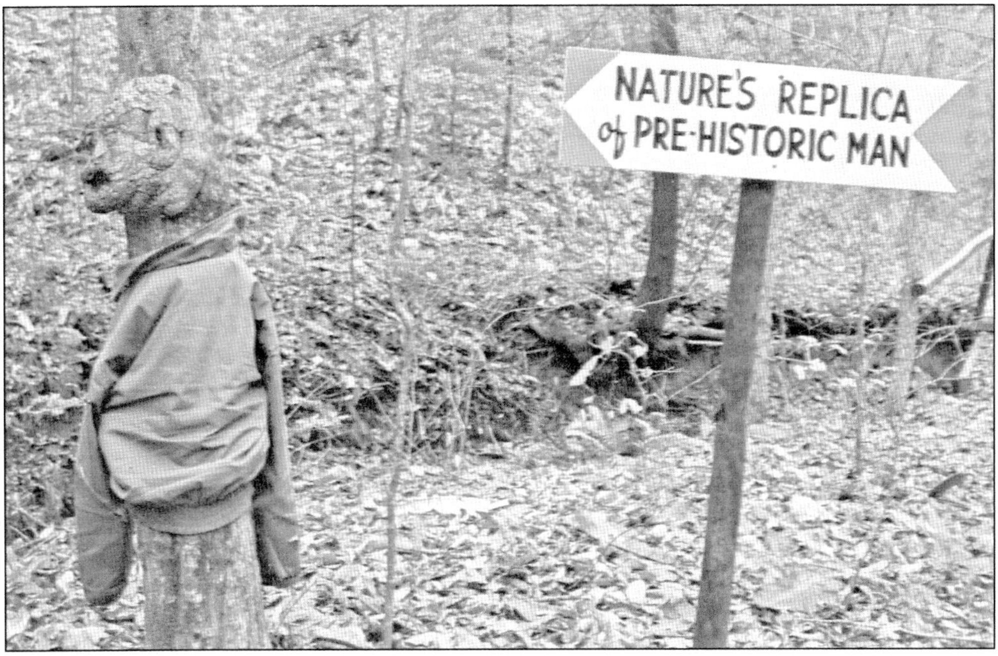

PRE-HISTORIC MAN TREE, NATURAL BRIDGE. An unusual natural phenomenon on one of the trails at the Natural Bridge of Alabama Park is this tree. It is just one of the many natural wonders associated with the park, which contains one of the largest rock bridges in the world. The area was the hunting grounds for the Choctaw and Cherokee for over 12,000 years.

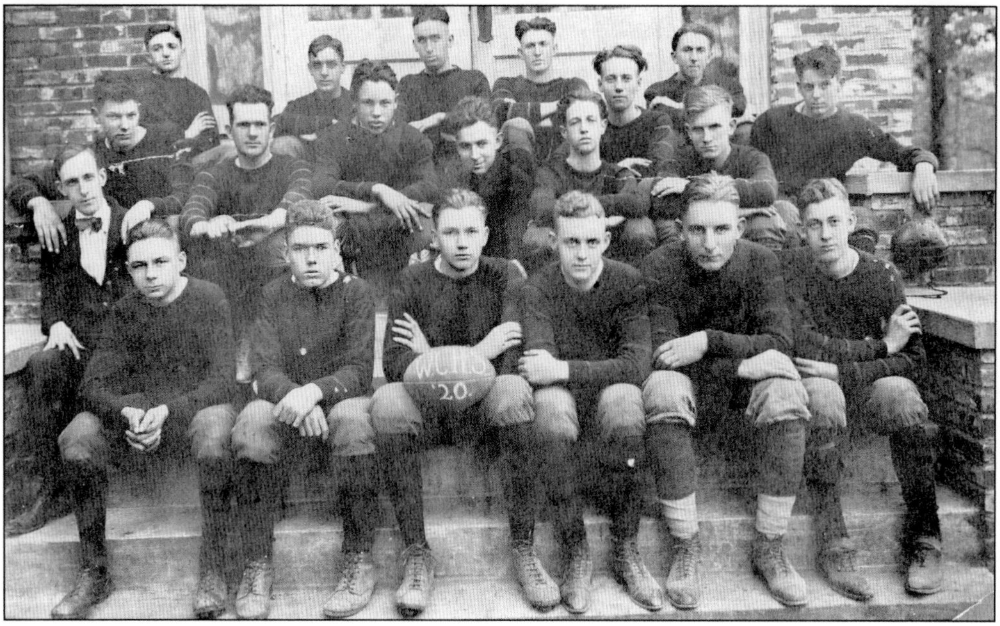

FOOTBALL, WALKER COUNTY'S FIRST TEAM, 1920. Pictured above is the first ever football team in Walker County, organized on September 3, 1920. This team did not win a game in 1920, but the next year they were undefeated and won the state championship. Pictured in the bottom row, second from right, is "Coop" Perry; at the far left in the second row is Coach Cranford Robinson; and behind him is Bruce Jones.

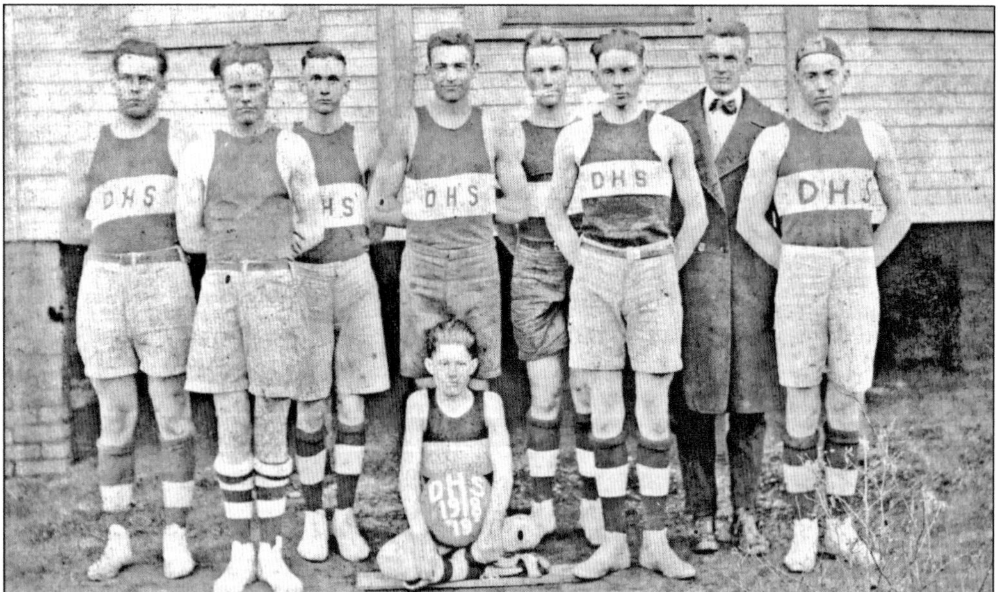

BASKETBALL, DORA, 1918–1919. The names are unavailable for the oldest known picture of a basketball team in Walker County. All basketball games were played on outside dirt courts until President Roosevelt's WPA built the city auditorium in 1936. Before that, basketball games were rained out and played on muddy fields just like football.

Six

Miscellaneous

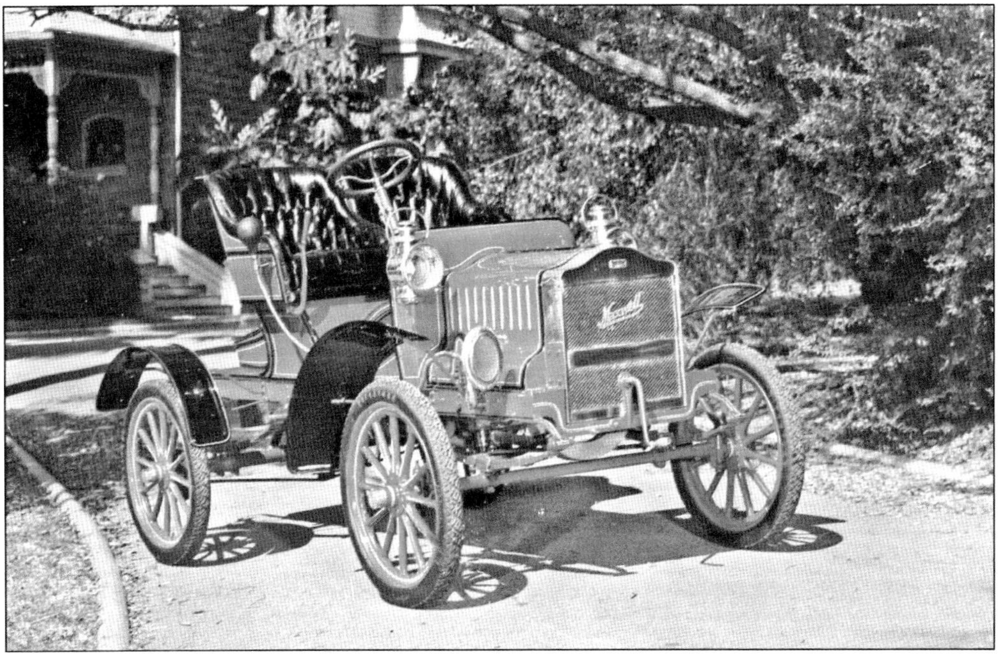

Walker County's First Car, 1907. This 1907 Maxwell, costing $850, is a replica of the first car ever owned and driven in Walker County. It was purchased by H.W. Cranford in 1907 in Birmingham and driven to Jasper in the record-breaking time of 11 hours. He then sped around the courthouse square at the amazing speed of eight miles per hour, scaring people and animals.

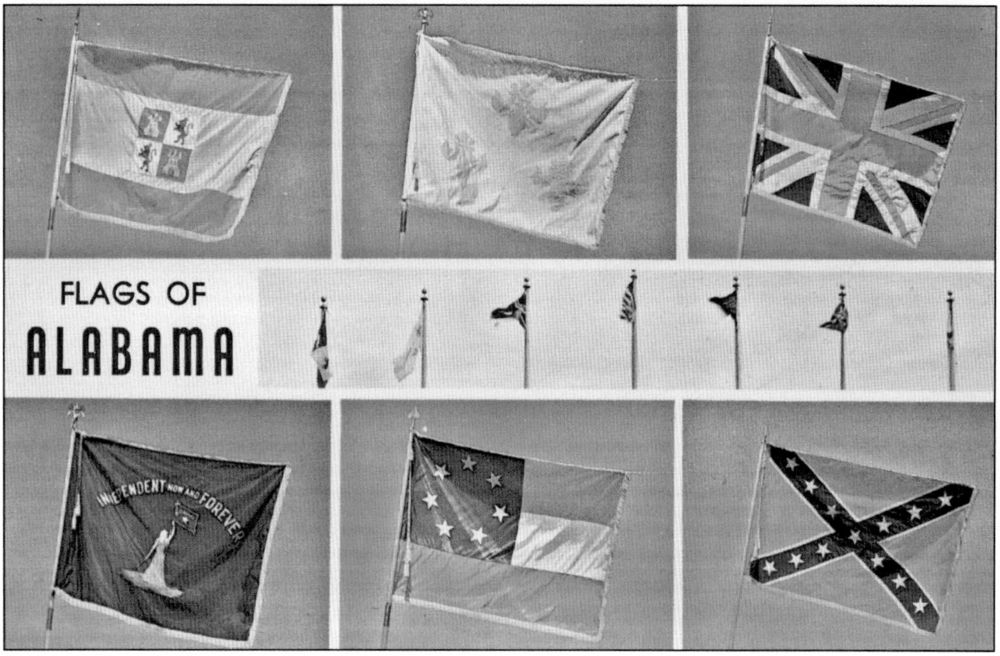

SEVEN FLAGS OVER ALABAMA. This card shows six of the seven different flags that flew over Alabama until the end of the Civil War. From left to right are (top row) the Spanish flag (1540–1699), the French flag (1699–1763), and the British flag (1763–1776); (bottom row) the Republic of Alabama flag (1861), the "stars and bars" Confederate Flag (1861–1865), and the Confederate Navy Jack. Not featured is the United States of America flag (1776 to the present).

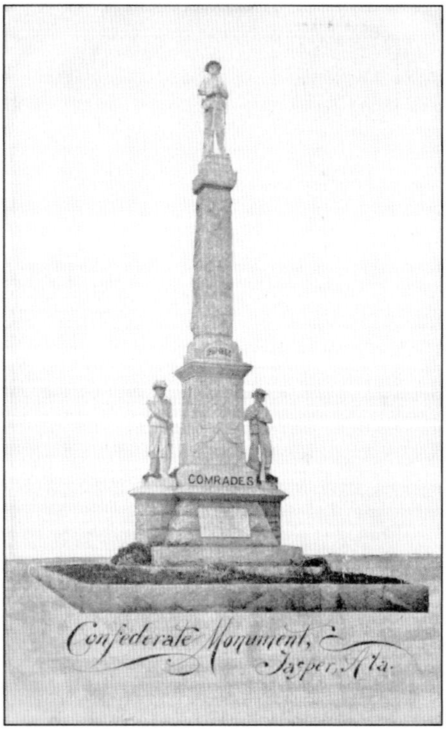

CONFEDERATE MONUMENT, 1908. The Daughters of the Confederacy began a campaign in 1907 to raise funds for a Confederate memorial to honor Walker County's soldiers who fought in the Civil War. This magnificent 30-foot monument of Italian marble was placed on the public square near the artesian well and is the only structure that remains from the 1908 courthouse square.

Hand Decorated Postcard, 1906. Cards like this one were produced for a time in the early 1900s and allowed the owners to send a personalized postcard to friends and family. They were produced in Germany and sold in America. This one, sent to Miss Siddie Sellers in Horse Creek, Alabama, has had glitter added with the addition of "Greetings from Carbon Hill, Ala."

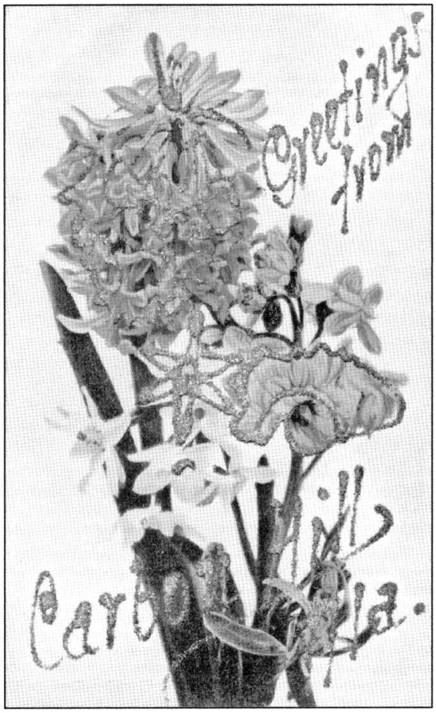

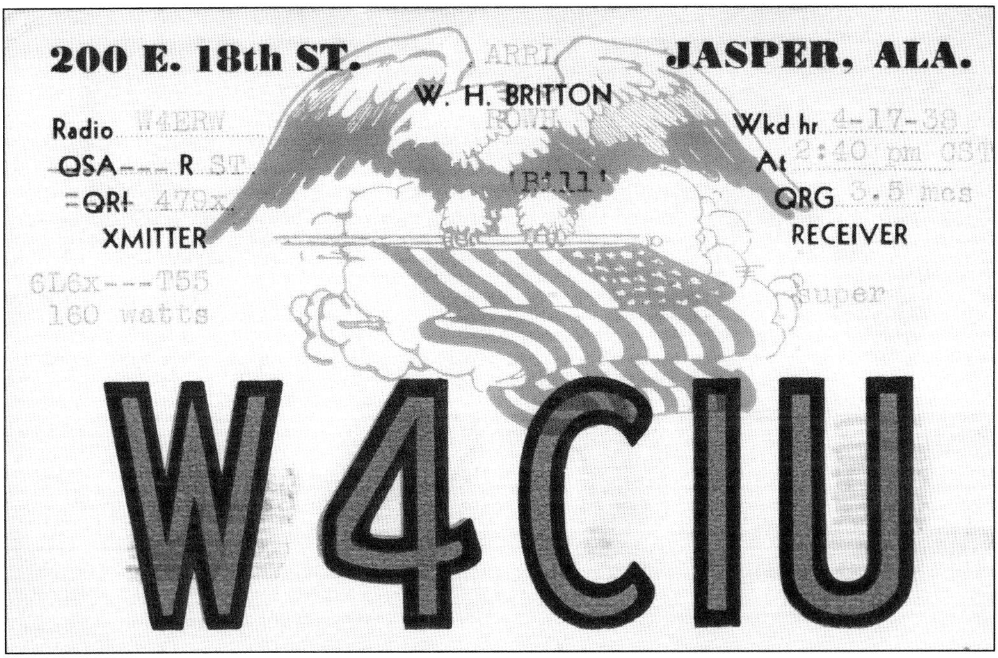

QSL Card, 1938. Produced by ham operators all over the world, these QSL cards gave pertinent information important to other operators. They would swap cards with each person they contacted over short-wave radios, and many operators had hundreds of these cards that were used like business cards are today. W.H. Britton, producer this QSL card, is recognized as the "father of ham operators" in the county. QSL is a code that literally means "I confirm."

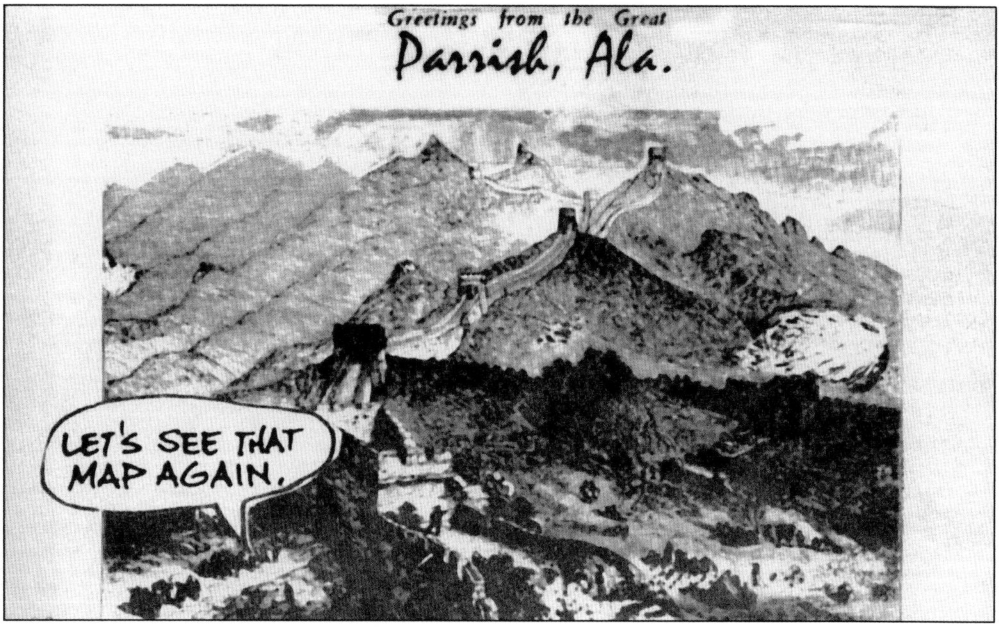

Humorous Postcard, Parrish. Distributed to local businesses by the Village Print Shop of Baldwinville, New York, these cards were sold as humorous advertisements for the town of Parrish, Alabama. The back reads, "One of a series of serious postcards done by a serious publisher in serious trouble." These postcards were sold at Wayne Gross's pharmacy in Parrish until 1974.

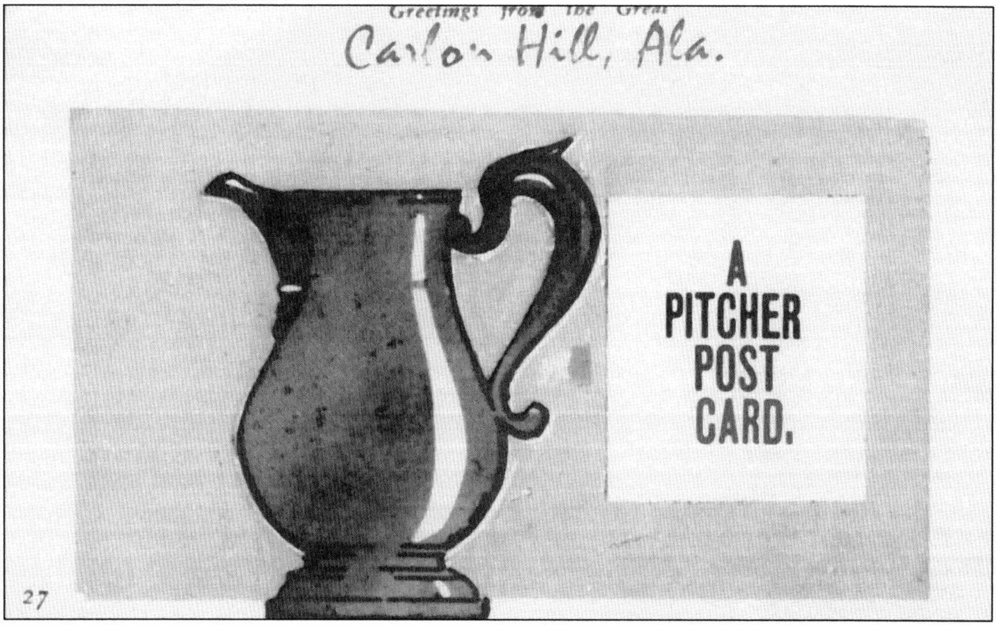

Humorous Postcard, Carbon Hill. This "pitcher postcard" is another example of a humorous advertisement by the Village Print Shop in Baldwinville, New York, which advertised small towns across America. This card was purchased from the Guin Drug Company in Carbon Hill, the only location in Walker County where these cards can currently be purchased.

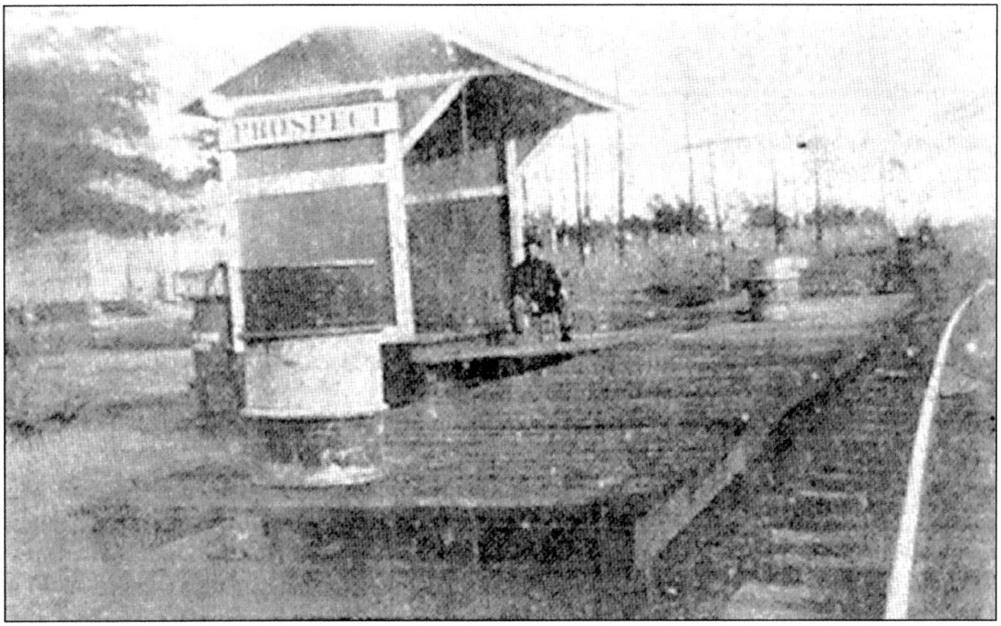

Southern Railroad Depot, Prospect. The small depot shown above was at Prospect, about 10 miles northwest of Jasper. Seated on the landing is Joseph William Smith who served as the postmaster of Prospect for over 50 years. Joe would hang the mail on a rack beside the tracks, and when the train came by, it would hook the mailbag and pull it in, thus avoiding the need to stop.

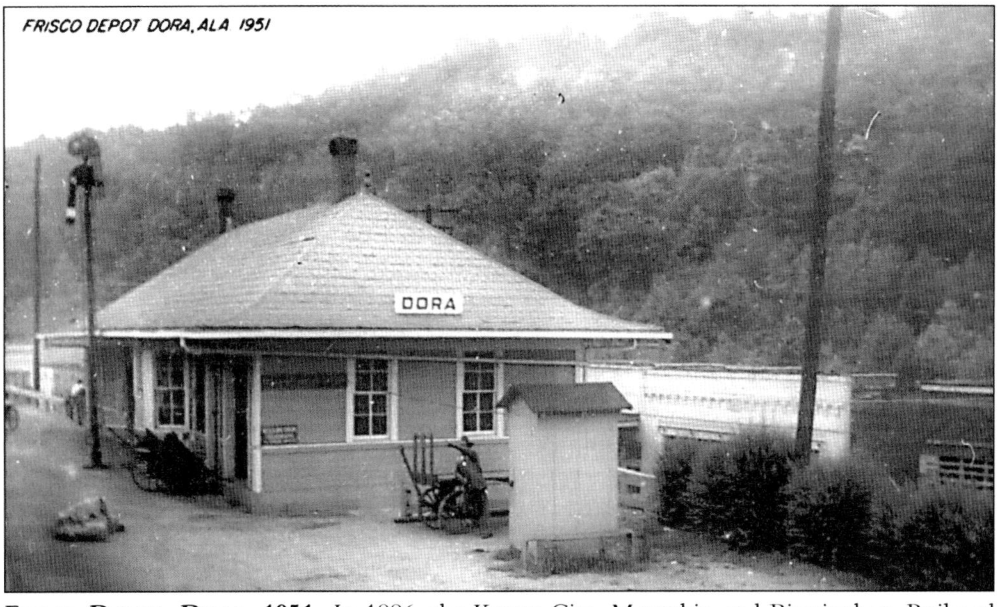

Frisco Depot, Dora, 1951. In 1886, the Kansas City, Memphis, and Birmingham Railroad (known as "Frisco") came through the little valley called Sharon. The name was later changed to Horse Creek in 1890 and then, finally, to Dora in 1906. The original depot was built in what is now the downtown Dora district on a foundation of railroad ties, which were later replaced by concrete.

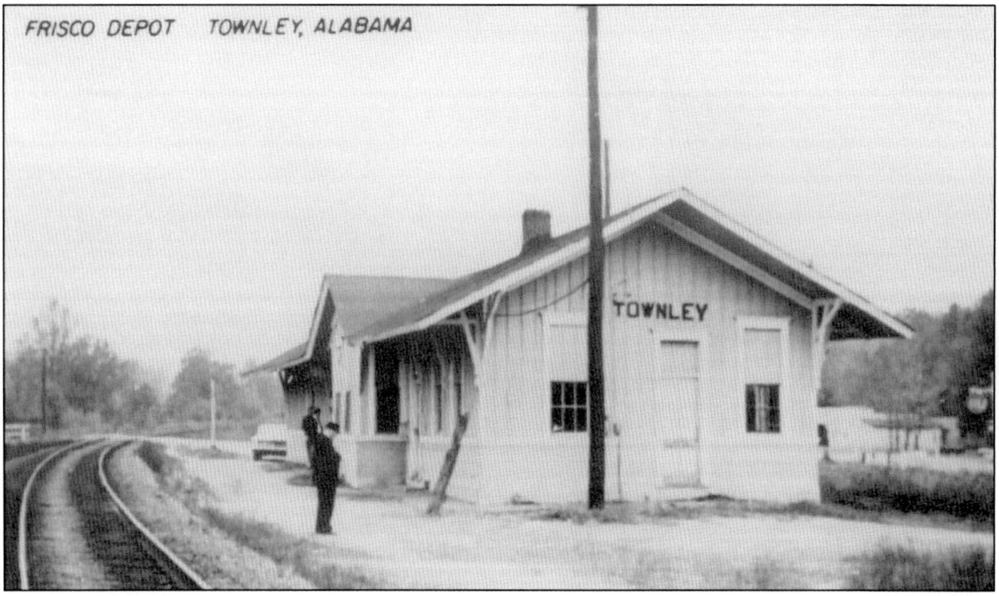

FRISCO DEPOT, TOWNLEY. Townley came into existence in 1886 when the new Kansas City, Memphis, and Birmingham missed the communities of Holly Grove and Pleasant Grove. Townley, which became a boomtown almost overnight, also became the market for farm products and lumber from the sawmills. The coal mines provided jobs for the rapidly growing community during its heyday.

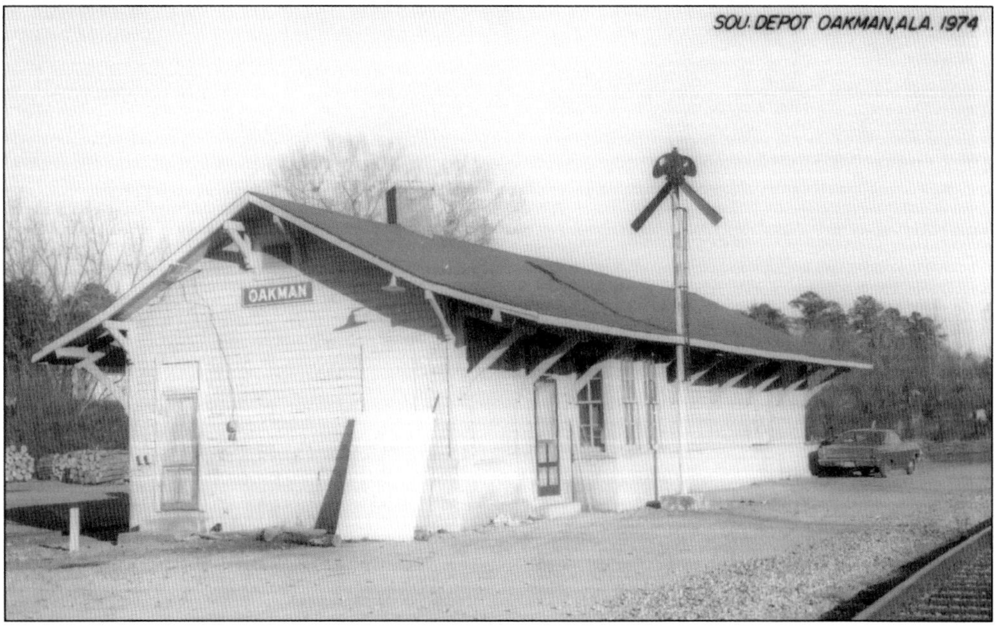

GEORGIA PACIFIC DEPOT, OAKMAN, 1974. Oakman is one of Walker County's oldest towns, and when the Georgia Pacific (known as the Southern or Norfolk Southern) came to Oakman in 1884, the town sprang into prominence. Serving as the distribution point for agriculture products, lumber, and coal, it gave passenger service to the county. The depot was moved to the Mining Museum in Dora, where it is now preserved.

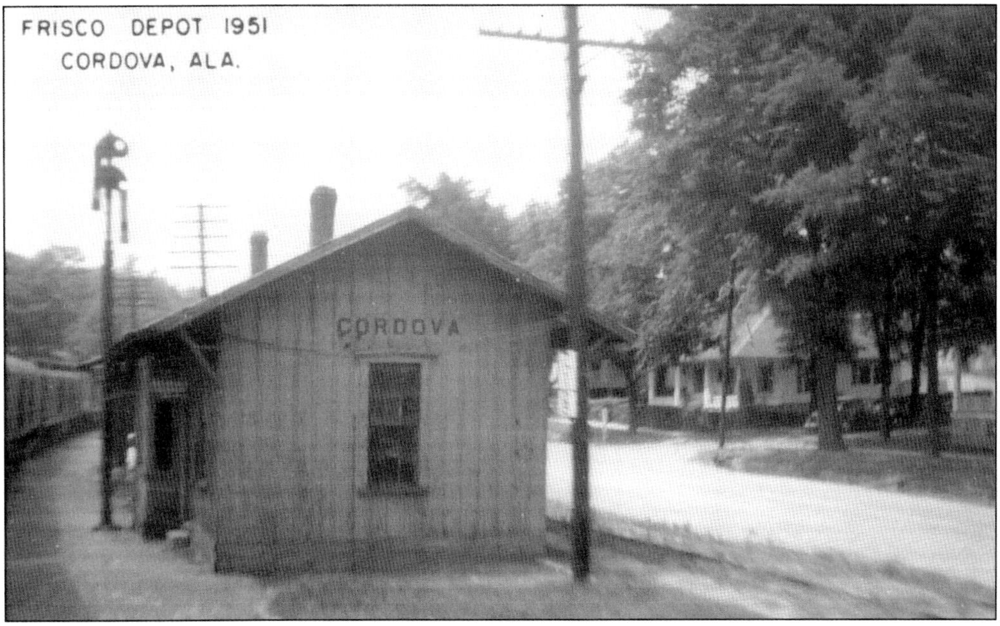

FRISCO DEPOT, CORDOVA, 1951. In 1886, Dent (later Cordova) jumped into prominence in the county with the laying of tracks by both the Georgia Pacific (Southern) and the Kansas City, Memphis, and Birmingham (Frisco), which gave the town direct connections with all markets across the South. Cordova remains a prominent point on the railroad, but the depot is now gone.

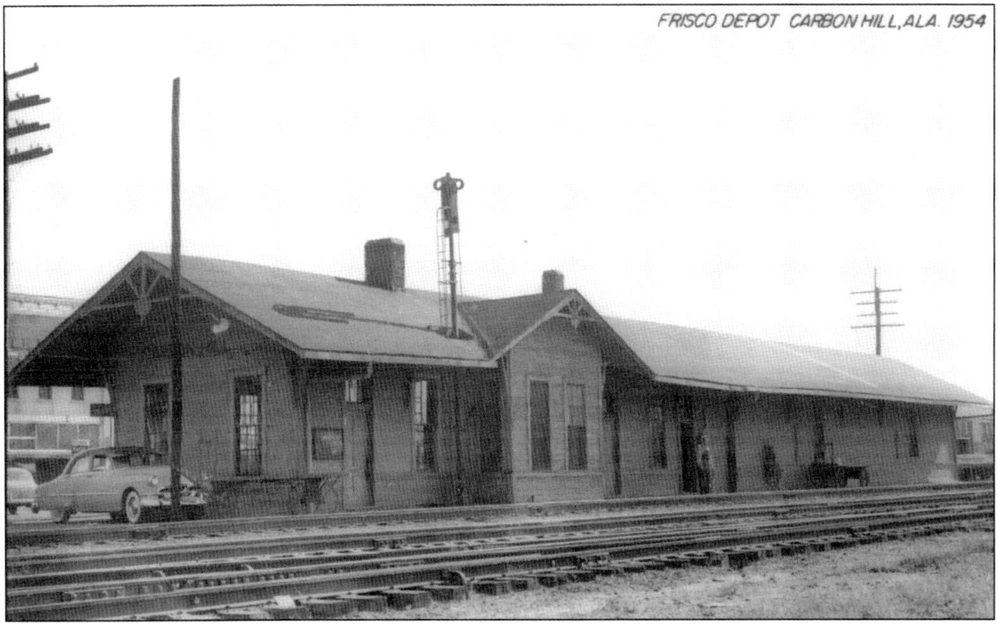

FRISCO DEPOT, CARBON HILL, 1954. Land donated for a right of way by Adeline and Timothy Barton brought the Kansas City, Memphis, and Birmingham (Frisco) to Carbon Hill. In 1886, the Frisco began construction of the railroad and coal was discovered, causing the little town to boom. Carbon Hill was born. The town developed the reputation of a rough weekend town.

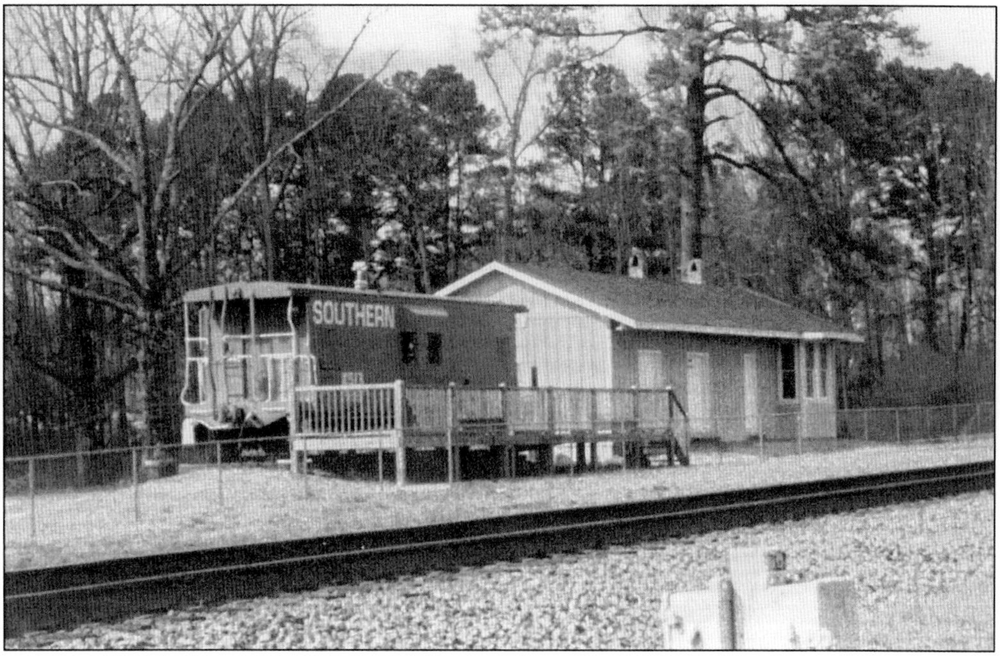

Southern Depot, Nauvoo. This replica of the original depot built in 1897 was dedicated during the Nauvoo Museum's grand opening exactly 100 years later in 1997. The depot was constructed under the direction of Eugene McDaniel. The Nauvoo Historical Society hired Mitchell McDaniel, a native of Nauvoo, to build it. The Southern Railroad brought prosperity to the little town, previously known as Ingle Mills.

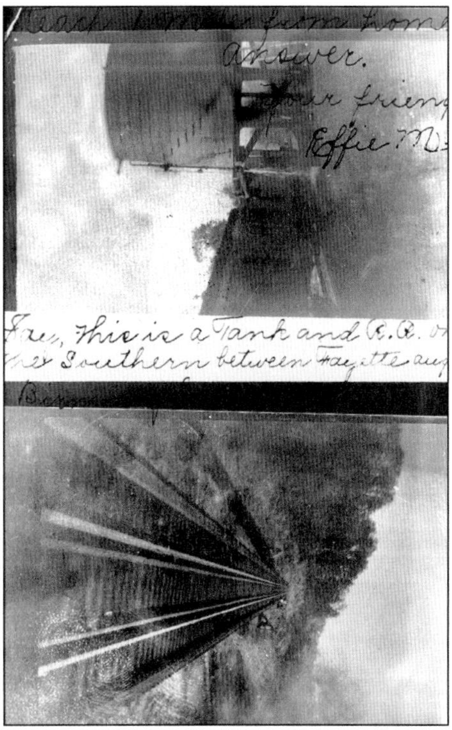

Railroad and Water Tank, Corona. This postcard shows the water tank and tracks at Corona, a mining town in western Walker County. The Southern laid tracks in 1884, and the Corona Coal Company shipped the first coal from Walker County in 1884. The largest single lump of coal ever recorded (40 tons) was dug at Corona. It broke two rail cars on its way to the New Orleans World Exposition.

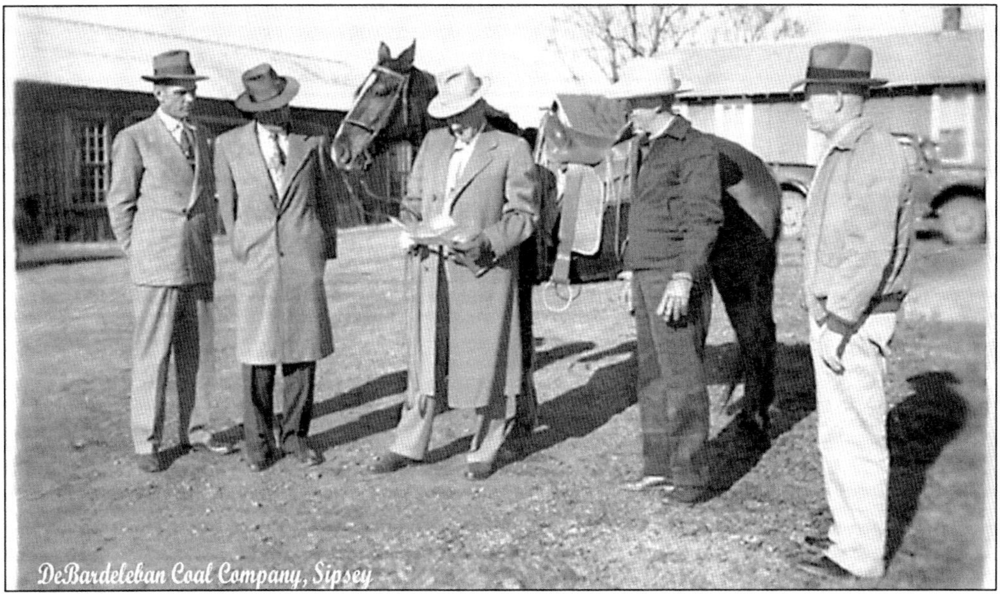

DEBARDELEBEN COAL COMPANY OFFICIALS, SIPSEY. The officials pictured above have just given Lattus Bishop a new horse for Christmas in 1949. Officials from left to right are Ned Strickland, ? Sides, Bishop, Henry Williams, and Roy Baxter. In the background, on the left is the repair building and on the right is the company eatery. This picture was taken at the DeBardeleben Camp in Sipsey.

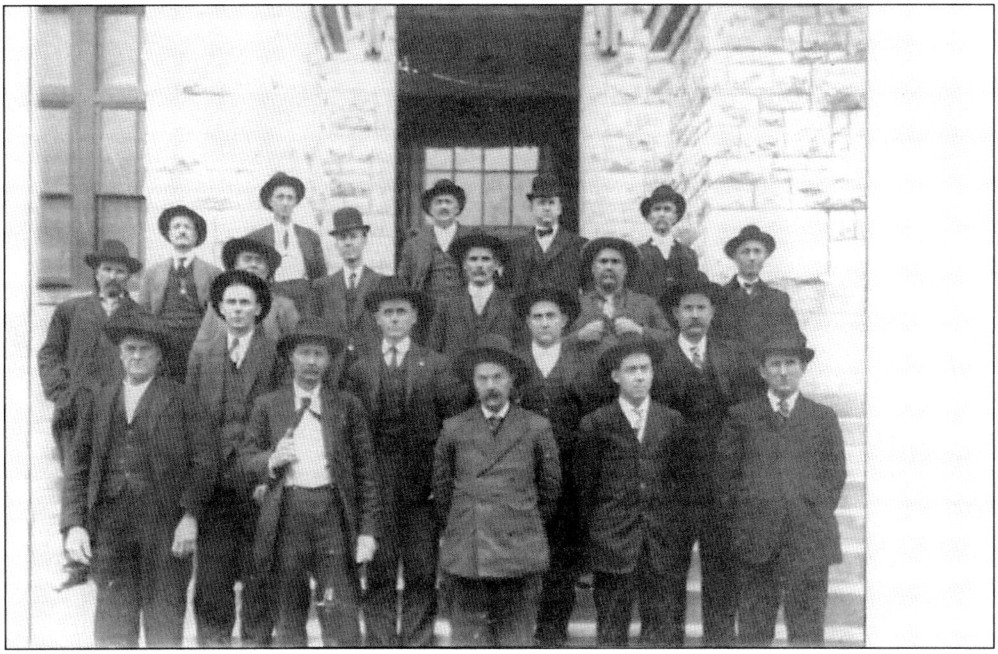

WALKER COUNTY GRAND JURY, JASPER, 1907. Standing in front of the new domed structure is reputed to be the first grand jury panel ever to convene in the new Walker County Courthouse. The only person positively identified is John Cranford Atkins, who was born in 1855. He is standing at the far left in the front row. This image was taken in the fall of 1907.

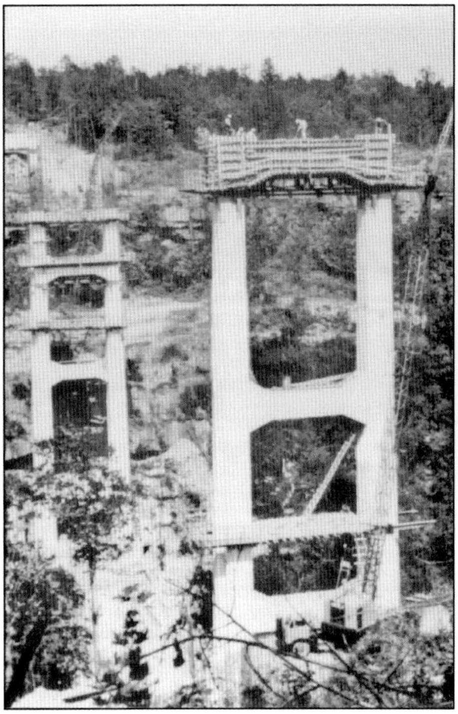

Duncan Bridge Under Construction, Curry. In 1959, construction started on an extremely tall bridge to span the Sipsey River, which later became Smith Lake. This new bridge replaced the small wood-and-metal bridge that had replaced the Old Lovell ferry. This ferry transported people and vehicles back and forth across the river until after 1934.

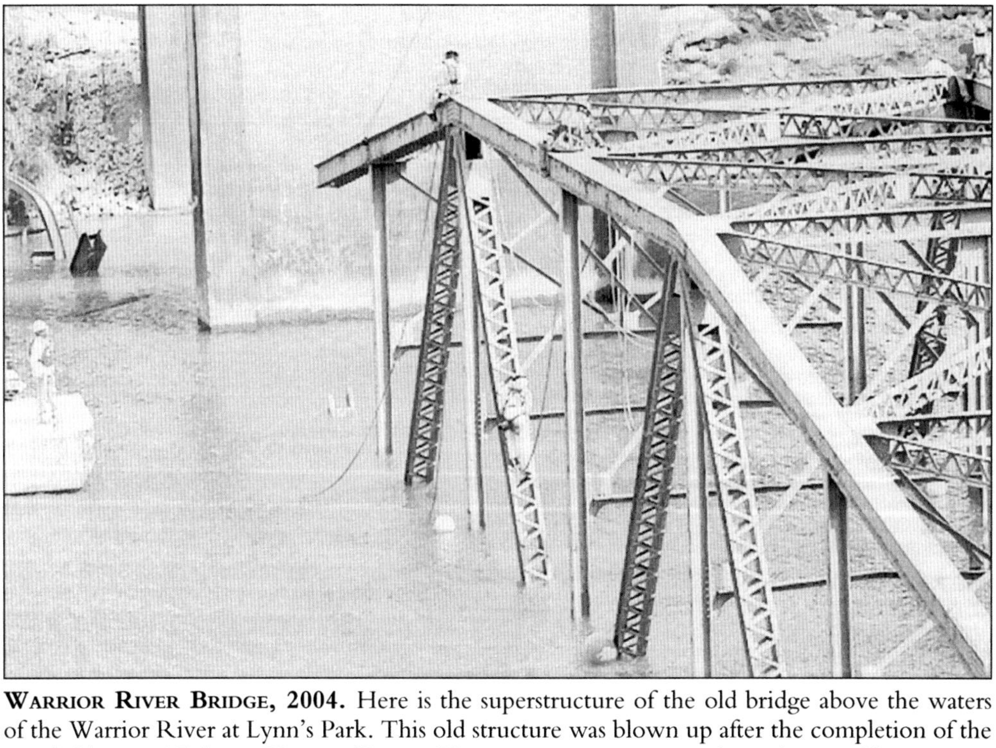

Warrior River Bridge, 2004. Here is the superstructure of the old bridge above the waters of the Warrior River at Lynn's Park. This old structure was blown up after the completion of the new bridges on Highway 78 east of Jasper. The superstructure was cut into pieces and large cranes on barges lifted the pieces out of the water.

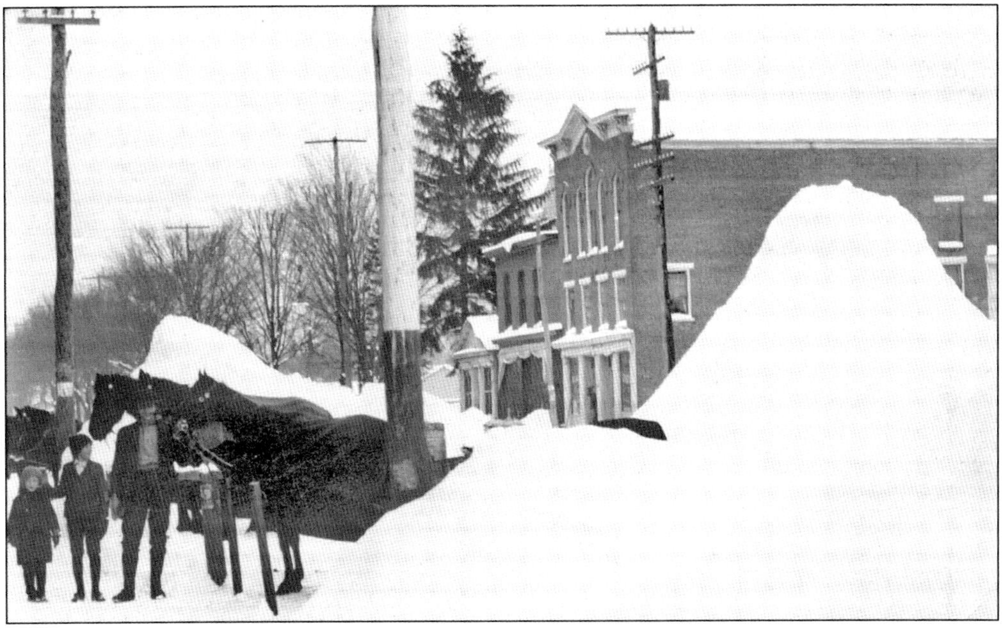

SNOW STORM, FLATWOOD. Snow is an occasion to celebrate and dread in Walker County, as shown in this early 1900s postcard. The snow is piled beside the road in Flatwood, a small town in Walker County near Nauvoo (not to be confused with the Flatwood near Oakman). A stagecoach stop and hotel made up the town. The only indication today that the town ever existed is the Flatwood cemetery.

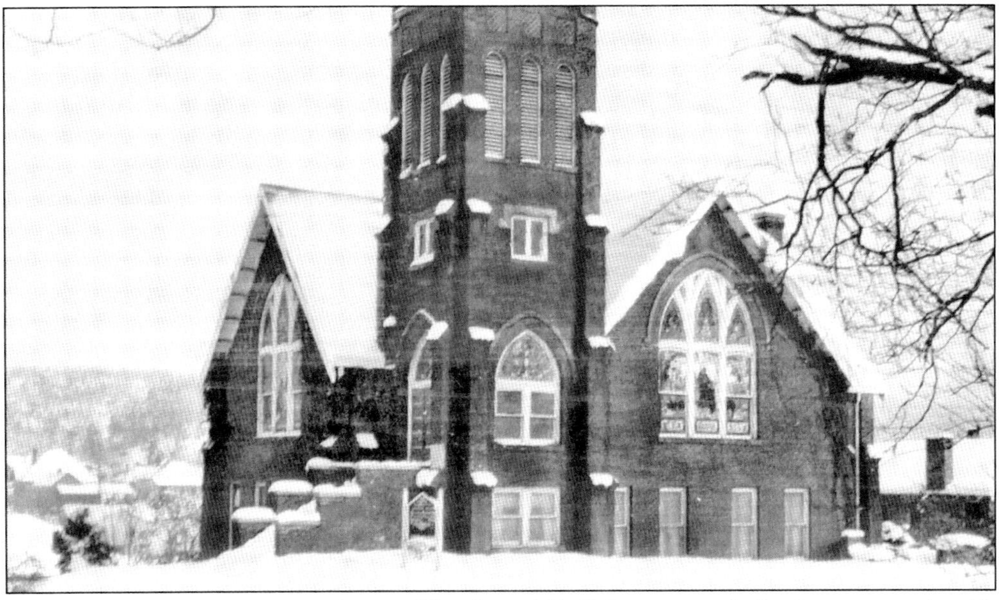

LONG MEMORIAL CHURCH, SNOW. The beautiful little town of Cordova covered with a blanket of snow is a paradise for the young and the young at heart, but it is considered a disaster for water pipes and unprepared driver. The winter of 1939–1940 was the worst on record, even freezing the Warrior River completely over and causing schools to be dismissed for almost a month.

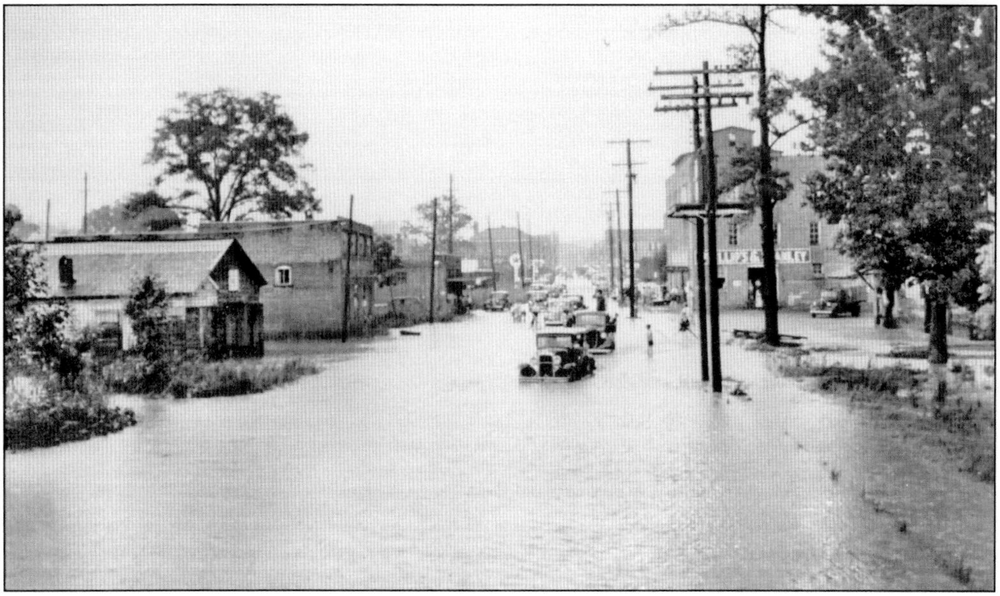

FLOOD, DOWNTOWN JASPER. Floods were a constant danger and a nuisance in the early days in Walker County. This view of Nineteenth Street looking east shows the completely flooded streets of downtown Jasper. Water covered the streets all the way to the Walker County Courthouse. On the right is the Phillips and Stanley Building, which served Jasper as a mercantile store.

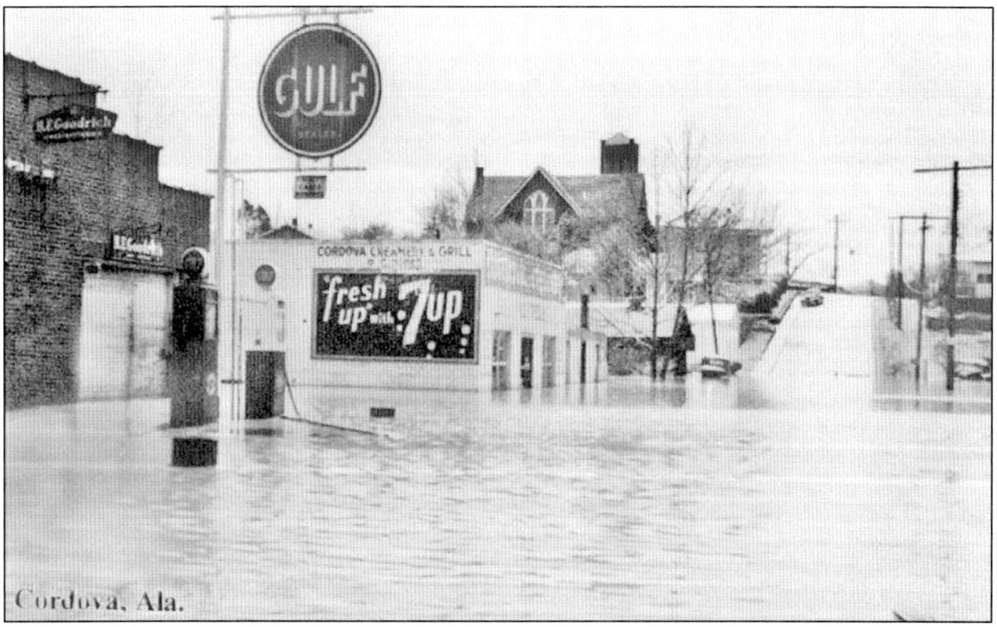

FLOOD, DOWNTOWN CORDOVA. This 1950 flood in downtown Cordova shows a view looking south down First Street. The building at the top of the hill in the middle of the card is the Long Memorial Methodist Church. On the left are Cummings Gulf Station and Oscar Dobb's Cordova Creamery and Grill. Dams on the Warrior River have reduced these floods but have not eliminated them completely.

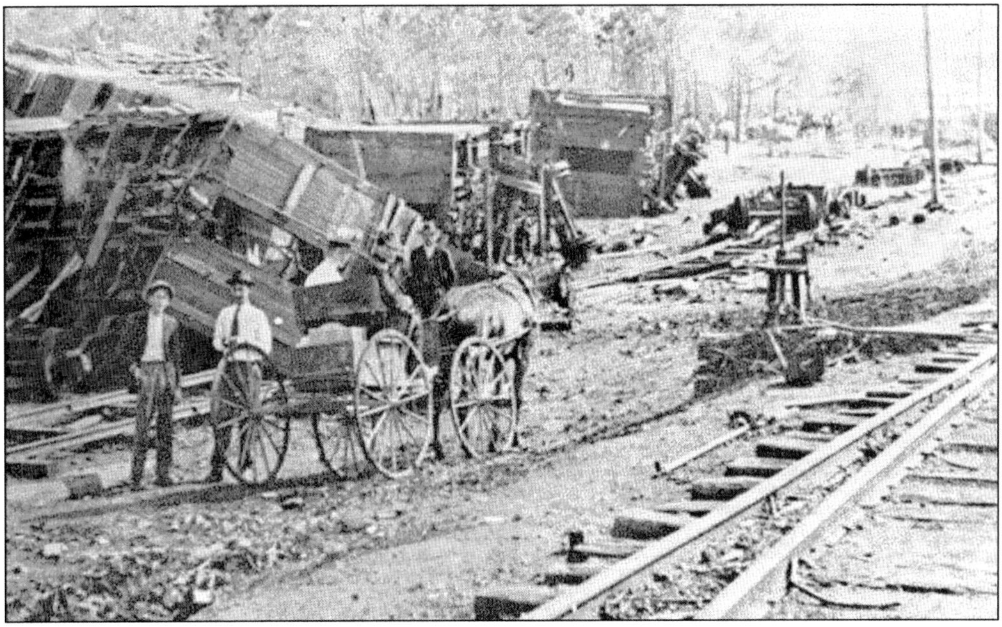

TORNADO, DORA MINE, 1908. The tornado of 1908 shows the type of destruction often caused each spring by storms in Walker County. In this card, it looks as if there has been a train wreck, where rail cars have been ripped apart and stacked on top of each other. There were a number of deaths caused by this tornado at Bergen in Dora, and the damage was extensive.

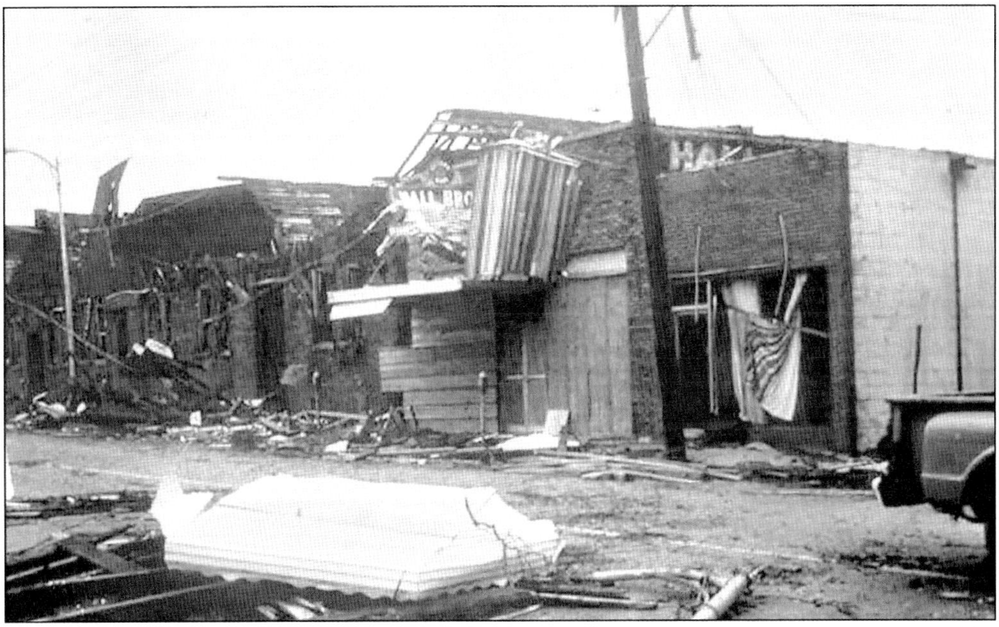

TORNADO, DOWNTOWN JASPER, 1974. The date April 3, 1974, will be long remembered by Jasper residents. At 7:55 p.m., the awesome power of nature was turned loose on downtown Jasper. The next morning the full extent of the tornado was evident. From Second to Fifth Avenue between Eighteenth and Nineteenth Street was massive devastation, including the Hall Brothers Sporting Goods Store, shown here.

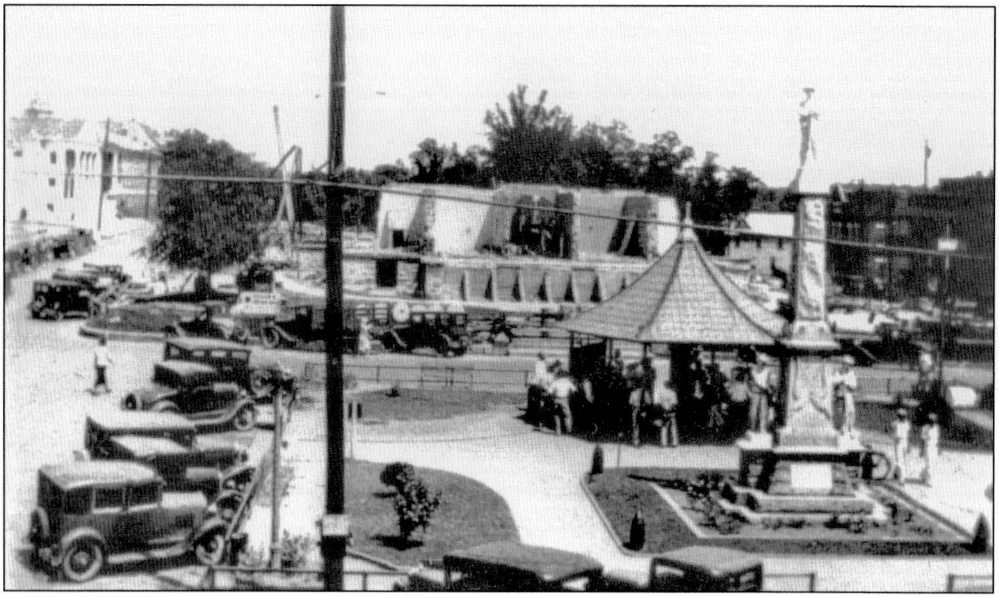

Walker County Courthouse Burned, 1932. At approximately 6:30 p.m. on January 12, 1932, a fire, believed to have started by lightening, destroyed the entire second story of the crowning jewel of Walker County, thus ending an era of unprecedented growth that had already been slowed by the Depression. This building was replaced by a much less aesthetically appealing courthouse.

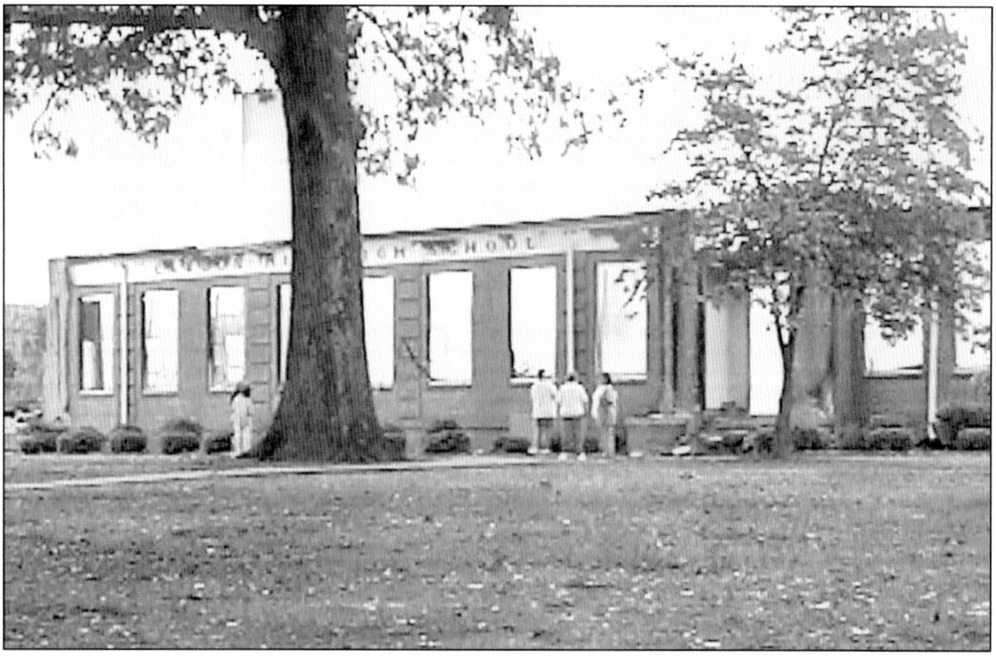

Carbon Hill High School Burned, 2002. One of the two major disasters to strike Carbon Hill in 2002 was the complete destruction of the high school by fire on June 20. The second was the tornado of November 10. The school had served the Carbon Hill area since 1972. The last principal of the Fifth Avenue N.W. School was Dr. Diane Jones.

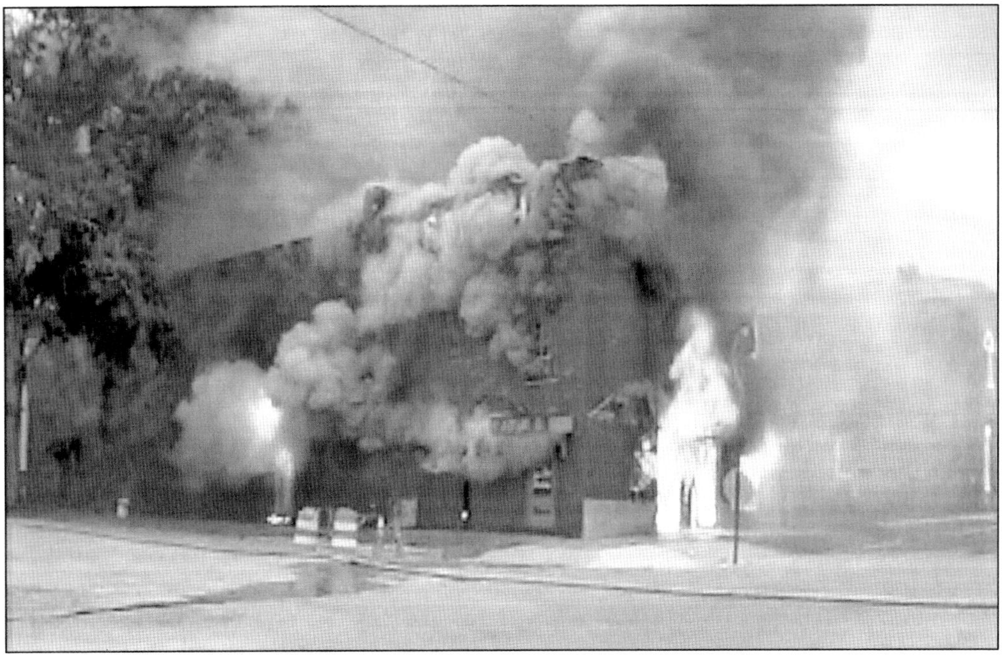

PASTIME THEATRE FIRE, CARBON HILL. Pastime Theatre, located on Second Avenue in Carbon Hill, was owned by Will and Minnie Thornton and was managed for years by Mr. and Mrs. Joe Allen. The Thorntons owned the home that was located next to the theater. The old theater was control burned in 2002 by the Carbon Hill fire department. It is shown here going up in flames.

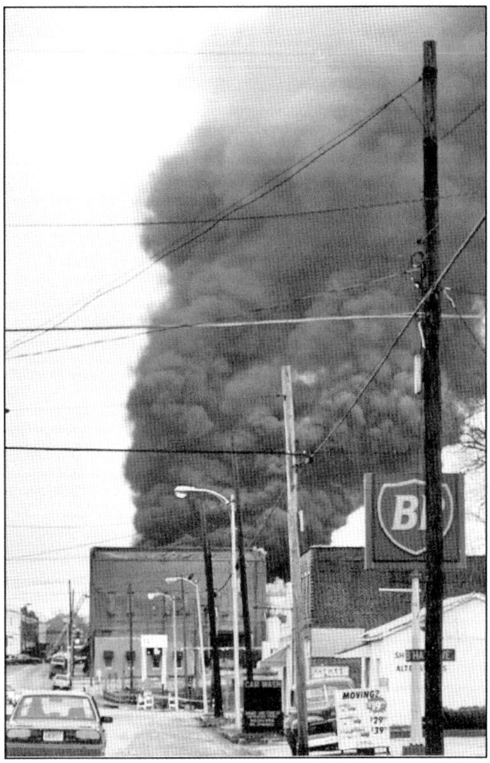

PEOPLES DRUG COMPANY FIRE, JASPER. On New Year's Eve, 1994, a Jasper landmark burned beyond repair. The remains of the building, including the basement, was torn down, filled in, and paved as a parking lot. At right is a western view from Nineteenth Street of black smoke billowing above the Burton Building, telling of the end of a Jasper institution. Below the Burton Building is the Jeff Donaldson Law Office.

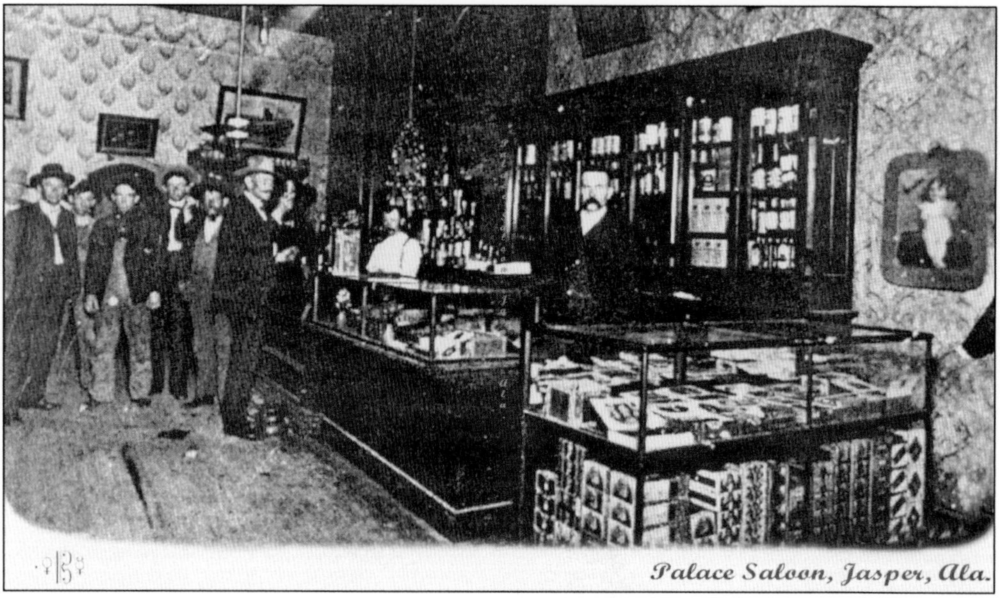

PALACE SALOON, JASPER, *c.* 1902. Located above the restaurant on the northwest corner of Third Avenue and Nineteenth Street in downtown Jasper is the Palace Saloon. S.J. Childers owned this unusual second-story saloon. Notice the glass-top bar and all the whiskey bottles in the cabinet behind the bar. The restaurant below was to later become the Peoples Drug Store.

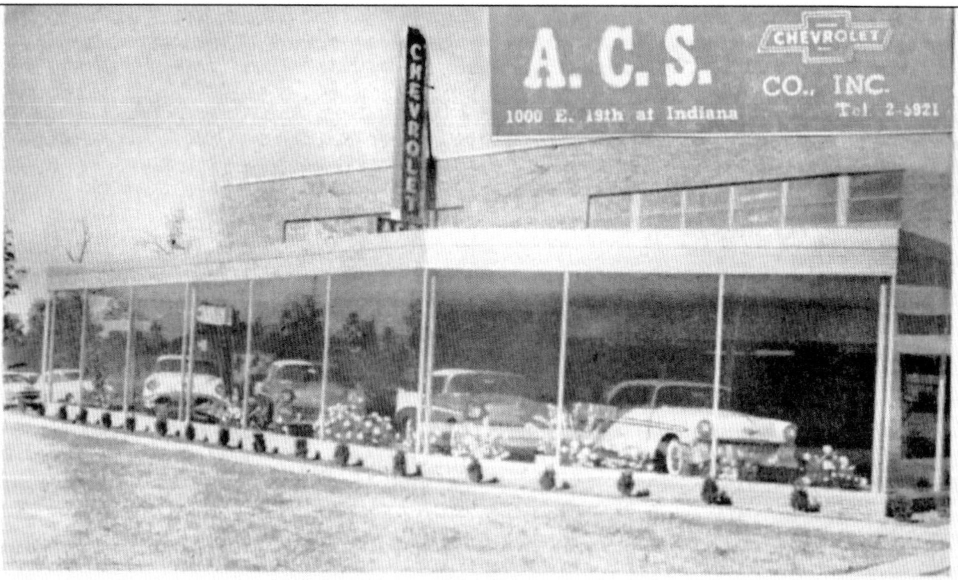

A. C. S. CHEVROLET CO., INC.
Organized Jan. 1, 1935

ACS CHEVROLET COMPANY, JASPER. The A.C.S. Chevrolet Company was organized in January 1935 in downtown Jasper, but it eventually moved to Nineteenth Street and Indiana Avenue south of Walker High School's Kiro Field. The Walker County Board of Education office moved into the old building, and the Walker County bus barn is housed in what was the service department.